★

"[NATIONS] ALL BEAR SOME MARKS OF
THEIR ORIGIN. THE CIRCUMSTANCES
WHICH ACCOMPANIED THEIR BIRTH
AND CONTRIBUTED TO THEIR
DEVELOPMENT AFFECT THE WHOLE
TERM OF THEIR BEING. IF WE WERE
ABLE TO GO BACK TO THE ELEMENTS
OF STATES, AND TO EXAMINE THE
OLDEST MONUMENTS OF THEIR HISTORY,
I DOUBT NOT THAT WE SHOULD
DISCOVER IN THEM THE PRIMAL CAUSE
OF THE PREJUDICES, THE HABITS, THE
RULING PASSIONS, AND, IN SHORT, OF
ALL THAT CONSTITUTES WHAT IS
CALLED THE NATIONAL CHARACTER."

—*Alexis de Tocqueville*, Democracy in America

DEFINING A NATION

Our America and the Sources of Its Strength

General Editor ★ David Halberstam

NATIONAL GEOGRAPHIC

WASHINGTON, D.C.

Table of Contents

CHAPTER FOUR: SOME STRUGGLES ALONG THE WAY

CHAPTER FIVE: OUR FELLOW AMERICANS

CHAPTER SIX: THE COMING OF AN AMERICAN CULTURE

Our America

by David Halberstam

SOMETIMES WHEN I'M OFF TO LECTURE here in New York and I'm in my finery, wearing a dark blazer and gray slacks and a very conservative tie, serious clothes for a serious man, I notice that the cab driver, usually newly arrived from the Indian subcontinent or the Middle East, will treat me with a certain respectful attitude, as though he is dealing with an older American, one whose family has been in this country for multiple generations. I always find this puzzling because I still think of myself as a new American, and I have clear memories of my paternal grandparents, the mark of the old country still very much on them, as they made their own difficult adjustment to this country, at once lovingly and warily, hoping against hope that it was as different from the old country as they believed when they first set off for its shores.

That duality of vision—the sense of the cabbies or the Hispanic superintendents on my block that I must be some figure off the *Mayflower*, and my own private sense, that Ellis Island is barely yesterday—seems to me to be wonderfully American. To be sure, we are, in terms of the bearers of our name, virtually the *Mayflower* Halberstams. My grandfather arrived in this country around 1890, to my knowledge the only Halberstam to come to the United States before the war; some fifty years later, after the war and the Holocaust, many other Halberstams, distantly related, came here and, like us, prospered accordingly. Both of my paternal grandparents came from around Brod, a part of Russia-Poland-Ukraine (depending on who was winning that year), outside Lvov. My father and his six siblings were, I believe, all born here.

Of my maternal grandparents less is known. They came from Vilno, in Lithuania, and thus in family disputes, my father's side were the Galitizianas, my mother's side, the Litvoks. My maternal grandfather made it as far as Jackson in west Tennessee, where other family members had already taken root. I do not think my grandfather fared very well, and at some point someone told him that part of the problem was his last name, Solinger, which was said to be too Jewish, and so he changed it in one great masterstroke—it's one of my favorite family stories—to Levy. It's a story that still helps make me modest when I deal with other, newer Americans.

My maternal grandfather, Abraham Levy, who was born in 1862, died very young, at forty-three, leaving his widow with six children, two of them infants, including my mother. When as a boy I listened to family stories from her side of the family line, my maternal grandmother seemed a distant figure, someone who never spoke or acted and in fact never even seemed to make an appearance; she always remained a figure in the shadows, as if her family's life had somehow gone on without her taking part. I later decided she had been so traumatized by the early death of her husband, the death of two other children in infancy, and the obligation to raise six children in a new and very alien world that she was dealing with serious depression in an age when people did not recognize what depression was.

Our family sagas were otherwise, I suspect, not that unusual for immigrant families of that era: a good deal of failure and hardship at first, some successes, followed by more failures. I sensed from the family stories that my paternal grandfather loved America immediately, even as he struggled with it, and that my grandmother, like the wife of many an immigrant, often said less and remained more wary of the new country but adapted more skillfully. Their store ("Harry Halberstam, Clothing, Boots, Shoes and Furnishings/Ladies' Cloaks, Suits and Furnishings") was hardly a smashing success; it opened and closed in Johnsonburg, Pennsylvania, and Springfield, Massachusetts, before finding some degree of permanence in Torrington, Connecticut. There were a good many family stories of my grandfather with his quick temper chasing customers out of the small store, and of Sarah Halberstam, my grandmother, deftly bringing them back in and completing the sale.

The more I hear of the immigrant experience, the more I am inclined to think that our story is fairly typical. In so many of these immigrant families in the very first generation, when the men hit something of a wall in adapting to a new culture with a new language and the most marginal—if any—jobs, it was the women who more often than not proved stronger and more flexible and held the family together, often under terrible hardships. They did this as discreetly as possible, careful to subtract nothing more in terms of pride from their men, who, no matter how great their courage when first starting on the adventure, could not deal with the sense of diminished self in a new country where it was turning out to be so hard to make a living, despite all the seeming new freedoms.

Of my grandfather's pride in being an American, and of his intentions for his family to be as American as possible, there can be no doubt. I recently came upon some of the letters he wrote to my father, then a sergeant with the American Expeditionary Forces (AEF) during World War I. He was thrilled that two of his sons had gone back to Europe to help settle the mess there; as they were now so American by dint of wearing his new nation's uniform in so patriotic a struggle, then so was he also that American. Perhaps my father would be on duty when President Wilson came to Paris for the Peace Talks. "Don't get into any mischief in Paris," he admonished my father in one letter, and above all else, he added, "don't disgrace the Halberstams in Paris."

There was gradually in our family, on both sides, a growing confidence about our place in America. The younger children in general were more Americanized and their education was better. They were permitted greater freedom of action—their older siblings often arguing on their behalf with the parents against the more traditional rules of the home, rules set in the old country. The anxieties of the grandparents, their fears that were rooted in the old country as well as their nervousness about how secure they were in the new one and their uncertainty about what to expect and how to behave, were passed on in ever smaller increments. Of course, there was a quantum change with the arrival of the grandchildren—the pull on them was the pull of their young American peers in the schoolyard, not the pull of the old ways in Russia and Poland and Austria.

My father, being the family's first professional man (he had, in typical American fashion, come back from World War I and, encouraged by the doctors there, gone to college and then medical school to become a surgeon), was the sun king of his family, a strikingly handsome man. He had great natural charm, and his graduation from Tufts Medical School marked our family's first stop toward the better part of the American dream. On my mother's side there was, after a time, a surprising amount of prosperity—her older brother Harry, after his father's death, had packed up the family, moved to Boston, opened up a commercial paint store, and soon prospered. In time he moved to a wonderful suburban home, bought Red Sox season tickets, and purchased a summer home in Falmouth on Cape Cod—all things virtually unknown in a family such as ours. Not surprisingly, neither he nor his older siblings got very much in the way of education after high school, but, because of his success, my mother went to Simmons College in Boston and got her master's degree in education at Boston University, and her younger brother Aaron, the baby of the family, went to Harvard and Harvard Medical School.

Our family has inevitably broadened out in the modern America. When I was a boy, all the members of my father's family lived within thirty or forty miles of my grandparents' house in Torrington, in the different industrial towns of north-western Connecticut, except for us, because my father practiced medicine in New York. My mother's family all lived in the Boston area, except for Aaron, my uncle, who seemed to be more attached to my father's family than his own and lived in Winsted, just a few miles from Torrington. Now we've branched out a great deal; moved all over the country, principally into the Sunbelt; and met and married people that we never would have met back in a more geographically and socially limiting and limited era.

The maiden name of my wife, Jean Halberstam, is Sandness and her people are Norwegian and Swedish, living mostly in the upper Midwest. Some have been farmers and some have been ranchers; they are Lutheran, serious, hard-working, incredibly purposeful, utterly admirable people. They tend to be much closer to the land than my side of the family; they can, unlike us, sing without being off key; and there is a far stronger sense of pacifism on Jean's side than on my side. Both her parents had died by the time we were married, but I did in time meet her people and liked them, especially her cousin Claire Sandness, her godfather and the son of her father's oldest brother. I was thrilled to meet him, not only because he is a lovely and good man who now raises quarterhorses, but because he has a marvelous face, looking much like Eliot Richardson, the former attorney general of the United States. I feel like we've needed a jawline like that in our family for a long time.

My daughter has both those bloodlines running through her. She has started off life more privileged than her mother or I and has gone to better schools at an earlier age, in many cases schools that neither I nor most assuredly my parents could have attended. Sometimes I am inclined to ponder how American she is (as my parents and grandparents must have pondered how American my brother and I were, so different in our more privileged young lives, with even a touch of the suburbs in our lives when we were teenagers, and so much more affected by peer friendships that must have been inexplicable to them). I sometimes think of how much my father, who died thirty years before she was born, would have loved this wonderfully funny, very modern, yet quite traditional young woman with her own powerful sense of obligation, her instinct to carry on without being asked, something of an unspoken tradition in our family—the idea that those to whom much is given must give back.

And I ponder as well where and when the Americanization of our family began: Was it when my father saw his first big-league baseball game and became an instant lifelong fan? Was it when he made the Johnsonburg High football team (at least I think it's the Johnsonburg team)? Was it when he volunteered for the AEF? Was it when my Uncle Harry moved the family from Tennessee to Boston and opened his store after his own father's death? But of course the real beginning was when they all first reached Ellis Island, the day they got off the boat. They were American because they chose to be American and had made that perilous journey to get here. I remember what Pat Moynihan, the New York senator and student of American immigration, once said about people like them. He had dissented from the famed Emma Lazarus poem about the tired and the poor—he spoke instead of what extraordinary people the immigrants who came here were, perhaps not in the material sense, but in their strength, their courage, and their willingness to journey into the unknown with so little except for their own willpower and their faith in the future.

◆ ◆ ◆

Over the years, like virtually every writer and social critic I know, I've had my own running arguments with my country, not surprising in my case for someone whose first reporting jobs were covering the early days of the Civil Rights movement in the South and then reporting on the beginning of the war in Vietnam. But I don't think I ever lost my love for America nor, perhaps even more important, something my parents taught me: my appreciation for its possibilities. As I've grown older I've become more convinced than ever that for all our contentiousness, we are always engaged in a great marathon debate and search for a just, democratic society, one that respects individual rights but allows the country to remain strong. The forces at play in this struggle, both exterior and interior, change and shift all the time, and thus the debate changes all the time. But the debate continues. The tensions in it—sometimes it's very ugly—do not mean we are less democratic than we think or than we used to be; rather it means that the terms of the debate and perhaps sometimes the technology of it are always changing.

As I enter my seventh decade I am intrigued that America, for all its flaws, for all the things I dissent from, remains so powerful a beacon to so many of the less favored of the world who understand the most elemental part of our social contract: If you come here and work hard, your children have a chance to rise above you in just one generation. The irony of that never escapes me—that at times when our own domestic disputes are sharper than ever, we remain more luminescent to the rest of the world than ever before. We offer, I think, an almost unique deal in the eyes of much of the rest of the world—come here and try it, remember that the first generation will have to sacrifice, but chances are that the next generation will have a far better chance of living a good life and enjoying far greater personal liberty than in the old country. Not everyone accepts the deal with equal enthusiasm. A few years ago I had a cab driver relatively recently arrived from Moscow. He had been a violinist in the old country and he played with various groups here, clearly in his estimation not to the level of his abilities, and therefore was also forced to drive a cab. He had, he said, been here all of two years. I asked him how he liked our country. "What's to like?" he answered. I asked if he had a family. Yes, two daughters. And how were they doing, I asked. Well, the older was at Yale on a full scholarship, and the younger had just been accepted at Harvard on a full scholarship. You're right, I thought to myself, what's to like.

We remain, for all our flaws, a place where for new Americans—as opposed to the descendants of slavery—the status and burdens of the past are more lightly imposed on the individual than anywhere else. Here more than anywhere else you are free to become the person of your dreams, to choose, with a bit of luck and hard work, your profession; you have the right to reinvent yourself and become the person you wanted to be rather than the person you feared you might become. Sometimes when I'm at a New York dinner party, where the guests are amazingly diverse, very successful, and represent in the truest sense the new post-war meritocracy, I like to imagine, instead of the company assembled, the parents or even the grandparents of those present, and the babble of voices and arguments that would ensue.

The best story along this line, about the chance to find your own talent level so quickly in this country, was told to me about I. I. Rabi, the famed physicist. Rabi was born in the old country, in Austria, and he had come here as an infant; his father had first worked on the Lower East Side in New York, making women's blouses in a sweatshop. But the son was a brilliant student who went on to college, became in time an integral member of the Manhattan Project, and in 1944, won the Nobel Prize. On the occasion of that award a journalist duly came out to interview him. What did Rabi think of this great honor? the journalist asked. "What do I think?" Rabi repeated rhetorically. "I think that in the old country I would have been a tailor."

Over the years, I have been increasingly impressed that we have been able as a nation to attain such high levels of personal freedom while remaining so strong as a nation; gradually I've come to believe that the two are directly connected, that the freer we are—the closer we come to using the talents of all our citizens—the stronger we are, not merely in the arts and in communications, where we monitor the quality of individual freedom so closely, but in business and in science as well. I believe that the business and industrial explosion of the latter part of the twentieth century was fueled by some of the same forces that drove the new independence and individualism of the counterculture spirit of the 1960s; and that any number of talented people, both from the business and scientific side, who in another age might have joined up with larger, more traditional, secure companies opted for more entrepreneurial incarnations offered in an increasingly iconoclastic America with high-tech start-up companies. There is, of course, no empirical evidence of this, but it's my strong hunch, nonetheless.

I do not, either in this introduction nor in the pages of the book, want to diminish the flaws of the society. A nation's own history casts a relentless, inescapable shadow over its daily life. No chapter in American history, I think, is as cruel as that of the slave trade, nor brands American so fatefully; if we could have a national plebiscite today and undo just one part of our past, I am sure it would be to prohibit slavery from the day the founding fathers first gathered. But history does not work like that; you do not, so to speak, get easy second chances to undo the miscalculations of the past. As such the mark of slavery is still on us, making us, no matter what our other strengths and successes, incomplete and flawed in a social and spiritual sense. Much of the first five years of my journalistic career were spent covering the early days of the Civil Rights movement in both Mississippi and Tennessee. Even now, thirty-eight years after the passage of the Voting Rights Act of 1965, the action that effectively ended state-sanctioned racism, I am more aware than ever of the duality of American citizenship, of journeys to full citizenship that are white and journeys to the same full citizenship that are black, and of how different they are respectively. Those of us who covered Civil Rights in those early days, back some forty years ago, thought in our innocence that it was mostly a matter of the courts and of politics. Looking back now on the nearly fifty years that have passed since *Brown v Board of Education*, it is clear that the psychological, economic, and educational damage inflicted over some two hundred years of racial suppression were as important or more important than the sheer legal-political burden.

Racism remains the darkest stain on us, and race is the issue we struggle with most fitfully, and not by any means always successfully. A few years ago I stumbled into an unpleasant and quite futile exchange of letters with a prominent British writer, who seemed so virulently anti-American to me that he had taken up the cause of Slobodan Milosevic, the Serb mass murderer. Attacking American policies in the Balkans (we were belatedly trying to end genocide there) was not quite enough for this writer, so he went on a prolonged tirade about America's racism. I wrote back that America was the only one of the developed nations that, for a variety of reasons—climate, richness, and abundance of fertile land—had experienced its colonial era on native soil. When the age of empire was finally over in the middle of the twentieth century, all the other colonial powers could pull back, announce they were out of the business of empire, and cut, as it were, the umbilical cord that bound colony to mother country. In America that, of course, was impossible, and the implications of it are overwhelming to this day: it means our evolution in the post-colonial era into one America is nothing less than the ultimate test of us as a democracy.

♦ ♦ ♦

The innate appreciation of country that is inherent in a book like this is, I hope, understated. We—the editors and, I believe, the writers as well—hoped to ruminate on the sources of America's strength and the forces that make it unique. I have always been a little uneasy with shows of patriotism that are too overt, many of them performed by people who in fact are neither more nor less patriotic than anyone else. This, too, is the legacy of my father, who went back in the service in World War II at the age of forty-five because he knew they needed surgeons in combat venues. Why you did it, he felt, was something you simply did not talk about. To me, wearing a pin in your lapel is not a sign that the bearer is a better (or for that matter a worse) citizen; it's merely a sign that he, or she, wears a pin in his lapel.

Patriotism, love of country, seems to me largely a private matter, something one can manifest privately. A few weeks ago, Lieutenant General Hal Moore, who commanded the American troops at the battle of the Ia Drang Valley and wrote what I think is the most brilliant book on combat in Vietnam, *We Were Soldiers Once . . . and Young*, invited my wife and me to a ceremony at West Point, where he was going to be given an alumni award—the voters being his peers. I did not know Hal Moore when I was a reporter in Vietnam, but I admire him greatly as an officer and a man (and I am delighted he was willing to write about the soldiers of a democratic society for this book). It was a glorious day for Jean and me—my friendship with Hal is one, given all the terrible pain of Vietnam, that I'm unusually proud of, and I love West Point; it's one of the most beautiful settings in America, and it is rich with living history. It was a lovely spring day, the corps of cadets marched, the band played, and it was all in all a remarkable morning. Though it was still close to September 11, and the major combat fighting in Iraq was just over, not a single word of bombast was uttered in any speech that day. If there were words, they were about duty and obligation. There was, of course, no need for bombast, for this was where it was all done, where the codes of obligation were etched into the character of the young men and women who marched in front of us; no one needed to *talk* patriotism; this, after all, was where they *did* patriotism.

My own definition of patriotism is somewhat broader, I suspect, than that of most people. To me, among the great patriots I've known were the young Civil Rights protestors whom I write about on page 178, and whom I first covered more than forty years ago when they challenged segregation at lunch counters in Nashville in the first sit-ins. If that was not dangerous enough, they then took it the next step by becoming Freedom Riders in the Deep South and challenging voting laws there. To me they were like the young men who had stormed ashore in France on D-Day; in this case they were risking their lives to make America whole, and they were doing it on native soil, in Mississippi and Alabama, the most dangerous venues in the country, and they were not carrying weapons.

◆ ◆ ◆

From the start we have seen this as a book that would reflect the forces that make America special—and dynamic. Many of the forces we describe in the book took place in the second half, or at least the second two-thirds, of the twentieth century. There is a reason for this. The America that preceded this time period was an America still coming to terms with its immense physical size (California was still more or less unsettled virgin soil); more than that, America's growth and settlement had been interrupted and damaged by a catastrophic civil war. On the eve of World War I, America was still growing into its body.

It was in the twentieth century that the forces that would set America apart became ever more distinguishable—others often identified them before we saw them ourselves. Winston Churchill, hearing of the Japanese attack on Pearl Harbor, noted the night that the deed was done, that the Allies would win, that it was now just a matter of time; that America would enter the war, that Germany would not be able to withstand American power, and that Japan, in his apt phrase, would be ground to powder.

America's twentieth-century ascent began with the advantages of geography. Two great oceans separated America from Europe in an era when European nations waged suicidal war on each other twice in a twenty-five-year period, leaving America rich in a world that was poor. That was an America just beginning to comprehend its own possibilities.

Gradually, as we've tried to reflect in these pages, a modern, new, infinitely more meritocratic and open America evolved in the post-war era. No country has ever changed so dramatically, I suspect, in so short a period of time from the America of 1900 to the America of 2000, from a predominantly rural nation of 76 million (some 46 million of them still defined as living rural lives of whom only 95,000 young people finished high school each year and about 30,000 went off to college) grown into a cutting-edge superpower of 276 million, of whom nearly 2.3 million enter college each year.

We have invited a diverse and talented group of writers and intellectuals to write about these sources of strength. I am deeply touched that so many agreed to take part in something that offered so little in terms of payback and took them away from their own more pressing projects. In editing, Jean and I have tried to be minimalists. That means the book has no one central voice—that is, the kind of smooth but bland uni-voice often found in encyclopedias. Rather, the voices are highly individualistic, as are obviously the viewpoints as well. We thought from the start that this would turn out to be an advantage, and that it would add to the texture and strength of the book. Now that the book is completed, we are all the more convinced that though we set the general direction, it is our colleagues who really became the guides on the most specific parts of the trip. In any number of instances, we had only a rough sense of what we wanted, and we got back—because of the passion and talent of our writers—something far richer than we ever expected. That made it fun for us, and we are grateful to all the writers for their willingness to be part of something we feel is quite special: a celebration of a country that is still a work in progress.

◆ ◆ ◆

Somehow miraculously, we as a nation remain young. We have, I believe, a certain elasticity in our processes that allows us to change, adjust, and deal with the changing pressures and needs of modern life, while holding onto the vision of those who went before us; newcomers, like my own grandparents, more often than not appreciate the unique vision of the founding fathers, in no small part because they have something much darker with which to compare it. I was thinking of this the other day when I went to my doctor's office for a routine blood test. The medical technician in his office who took my blood sample is a young woman named Mihaela Opritoiu, who came here some eight years ago from Romania. She had taught philosophy in high school, and her husband had been an electrical engineer, and they had been through the worst of the Ceausescu years, the cruel totalitarianism of the old Communist order. Then she had high hopes for the new post-Communist era, but the transition had been slow and hard; democracy did not arrive readily and unblemished. There had been a day when her young son had pointed at a candy bar in a store window and said he wanted it, and she had checked the price and found it was prohibitive. On that day Mihaela and her husband had decided to apply for the lottery for visas to America, and they had won. And so she and her family had set off by plane from a country and a world where, for most of her lifetime, the authorities had told people what they could do and what they could think, where they could live, and where they could travel to. (Owning a passport and settling in the city of your choice was not, in much of Eastern Europe, a citizen's right.) And so, knowing no one here and without anyone to meet them, they landed at Kennedy Airport on July 29, 1995 ("a date I never forget," she called it), and began the long and complicated process facing new immigrants, including the fingerprinting and the myriad forms to be filled. And finally they were done. Completely unsure of herself—what should she do now, surely there were more orders to be obeyed?—Mihaela turned to the last of the immigration officials and asked him, "Where should I go now?" He looked at her and answered, words she will never forget, "Lady, it's a very big country and it's a very free country—go wherever you like." ★

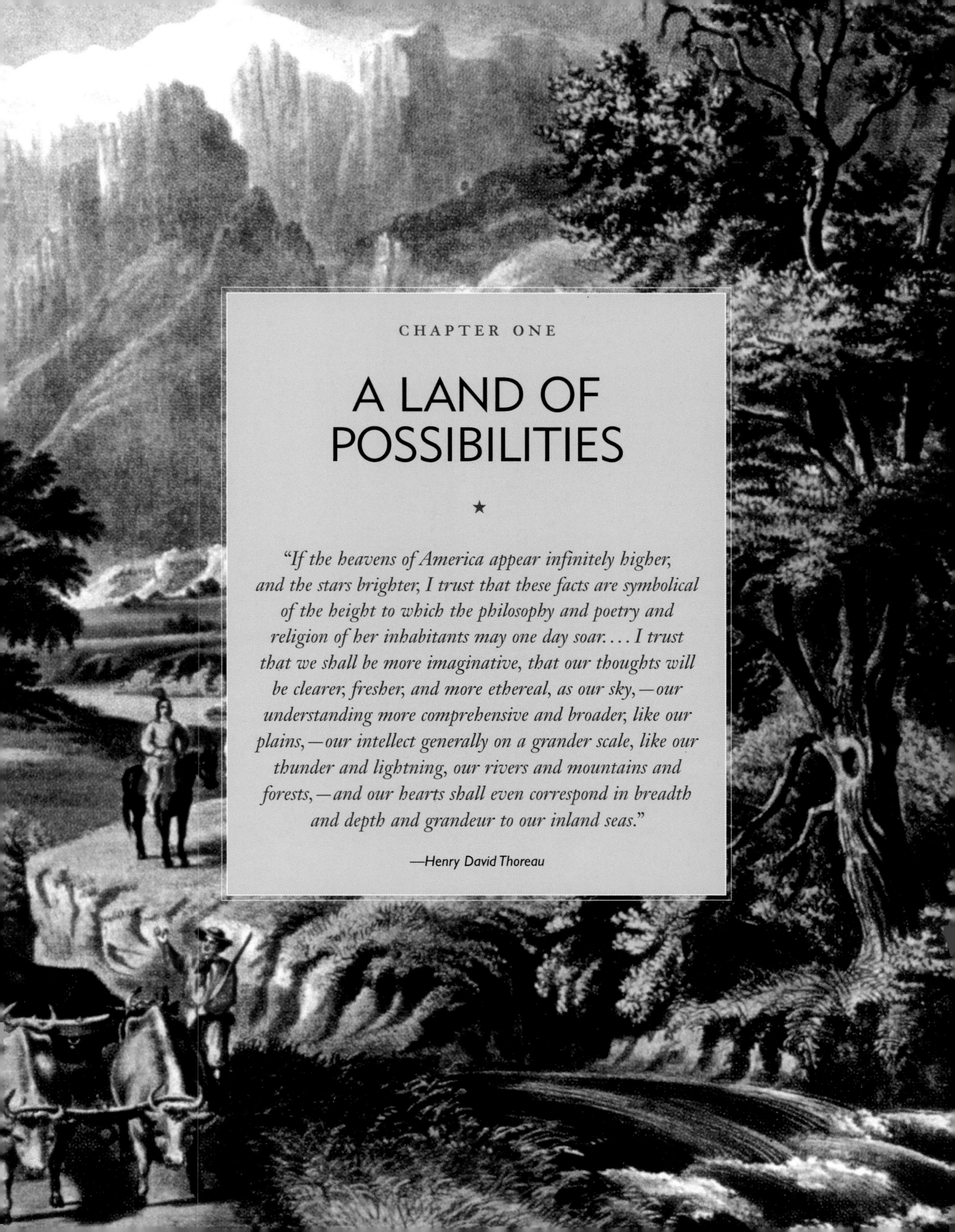

CHAPTER ONE

A LAND OF POSSIBILITIES

★

*"If the heavens of America appear infinitely higher,
and the stars brighter, I trust that these facts are symbolical
of the height to which the philosophy and poetry and
religion of her inhabitants may one day soar.... I trust
that we shall be more imaginative, that our thoughts will
be clearer, fresher, and more ethereal, as our sky,—our
understanding more comprehensive and broader, like our
plains,—our intellect generally on a grander scale, like our
thunder and lightning, our rivers and mountains and
forests,—and our hearts shall even correspond in breadth
and depth and grandeur to our inland seas."*

—Henry David Thoreau

The Promise of America

by Vartan Gregorian

THE FIRST CONCEPTION I ever had of America was of a beautiful, faraway land, where I was told that my mother, Shooshanik, had gone, undertaking a journey on which I could not accompany her. I was a young boy, an Armenian living in Tabriz, Iran, in the years before World War II and I did not understand that I was being told this because my gentle, dark-eyed, and beloved mother had died. No one in the family had the heart to reveal the truth to me. I had no real idea of what death was, and I believed what I was told. So, for many years, America to me was a place of dreams where my mother was living and from where, one day, she might return to me.

Later, when I could scrape up enough money to go to one of the three local movie houses, America became the fantasyland I saw in moving pictures—all of which, by the time they got to Tabriz, were already out of date. Still, I became a movie addict, convinced that what I saw onscreen painted a true picture of American life: surely, in America, the good guys always wore white hats and the bad guys black ones (and when the good guys were knocked off their prancing steeds, they jumped right back on, their spotlessly clean hats still perfectly balanced above their noble brows); surely in America justice prevailed, goodness triumphed, and all stories ended happily. The movies were a respite, for me, from the monotonous routine of life in Tabriz, where my family—led by my extraordinary, indomitable grandmother, who became my protector, advocate, and surrogate mother— struggled to keep food on the table and a roof over our heads. America was where the Keystone Kops frolicked, along with Laurel and Hardy, Charlie Chaplin, and Abbott and

> "BUT PERHAPS WHAT IMPRESSED ME MOST ABOUT THE COUNTRY WAS THAT IT TRULY IS THE LAND OF OPPORTUNITY. IT IS ALSO—AND I SAY THIS FROM PERSONAL EXPERIENCE— A LAND OF GREAT GENEROSITY."

Giddy immigrants react with joy to their first glimpse of the Statue of Liberty, opposite. Between 1900 and 1910, some nine million people arrived from abroad. Most could not speak English and had acquired what knowledge they had of the United States largely from American pop culture—like the Lone Ranger.

Costello; it was the home of cowboys like the Lone Ranger, Tom Mix, Hopalong Cassidy, and heroes like Douglas Fairbanks, John Wayne, Clark Gable, and Randolph Scott. In America, even the dogs were brave and resourceful: I was a big fan of Rin Tin Tin. There were gangster movies, too, full of excitement and centered around liquor, "dames," and bank robberies. The movies also showed me that America was a place where individuals stood up for their rights, where good people defended each other and respected each other's land and property, where kindly teachers and doctors staffed schools and hospitals, where even the policemen were kind and everyone was willing to help those who were hard-pressed to help themselves. Another image I had in my mind about America was that it must be a clean country—so clean that there weren't even any ants!

That was my idea of America when I was growing up. I also had a few encounters with "real" Americans, such as the occasional GI, for example, and a handful of American missionaries; the latter all wore glasses, which gave me the idea that America must be a country of such avid readers that everyone strained their eyes by reading lots of books! There were some tombstones of Americans who had died in Tabriz and were buried in the Armenian

In a swirl of light and noise, cabs navigate New York's Times Square. Early immigrants here sometimes faced a backlash: "No Irish Need Apply" appeared in job ads.

cemetery, which made me think that all Americans were Christians. In addition to these brushes with Americans, my father had graduated from the American Memorial High School in Tabriz, and I made one visit to the American hospital in town when my sister had an appendectomy. But that was my total knowledge of all things American.

Hollywood, of course, had not prepared me for the reality of America. When I finally arrived in New York—as a poor student miraculously headed for Stanford University—I was totally overwhelmed. The city was huge, massive, powerful. The varieties of sounds, colors, and shapes dazzled me. I had never seen so many cars, buses, ambulances, so many fire engines, police cars, taxis, or people in one place. The nonstop action on Broadway and in Times Square stunned me; I had never thought it possible for a city not to sleep or to have so much entertainment, so many bars and theaters, so many nightclubs, so much nudity, so many stations of sin and fantasy. But most impressive of all, I had never imagined seeing so much light and electricity in a single city. I saw New York as the City of Cities, the embodiment of Power and Sheer Energy.

This was the America of abundance, a land of wealth and possibility. But when I began my studies, for the first time I also began to learn about the structure and ideals that undergird the nation: I read, for example, *But We Were Born Free*, by Elmer Davis, a defense of the freedom of speech in America. I also studied the debates about ratifying the Constitution immortalized in the Federalist Papers and anti-Federalist writings, both sides of the argument rich with proposals for how a fledgling country should delegate power and protect human rights. What kind of a country did the Founding Fathers want? They wrote passionately about their ideas and then refined them in the Bill of Rights. I read about the moral issues surrounding the toleration of slavery and the final elimination of this abominable institution, which nearly split the nation apart, and about the practical exigencies of preserving the Union after the Civil War. And I was deeply impressed when I read Alexis de Tocqueville's writings about America and agreed with the term he coined—"individualism"—to describe the American character. I also concurred with de Tocqueville's belief that at their best, Americans combined self-interest with public interest, and that they had laid down the foundations of participatory democracy and taken hold of the very life and fabric of America through the creation of both local and national organizations—community action groups, associations, committees, volunteer agencies, and other entities—all designed to improve society through the joint effort of free citizens. This was, and continues to be, one of the country's greatest strengths.

It was at Stanford that I also began to understand that perhaps America's greatest wealth is its educational system. As I went through my years of schooling and later became a professor and university dean, provost, and president, I was, in addition, deeply impressed by the range of America's public schools and public libraries, but particularly by its vast array of colleges and universities, which have opened, gradually, to almost all Americans, but also to the international community. This welcoming of students from abroad meant that people like me, who at one time could only dream of studying in America, could actually be accepted not only to public universities but to private institutions like Stanford, as well. The research and knowledge generated by America's network of higher-education institutions, which is disseminated throughout the world, is another of the nation's greatest strengths and an international gift that benefits not only Americans but also people all across the globe.

When I discovered the works of Frederick Turner, I discovered yet another America: the "endless frontier," the restless

"westering" and expanding country that was irrepressible in its mobility, unstoppable in its endless quest to keep growing, moving, building, and changing. That eager, impatient country also became part of my growing storehouse of ideas about America.

Students at Oberlin College in the 1970s experiment with life in a coed dorm. The chance of an American education was a large draw for immigration.

There were, however, some troubling and disappointing realities about America that confronted me, too. While I was impressed by the fact that America was indeed the land of immigrants, a "nation of nations," and a microcosm of humanity, it didn't take long for my experiences to dispel any notions I had that in America all the ethnic groups and races lived in peace, harmony, and equality. Naively, I had thought that all the racial issues in America had been settled in the aftermath of the great Civil War and with the issuance of Abraham Lincoln's Emancipation Proclamation, so I was shocked to see segregation, discrimination, ghettoization, and poverty—especially in a land that provided such a wealth of opportunities to immigrants. It was tragically ironic, I thought, that immigrants from distant lands should, in many cases, be welcomed and treated better and find more doors open to them than native-born African Americans and other Americans of color.

Still, for me, in America there was always much more good than bad, because Americans always attempted, in good faith, to deal with vexing issues. In addition, I found that in America, work had dignity and hard work was rewarded with recognition. Work also had variety, and individuals had much more ability to choose work that would satisfy and interest

them than I had ever dreamed possible. But perhaps what impressed me most about the country was that it truly is the land of opportunity. It is also—and I say this from personal experience—a land of great generosity. Recently, when I wrote about my life in a book called *The Road to Home*, I thought about the idea of calling it, instead, "With the Kindness of Strangers," because my life in America has been blessed by the benevolence extended to me by total strangers. Indeed, when I first arrived in New York I stayed in the home of a stranger, an Armenian American who was the director of the Taft Hotel's auxiliary services, and when I arrived in San Francisco, on the last leg of my journey to Stanford University, I lived in the home of another Armenian American. Even the story of how I traveled from the east coast to the west is a story of a goodhearted stranger: arriving at the airport in New York, I realized that I had lost my airplane ticket and I became desperate, since I was due at school the next day. Of course, I also had no money to replace the ticket. Horrified, angry, full of self-pity, shame, and desolation, and with tears streaming down my cheeks, I was at a loss for what to do. Seeing my desperation, a ticket agent told me, "I have never done what I am about to do: I will stamp this empty envelope, marked New York to San Francisco, without a ticket in it. You can board the plane. But you must stay on board all the way. Do not disembark. Stay on it until you get to San Francisco." Grateful, yet fearful, I

An African American drinks at segregated water cans in Oklahoma City in 1939. Many immigrants found discrimination against blacks shocking.

Beflagged spectators line the route of the 1993 Dominican Day Parade in New York City. In recent decades, the ethnic populations of New York, growing in size and confidence, have increasingly found ways to demonstrate pride in their heritage and backgrounds.

boarded the midnight plane. The fourteen-hour flight stopped in Chicago, Kansas City, Phoenix, and Los Angeles before arriving in San Francisco. At each stop, I told the stewardess that I did not feel well and would rather stay aboard. The generosity of the airline clerk, one of my first encounters with an American, had a lasting impact on me. Even in New York, this massive metropolis, individuals mattered.

It was around this time, in 1958, that I received my first practical lesson in democracy. I was standing in line at a Howard Johnson's restaurant, and a military officer, a colonel, was standing behind me. Instinctively, I attempted to give my

place to him, as was the practice in the old country, but he refused. He simply said to me, "There is a line."

It was in America that I also realized how diasporas—Jewish, Polish, Italian, Greek, Indian, Irish, and many others—were not necessarily simply parochial entities but served as bridges of acculturation to America. The ethnic press, for example, that served the many immigrant groups in the United States were also transatlantic links that helped to commingle the heritage of the "old country" with the dynamism of the new. For me, being both an outsider—an immigrant, a child of the Armenian diaspora—and, eventually, an insider, provided a unique perspective on this nation, which is constantly reinventing and renewing itself, as well as a deep appreciation for its resiliency, its ability to emerge from each danger, each downturn, seemingly stronger than before. Most of all, coming from a traditional society, a region ruled by monarchies, I especially appreciated the mobility—both social and geographical—provided, even encouraged, by American society. I found that, among Americans, social mobility is an article of faith: they deeply and truly believe that with enough education and effort they can change their circumstances for the better and improve not only their own lives but the lives of their families as well. Often, they are exactly right: they can reinvent themselves, change careers and localities, ascend the social ladder or decide not to climb it at all, if that's what they prefer.

A 1919 poster entices immigrants to America, offering a better chance to "earn more, learn more," and "own a home." A golden city rises beyond the Statue of Liberty.

I was also touched by a new phenomenon I found in America: philanthropy. And I was stunned by the extent and scope of American philanthropy—how ordinary citizens gave so regularly and freely as a way of investing in their society and its future.

All the freedoms America stood for —the freedoms of speech, of thought, of assembly and dissent, along with an individual's right to his or her privacy—are all luxuries in many countries and on many continents. I have always cherished and

believed in these freedoms. Indeed, when I became a citizen of the United States in 1979, I invoked many of these ideals in a speech I delivered at my naturalization ceremony, which involved seventy-seven other immigrants from twenty-seven countries. Addressing my peers on this momentous occasion, I said:

"We, America's newest citizens, are immigrants like our forefathers who founded this nation of nations. We come from dozens of countries, from many cultures, from many continents, many faiths, many colors, many languages, many accents, many races. We come from different social and economic backgrounds and from different political persuasions. Whether we came to the United States for economic opportunity, political or religious asylum, education, security, or reunification with our families and relatives, we share a common faith in this country.

"We share James Madison's vision of a country built on diversity and idealistically guided by its motto, *E Pluribus Unum*—out of many, one. This is a land where faiths, cultures, races, and ethnic groups coexist and contribute to America's democracy as well as to its dynamism and creativity.

"We, the newest citizens in the U.S., like so many of our immigrant ancestors, have come not only to enjoy the benefits of America but also to work for its development and welfare. We have come to lend a hand in reaching out for democracy's ideals. We know that the American

New American citizens take the oath at a New York baseball stadium, left. Freedoms taken for granted in America— of speech, of thought, of assembly, of privacy— dazzled immigrants who were fleeing more restrictive cultures.

dream is not only about making money, advancing in careers, or finding opportunity. We know that, above all, the American dream is about living in a land that has a profound respect for human dignity, freedom, and for men's and women's potentialities. We have come to share America's legacy and mission and to contribute to that 'perfect union,' as envisaged by our Constitution."

But even with all the potential for individual achievement that is inherent in American society, if anyone had told me, long ago, that a foreign student like me, a young man who came to the United States with a limited ability to speak English and a limited knowledge of what kind of country America truly was, would have the opportunity to accomplish all that I have—from being the first person in my family to attend a university to becoming president of an Ivy League university—I would have considered all that to be an impossible story conjured up by a fantastic and possibly addled mind. But these things happen in America, and these things happened to me.

But what would my life have been like had I not come to America? Gabriel García Márquez, in his novel *Love in the Time of Cholera*, speaks of the conviction that human beings are not born once and for all on the day their mothers give birth

Another cherished freedom—of religion—allows a Muslim street vendor in New York City to take a moment to pray in December of 2001.

to them, but that life obliges them over and over again to give birth to themselves. I have often speculated about what I would have made of myself, given my circumstances. I am not certain, for example, that I would have finished high school because of the unpredictable state of my father's finances. Perhaps I would have become a famous thief, like one of my friends. Or perhaps I would have been an assistant clerk in the Armenian prelacy, or a subdeacon in the church. Beirut changed all that. The Collège Arménien gave me both an Armenian and a European education; it internationalized my outlook and broadened my horizons.

But what if I had gone no further than that, if I had not been accepted by Stanford and gone to America in 1956? I still would have been a teacher—I know that for a fact. When I graduated from the Collège Arménien in Beirut, Lebanon in 1955, there was a distinct possibility that I would have gone to Brazil to become director of the Armenian high school in São Paulo. If that position did not materialize, I could have stayed in Beirut, teaching Armenian history and culture, and I would have continued to write about these subjects for Armenian periodicals. In either case, whether or not I would have been able to receive a university education is a question mark that must remain to this day. Certainly, I would have had a different family, because I would never have met my wife at Stanford, and so never have fathered my sons. I would have had a much more ethnically homogeneous group of friends. I certainly would have been a person with a parochial outlook and would not have met all the eminent professors, scholars, men and women of letters, journalists, artists, diplomats, leaders of republics, monarchs, even presidents of the United States it has been my privilege to know and sometimes work with. My perspectives would not have been international and there would have been, as García Márquez has said, no possibility to reinvent myself.

So America not only allowed me to transcend myself and my fortunes but helped me—indeed, forced me—to cross cultural borders, to know people different from me, with different backgrounds and different ways of life. As I said in my naturalization speech, America is about possibilities. My life as a teacher in Lebanon would have been predictable. Here, my life has been a series of adventures. What more could I ask for than that?

Because of America's many gifts to me—including the fact that it was in America that I married and started a family—I have always been concerned with how I can repay some portion of the opportunities provided to me by so many individuals and institutions in this country. Early on, it seemed to me that the best way to do this would be to become a teacher, and now, after having taught some twelve thousand students over the course of my career, it has always been my ardent hope that I have been able to impart them some sense of the extraordi-

nary ideals and ideas upon which this country is founded, making it truly the "noble experiment" that Thomas Jefferson so fervently believed in. Equality, justice, the supremacy of law, a representative government predicated on true democracy, the promise of "life, liberty, and the pursuit of happiness" celebrated in the American Declaration of Independence, the respect for the intrinsic worth of the individual and the acknowledgment of individuals' rights embedded in the Bill of Rights: these uniquely American values must be taught, discussed, and remembered time and time again.

A lone voter in Chicago in 2000 makes his preferences known. The children of immigrants— especially the Irish— often found their way into politics, notably in large cities like Boston and here in Chicago.

I have always believed that America is a work in progress, a nation of individuals still pursuing a vision of that "perfect union" of humanity, ideals, freedom, justice, and equality first contemplated by our Founding Fathers. The nation certainly has problems and faces many challenges— particularly, in finding ways to close the gap between the ideals enunciated by leaders and the practical realities of day-to-day life in America, as experienced by its citizens—but we are a free people, good hearted, well intentioned, and able to deal with whatever lies ahead of us. As I noted in my speech of July 4, 2001, which I delivered at Monticello, the home of Thomas Jefferson, though America is not perfect, it is definitely "perfectible."

Expanding Horizons

by James Hoge

FROM PIONEER DAYS to the present, a sense of geographic security has shaped the American imagination. The early settlers were keenly aware that keeping a certain distance from the Old World was critical to their hopes for a more equitable society. In the New World, they had to contend with untamed forests and hostile natives but not with oppressive aristocracies or powerful neighbors to the north and south. To the east, the vast Atlantic Ocean limited intrusions from Europe's naval powers, and the Pacific Ocean provided similar protection once westward expansion was completed.

Physical separation and bountiful nature were the ultimate luxuries for the new nation. It could forge a path-breaking democracy and get rich with only limited threats from established great powers. Such dangers as there were arose most frequently in the early years of the American republic when Great Britain, France, and Spain continued to vie for stakes in the New World. America parried their acquisitiveness by staying clear of Europe's political rivalries and, through the Monroe Doctrine, keeping them from spilling into the western hemisphere.

America ventured forth mainly to advance its trade. A feisty U.S. Navy sailed as far from home as the Mediterranean, but primarily to destroy marauding pirates. Except for the short-lived disaster of 1812, war was avoided. Instead, skilled diplomacy and a bit of luck secured a number of the young republic's interests. None was more significant than the purchase of the Louisiana territory from France in 1803. For $15 million, President Thomas Jefferson doubled the area of the United States. That diplomatic masterstroke,

> "CLEARLY, THE GEOGRAPHY OF SECURITY WAS NOW GLOBAL. . . . THE OCEANS WERE NO LONGER BARRIERS BUT HAVENS FOR MISSILE-LAUNCHING SUBMARINES. AND THE SKIES WERE PATHWAYS FOR NUCLEAR-TIPPED MISSILES."

A jagged coastline guards America's Pacific shore, opposite; an early nineteenth-century navy frigate, below, does the same in the Atlantic. By the 1890s, when Indian resistance finally ended, the nation had realized its Manifest Destiny and stretched from sea to sea. A period of isolationism followed that lasted until World War I drew America into international affairs.

America's domain reaches into Paradise: Mountains and sugar-cane fields edge a harbor on Maui, Hawaii, right. The Hawaiian islands were a commercial outpost early in the twentieth century but would become an important base of military operations for the United States. A Japanese attack on Pearl Harbor on Oahu precipitated the nation's entry into World War II.

coupled with the Lewis and Clark cross-country exploration, gave the fledgling nation its "manifest destiny" to build a continental power. And build it did with constant government support throughout the nineteenth century. A series of congressional acts offered cheap land grants to farmers willing to settle the West, and other federal funds spread colleges and libraries through the new territory. One-sided acquisitions of Mexican and Indian lands were also essential to the conquest of the West.

After the Civil War, America rose swiftly to the first ranks of economic powers. By the last decades of the century, it was also a military power that embraced the imperial spirit of the times by seizing the Philippines from Spain in the brief war of 1898. The republican idealism on which the nation was founded restrained further imperial adventures, but it did not altogether impede assertive engagements with the world. President Theodore Roosevelt sent the White Fleet around the globe to give notice of America's new eminence. And he made available his big stick and soft voice to mediate the Russo-Japanese war in 1905. During those turn-of-the-century years, America was also busily acquiring or leasing the Panama Canal and overseas islands like Hawaii, eastern Samoa, and Guam. The purpose was not to establish beachheads for advances into Asia. Rather, it was a defensive check against further Russian or British penetration of the Pacific.

Continental defense was the motivating idea for these offshore sallies, and it remained America's basic security doctrine well into the twentieth century. Its enduring potency floated on the two oceans that constrained meddling by Eurasian powers. The preference for staying at home and avoiding foreign entanglements was also reinforced by strong social biases. The European and Irish immigrants who flowed into America during the nineteenth century were sentimental about their cultural roots but hostile toward the elites and governments of their countries of origin.

They rekindled the antipathy to the Old World of the early settlers. When coupled with the enduring faith in geographic security, the ground was laid for sturdy resistance to involvement in World War I, even though America was a major power by then. Woodrow Wilson campaigned against participating in the European conflagration. Once in the presidency, he held off committing American troops for two years. His hand finally was forced by mounting attacks on U.S. cargo ships and a growing fear that a German-dominated Europe would endanger American interests.

President Woodrow Wilson addresses the assembled houses of Congress on April 6, 1917. Resisting isolationist impulses, Congress voted for war with Germany.

This was a dent in America's belief that continental isolation provided sufficient security. But it was only a dent. The American public and military brass remained wedded to continental defense. Even Wilson's dramatic championing of a

League of Nations could be viewed as an effort to make the world safe for democracy and for American self-absorption. The League was supposed to end war and assure perpetual peace through international regulation.

Senatorial rejection of the League not only signaled skepticism of such a utopian project, it also registered anew America's intent to avoid overseas entanglements in the lethal rivalries of other powers. Continental defense, based on favorable geography, was still the favored route to preserving America's uniqueness. In the buildup to World War II, America's potential participation was again strongly resisted by inward-looking military strategists and a wary public. To transform America into a globe-spanning fighting machine, it would take a major provocation. Japan provided it by attacking Pearl Harbor on December 7, 1941. Five days later, Germany and Italy made the provocation global by declaring war against the United States.

Even then, the initial public demand was an insular one of assuring that U.S. territory was never again attacked. Only late in the war did a larger view emerge. On the military side, a rising generation of officers saw the inadequacy of continental defense in an era of airplanes and missiles. For the post-war era, they concluded that American security required forward positioning of forces in Europe and Asia. Political thinking underwent a similar revision. The United Nations came into being largely because of American support that had not been there for the League of Nations. That support was not just based on war-bred fears. The public was also growing more cosmopolitan. Millions of GIs, overseas for the first time, returned to cash in on the GI Bill of Rights that sent them to college in unprecedented numbers. Similar educational benefits would be available for veterans of the Korean and Vietnam wars.

Isolationism never fully dissipated but was decisively surpassed by a newly minted internationalism, most strikingly captured in the "American Century" manifesto of *Time* magazine's powerful founder, Henry Luce. He inflated the nation's "manifest destiny" from continental to global dimensions. Americans, Luce wrote, should "exert upon the world the full impact of our influence, for such purposes as we see fit and by such means as we see fit." Less stridently, U.S. statecraft set about erecting international institutions to maximize cooperation and minimize interstate frictions. Clearly, the geography of security was now global. The old continental version was a casualty of the world war and the Soviet threat. The oceans were no longer barriers but havens for missile-launching submarines. And the skies were pathways for nuclear-tipped missiles.

Thus the armed forces that were hastily cut back in 1945 were dramatically

Listening for Japanese planes, the American military turns metal ears skyward late in World War II. San Francisco's Golden Gate Bridge rises beyond.

expanded once the conflict on the Korean peninsula crystallized the global threat of the Soviet Union and its fellow communist states. Large, steady expenditures produced the most advanced ships and planes, missiles and warheads. Ground troops were mechanized. Lift capacity mushroomed. And bases were manned around the globe. The Korean War of 1950 to 1953 was only the first of a series of big and little proxy clashes. The most traumatic was the war between South and North Vietnam that ended with the fall of Saigon to the communists in 1975, two years after America ceased its twelve years of military support for the South. Among the many consequences of America's failed involvement was a rekindling of the old desire to retrench to our continent. The 1972 Democratic presidential candidate, George McGovern, epitomized widespread public despair with his convention call, "Come Home, America."

But it was not to be. Continental defense and limited political engagement were no longer possible in a globalizing world. Military budgets and diplomatic activity receded only a little and not for long in the post–Cold War era. Unleashed by the demise of superpower rivalry, ethnic clashes and terrorists acts increased and so did America's efforts to impose stability. The efforts were tiring, often unsuccessful. The armed forces were stretched thin and resources depleted without a clear sense of what national interest was being served. As the twenty-first century began, presidential candidate

George W. Bush found a public appetite for his advocacy of a more selective role for America in international affairs. There were to be fewer interventions in conflicts and no nation building. This was yet one more turn of the dial toward insularity.

And then the terrorist attacks on America of September 11, 2001, prompted the quickest and most far-reaching return to interventionism since the Korean War. Terrorism took the place of communism as an overarching threat, and Bush promised to go everywhere and use all means to eradicate terrorists and the states that support them. Within two years, Bush reorganized the government and the nation's legal code, ramped up the military budget, and launched two military campaigns. Coun-terterrorism was the driving force for these actions and many others, including nation building, in practice if not in name.

Delegates mingle prior to a meeting of the United Nations Security Council on March 19, 2003, at which they will discuss the developing American–Iraqi situation. The UN represents an attempt by the world's nations to police themselves.

Many citizens found much to oppose, ranging from the military actions to the administration's tough style. But very few argued for a return to continental isolation.

The world was smaller and engagement of one kind or another was unavoidable. The comforts of benign borders and barrier oceans were fading from the American imagination, unlikely to be revived again.

The Manifestations of Destiny

by *Félix F. Gutiérrez*

UP THE STREET and around the corner from our early twentieth-century Craftsman home in South Pasadena, California, is an older home that may have impacted my life even more than the wood-frame house my family has owned since 1956.

A single-story adobe home framed by red roof tiles and a cactus garden, El Adobe Flores seemed just an out-of-place curiosity near the modern apartment houses to which I delivered newspapers in the 1950s. Only later did I learn how much what happened there in January 1847 affected my life, the lives of my ancestors, and my children's lives.

It was in that adobe owned by Manuel Garfias on the Rancho Rincón de San Pascual on January 11, 1847, that Californio militia and volunteers led by Mexican captain José María Flores met to discuss whether to make peace with invading United States armed forces. Driven by a hunger for new lands to fulfill its self-proclaimed Manifest

"BORN IN 1943, I'VE ALWAYS LIVED IN A WORLD OF MORE THAN ONE LANGUAGE, CULTURE, AND NATION. I LIVE IN WHAT USED TO BE MEXICO."

Destiny, the U.S. military had prematurely proclaimed its conquest of California the previous summer shortly after learning the United States had declared war on Mexico. Mexican military units were transferred to fight closer to Mexico City, taking with them the weapons of many Californios. Mexico's leaders focused on defending the central territories, not distant outposts on the northern and western edge of what was once the Spanish Empire.

So the Californios took matters into their own hands. Outnumbering the occupation forces that imposed harsh martial law, the pobladores in Los Angeles struck back in September 1846, forcing the U.S. military to seek shelter on a merchant ship anchored at San Pedro. The Californios enjoyed "a long winning streak, from late September to mid-December—capturing the Americans at Chino . . . defeating the navy at San Pedro . . . and exacting a grim toll at San Pasqual

A Mexican-American mural dominates a sidewalk in a predominantly Latin American section of Los Angeles. About 39 million Americans now identify themselves as Latinos.

U.S. General Zachary Taylor, "Old Rough-and-Ready," leads troops attacking Mexican forces under General Mariano Arista at Palo Alto, Texas, on May 8, 1846. The battle occurred five days before the United States officially declared war on Mexico.

and La Natividad" among other battles, one historian noted. Effectively employing lances, lassoes, and superior horsemanship, the Californios restored their own order.

They faced an impressive opponent prepared for war. U.S. naval vessels could easily move troops and munitions up and down the coast. In December 1846, General Stephen W. Watts Kearny's Army of the West ended its desert trek following battles in New Mexico to join with Commodore Robert F. Stockton's forces in San Diego. Later that month their combined forces of about six hundred men prepared to move north to recapture the Pueblo of Los Angeles.

After U.S. troops attacked Mexico City in 1847, 1,193,061 square miles of land was transferred from Mexico to the United States.

Ahead of them was Flores's force of about five hundred Californio militia and volunteers, a homeland defense facing heavily armed invaders. Flores's troops' "courageous determination to defend and preserve their nationality offset the disparity of weapons, munitions, and numbers of soldiers. Even though they were at a disadvantage, they were not frightened as they were lying in wait to see if they could strike a decisive blow when the commodore approached," wrote Californio Antonio María Osio in his 1851 history of California.

U.S. military leaders had learned the hard way that the Californios were smart strategists and tough fighters. Heading north from San Diego on January 3, 1847, Commodore Stockton warned Lieutenant Colonel John Charles Frémont, inching south toward Los Angeles from San Juan Bautista, that his force of 350 men "had better not fight the rebels until I get up to aid you or you can join me on the road to the Pueblo."

These fellows are well prepared, and [U.S. Navy Captain William] Mervine's and Kearny's defeat have given them a deal more confidence and courage," Stockton wrote. "They will probably try to deceive you by a sudden retreat, or pretended runaway, then unexpectedly return to charge you after your men get in disorder in the chase. My advice is to allow them to do all the charging and running and let your rifles do the rest. In the art of horsemanship, of dodging, and running, it is in vain to compete with them."

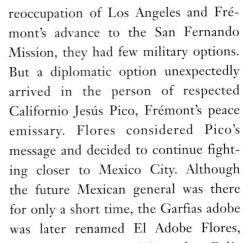

As Stockton and Kearny approached Los Angeles from the south, Flores carefully chose a battlefield. But his forces were outgunned on the banks of the San Gabriel River on January 8 and at La Mesa on January 9. To avoid damaging the pueblo and its inhabitants, the Yanquis were allowed to enter Los Angeles peacefully on January 10. Regrouping northeast of the pueblo, Flores and Californio leaders met at the Garfias adobe in present-day South Pasadena to decide their future.

Outnumbered, outgunned, and caught between Stockton and Kearny's reoccupation of Los Angeles and Frémont's advance to the San Fernando Mission, they had few military options. But a diplomatic option unexpectedly arrived in the person of respected Californio Jesús Pico, Frémont's peace emissary. Flores considered Pico's message and decided to continue fighting closer to Mexico City. Although the future Mexican general was there for only a short time, the Garfias adobe was later renamed El Adobe Flores, recognizing the Californios' last Mexican commander.

Flores's successor, Andrés Pico, and fellow Californios had faced Stockton and Kearny in battle and feared the worst if they tried to negotiate with them. In early December, Andrés Pico had beaten Kearny at the Battle of San Pasqual outside of San Diego. Eighteen U.S. troopers were killed and Kearny himself suffered lance wounds. Having never formally battled Frémont, the Californios in the adobe decided to negotiate with someone who might consider their terms.

Though outranked by General Kearny and Commodore Stockton, Lieutenant Colonel Frémont received the Californios' "propositions of peace or cessation of hostilities," and on January 12 ordered a one-day armistice to negotiate with the Californios.

Guided by terms discussed at the Garfias adobe, Andrés Pico's "Californian Forces under the Mexican Flag" met the U.S. commissioners in the home of Don Tomás Feliz at the northern end of Cahuenga Pass.

Signed on January 13, 1847, near the site of today's Universal City in the San Fernando Valley, the Treaty of Cahuenga marked the official end of military operations between Mexico and the United States in California. The Californios agreed to deliver to Frémont "their artillery and Public Arms, and . . . return peaceably to their homes conforming to the Laws and Regulations of the United States." Frémont anticipated he would need help from Californio leaders if he were appointed governor of California, a title conferred on him by Stockton three days later. So the treaty imposed no sanctions on the Californios and promised "equal rights and privileges are vouchsafed to every citizen of California as are enjoyed by the citizens of the United States of North America." However, this and similar promises in the Treaty of Guadalupe Hidalgo that ended warfare between the two nations in February 1848 were not respected by all newcomers after California joined the union. Tense relations and violence between Anglos and Californios continued well into the latter half of the nineteenth century.

El Adobe Flores is barely a footnote in history books. But its importance in the United States expansion into Spanish and Mexican territories ranging from Florida to California is more than symbolic to me. My ancestors, who came to Alta California's San Gabriel Mission before the American Revolution, were among the Californios who fought the U.S. military and others who supported their California conquest. Like most Latinos, my presence in the United States today is inextricably linked to this country's nineteenth century territorial ambitions.

Early in the 1800s, President Thomas Jefferson expressed a vision of predestined expansion into Spanish territories. This vision became a reality with the addition of Florida and part of Alabama in the Adams-Onis Treaty of 1819 and the taking of Mexico's territory from Louisiana and Arkansas west to the Pacific Ocean and as far north as Wyoming in the Treaty of Guadalupe Hidalgo of 1848 and Gadsden Purchase of 1853. After the Spanish-American War of 1898 the United States kept Puerto Rico, established governments friendly to its interests in Cuba and the Philippines, and set the stage for future

Another imperialist adventure takes troops south once again. Left, American soldiers bound for Cuba in 1898 board a train in Tampa, Florida.

military actions in the Dominican Republic, Nicaragua, Mexico, Panama, and other Latin American nations. U.S. leaders saw expansion of territory and influence as the nation's Manifest Destiny, but focused more on adding real estate than assessing the social legacy of the people on or near newly acquired lands. Along with the territories came the Latino people who lived on them, including my Californio forebears.

When I was a boy my father told me the straight facts without rancor or anger: "The Anglos came. We welcomed them. And then they turned against us." He could just as easily have said, "We didn't cross the border. The border crossed us."

The treaties allowed Mexicans in conquered territories to head south across the new border. But my ancestors had no Mexico to go back to. Their homes were now in the United States and, like most, they stayed put. Though homes have changed, we still live and own property in the San Gabriel Valley.

San Gabriel Mission, Faunded 1771 near Los Angeles, California

On an early postcard, palms front the San Gabriel Mission. From this site in 1781 a multiracial group of Spanish colonists set off to found the Pueblo of Los Angeles.

After the war my great-grandfather became a blacksmith in El Monte, repairing covered wagons and shoeing horses of Anglos reaching the Santa Fe Trail's end.

My grandfather was baptized at the San Gabriel Mission in the 1870s and became a cement contractor, laying irrigation ditches and sidewalks as agriculture and housing boomed in the San Gabriel Valley into the 1920s. Born in 1918, my father grew up in Monrovia, east of Los Angeles, was sent to segregated schools before attending high school, and then attended college on his way to becoming a junior high school teacher in the late 1940s.

Along the way we learned from the Anglos who came to California and offered them our ways, even though many felt the only meaningful remnants of Spanish and Mexican California were the names of mountains, rivers, and cities. Most felt they could offer us more than we could offer them. But my ancestors absorbed from both sides, learning the language and ways of the Anglos without rejecting their own.

Born in 1943, I've always lived in a world of more than one language, culture, and nation. I live in what used to be Mexico. Nearby is a Mexico from which people have long come north across borderlines to reinforce multicultural borderlands. My Mexican-born mother, who grew up and graduated from college in the United States, began teaching school in the 1930s. Though proudly a naturalized U.S. citizen, she strengthened our interest in the country of her birth and also a pride in recognizing our identities as Latinos in a nation of people of all races and cultures.

We Latinos who find ourselves living in territories now held by

the United States are helping to reshape America's Manifest Destiny. Though many are immigrants, we don't fit into the assimilation melting pot that once defined what was expected of newcomers. Instead, our American stew pot—in which we have retained our identity while also contributing to and absorbing the flavors of others—is becoming the prototype for the future. Though some of us are of darker shades, we also do not fit into the racial dynamics of a nation that long has seen race relations mainly as a matter of black and white. At 38.8 million people and growing, U.S. Latinos can be white, brown, black, and even Asian Pacific. We can be Catholics, Protestants, Jews, and Muslims and still be full-blooded Latinos, if there is such a thing.

African Americans, Asian Pacific Americans, Latinos, and Native Americans comprise more than a third of the nation's population and are projected to become the majority by mid-century. Americans of all colors are understanding it is to their advantage to learn about more than one language, one culture, and one nation. Latinos have been doing so for generations. And others might help themselves by taking a closer look at how we have done it.

The Nation's Backbone

by Alex Kotlowitz

I'M AN ACCIDENTAL midwesterner, lured here from New York City by a job at a small newspaper in Michigan. I assumed I'd eventually find my way back east, but seduced by the sense that from this perch I could peer into America's heart, I've lingered, planting roots, though it's rare that I identify myself as a midwesterner. Indeed, the Midwest is no longer a place of destination, a place one seeks out. It is a place where one ends up, a place where one simply finds oneself.

If one were to ask a Detroiter or a Nebraskan where he is from, it is highly unlikely that he would tell you "from the Midwest." It's a region with little cultural identity. The South, which people can lay claim to simply by their shared dialect, has spawned a school of writers and claims a common history, most of which centers around race. Or, consider the West, a territory marked by its confrontation of such urgent matters as immigration or oil exploration or the shortage of water. Here in the Midwest, a Nebraska farmer feels little kinship with an Indiana steelworker. The landscape, which is as flat as a hardwood floor, is difficult to love. The harsh Chicago "dems" and "dose" sound nothing like a Minnesotan's sprawling vowels. I dare you to find a writer who identifies him or herself as "a midwestern writer." In fact, the area's best usually leave: Sherwood Anderson, Saul Bellow, Willa Cather, Ernest Hemingway, Theodore Dreiser, Sinclair Lewis. Or others, like Richard Wright, simply pass through.

> "THE CLICHÉS HERE APPLY. THERE IS A HEARTINESS ABOUT MIDWESTERNERS. A PERSEVERANCE. AN AVERSION TO FEELING SORRY FOR YOURSELF."

Yet, this amalgamation of wine-colored wheat fields and belching foundries, of sleepy north lake country and sprightly Mississippi River coastline has come to symbolize America and what it strives to stand for: ingenuity, social cohesion, egalitarianism. A democratic temperament, if you will. It's a place, though, that is also filled,

The American Midwest provides a pair of disparate symbols: A lonely trail threads Agate Fossil Beds National Monument in Nebraska, opposite, and Chicago's Sears Tower reaches skyward, below.

as one writer has suggested, with its share of paradoxes: idealistic and populist on the one hand, materialistic and socially conservative on the other. That stew of internal contradictions personifies the American character, determined, grappling with its promise, alternately sure and unsure of itself. Nelson Algren, yet another writer who eventually emigrated for one of the coasts, wrote of Chicago, the heart of the heartland, "once you've come to be part of this particular patch, you'll never love another. Like loving a woman with a broken nose, you may well find lovelier lovelies. But never a lovely so real." He might as well have been writing about the entire Midwest.

When I arrived here in the late 1970s, the region was tottering. The family farm was disappearing and thousands of hard-working, industrious farmers were displaced, thrown off land that had been plowed by their parents and grandparents. Its industry—mostly auto and steel—was laid up, sickly and aging. Factories by the score were being shuttered. Workers were laid off. Unemployment in some places reached well into the double digits. The region acquired a new label, "the Rustbelt." People felt lost. In Flint, Michigan, once the embodiment of the nation's industrial might—it

Reflecting a diminished manufacturing base in the Midwest, out-of-work auto workers line up at an unemployment office in Detroit in the summer of 1980.

lays claim to being the birthplace of both General Motors and its adversary, the United Auto Workers—civic fathers desperate for revival sought to build a theme park called AutoWorld, a monument to the very industry that had abandoned the town. It closed within six months. It was not a good time for the Midwest. It was not a good time for America.

The clichés here apply. There is a heartiness about midwesterners. A perseverance. An aversion to feeling sorry for yourself. While in Flint, I met Mike Bennett, a sad-eyed, soft-spoken Vietnam veteran in his thirties who wore an outdated Beatles haircut. He was, to say the least, embattled. As president of a UAW local, he was fighting GM's demands for wage concessions, but he also absorbed the anger and bitterness of his members. They accused him of being a company stooge, of not fighting hard enough. He was, after all, the bearer of bad news. Moreover, they were indignant that this behemoth of a company wanted them to pay for its wrongheaded decisions over the years. And, yet, Bennett invited his coworkers—beefy, beer-bellied men and blunt-spoken women—at meeting after meeting to essentially harangue him. They argued. They disagreed about how much to give in to the company's demands. They whistled Bennett down. He'd shout over them. They'd hurl insults. He'd deflect them, and fling them right back. It was a thing of beauty—this open debate, searching for what felt just, for what felt right. Eventually, the Midwest brushed itself off and found its way to its feet. Nothing spectacular. Not a new mode of life. No new new thing. But it's the manner here, to move on, without much fuss, just finding a way.

It's the story of this place. Making do. As historian Donald L. Miller points out, when Chicago was first settled, in the early 1800s, it was "a mudhole," a "windswept prairie marsh" so inhospitable that the Miami Indians chose to settle elsewhere. Its very name is derived from an Indian word meaning "the place of the wild onion," or skunkweed. The early explorer René-Robert Cavalier, Sieur de La Salle, wrote that "the typical man who grows up here must be an enterprising man. Each day as he rises he will exclaim, 'I act, I move, I push.'" Which is what happened. Chicago became, as Miller's book title suggests, the city of the century. It became the nation's hub, its geographic and spiritual center. Crops and cattle from the plains made their way to Chicago by train, where they were stacked and butchered, and sent along to the coasts. "Modern Chicago," Miller writes, "was a triumph of engineering over nature's constraints." When it became apparent that the sewage flowing from the Chicago River into Lake Michigan might contaminate the drinking water, the city reversed the flow of the river. By the turn of the century, it was a place awash in newness, in inventiveness. You could find the daring architecture of Frank Lloyd Wright and Louis Sullivan, the bold reforms of Jane Addams and Ida B. Wells, and soon the brazen exploits of Al Capone and John Dillinger.

The Midwest was not only the place to come if you were of an enterprising nature; it became a place of refuge. Indeed, the region has been a kind of beacon for the oppressed. In the mid-nineteenth century, Germans fleeing religious and political persecution found their way here, buying farmland and settling in the cities. Norwegians and Finns fled the poverty of their homeland to become loggers and ironworkers in the north woods. In the mid-twentieth century, African Americans fleeing the legal apartheid of the South traveled by train and by car to what came to be called "the promised land." It was seen as a place in which neighbors felt a responsibility for each other but where self-reliance (or so most believed) could pay off. The northern Midwest states are characterized by a persistent liberalism, a sense of obligation to people who aren't necessarily in their midst, a commitment to the democratic ideal. Wisconsin's Bob LaFollette took on the monied interests, especially the railroads, which so dominated the region's economy early in the twentieth century. Indiana's Eugene Debs in 1893 helped form the nation's

"Stormy, husky, brawling, City of the Big Shoulders," Carl Sandburg called Chicago. Here, on a 1911 postcard, State Street bustles with citizens, many of them immigrants drawn to the city's booming factories.

first industrial union, the American Railway Union, and then went on to edit the populist Kansas-based *Appeal to Reason*. Minnesota's Farmer-Labor Party and Michigan's United Auto Workers secured the rights of working people. More recently, champions of civil rights—Eugene McCarthy and Hubert Humphrey from Minnesota, George McGovern from South Dakota— emerged from states with minuscule African-American populations.

But, again, peel the folds back, and the Midwest's contradictions emerge. You can't overlook the fact that this land also spawned the likes of the anti-Semitic Father Charles Coughlin (himself a bar of discordant notes, a defender of the ordinary man, and yet an apologist for Mussolini and Hitler) and the scapegoating, anti-communist Joseph McCarthy. Indiana harbored Ku Klux Klan chapters as strong and as frightening as anywhere in the deep South. And when Martin Luther King in a campaign for open housing made his major foray north, to Chicago, he left defeated and forlorn. This is, of course, America. Faltering, rocking back and forth, foraging for its moral compass.

A friend recently suggested to me that Chicago—and by inference the rest of the heartland—might be passé. The west coast boasts new technologies. The east coast lays claim to the center of finance, politics, and fashion. Chicago is no longer hog-butcher to the world. Now with over one hundred sweets manufacturers, it has become the candy capital of the world. The city's mayor, Richard M. Daley, is of the old school, the kind of politician who in the cover of night sends a batallion of backhoes and bulldozers to tear up a small airport he wants as a park. King Richard the Second, Chicagoans joke. Chicago still fights the battles of the twentieth century. Race—as in black-white relations—remains the deepest fissure here.

Even the city's one claim to edginess, *Playboy* magazine, has packed up shop and moved. "I love Chicago," the magazine's new editor, who's now based in New York, told a reporter. "It's my second favorite city."

The Midwest is like a parenthetical thought, a land and a people not certain—frankly, not caring—how or even whether it fits in. Midwesterners are a modest people. Defensive perhaps, but not showy. Even our rogues and roustabouts avoid the limelight. The most accomplished bank robbers of modern times are two droopy-eyed men from Kansas City, Missouri, who no one's ever heard of. Ray Bowman and Billy Kirkpatrick—or the Trenchcoat Robbers, as they came to be known because of

their sartorial tastes—liked it that way. Some may think the Midwest passé, out of touch, perhaps a backwater. And yet if you want to know what's tugging at the nation, this is the place to come. Marketers and producers still ask, will it play in the heartland, "Will it play in Peoria?" (A line, incidentally, derived from the town's demanding vaudeville audiences.)

In 1929, Robert and Helen Lynd published their landmark study of American habits and values, *Middletown*. It was an overnight sensation. The Lynds explained that they chose Muncie, Indiana, because "it's as representative as possible of American life." And what they found were a people wrestling with who they were, and who they wanted to be. They were a people, the Lynds found, who deeply believed in the notion of egalitarianism and in the possibilities arising from hard work; they embraced the Horatio Alger myth. And yet the Lynds also discovered the scandal of class, the deep divisions that ran through this typical American town. That is the Midwest, a land of dreamers and pragmatists, a grounded people struggling to reconcile promise with reality. As Algren wrote of Chicago: "Out of Man's endless war against himself we build our successes as well as our failures."

Storefronts of Main Street in Galena, Illinois, preserve the small-town ideal of midwestern cities, left. A similar midwestern town—Muncie, Indiana— was featured in Middletown, a 1929 work of social anthropology that documented midwesterners' egalitarianism and work ethic but also their anxieties and class divisions.

AGRICULTURE

The Bountiful Land

by Nick Kotz

FROM A HILL HIGH above Harper's Ferry in 1783, Thomas Jefferson looked out at "one of the most stupendous scenes in nature—in itself worth a voyage across the Atlantic." What Jefferson viewed with such awe was the natural beauty and fertile land stretched out below him at the confluence of the Shenandoah and Potomac rivers. The author of the Declaration of Independence had inhaled deeply the heady ideas of individual liberty in the New World. He was equally intoxicated by the wonders of its bountiful land.

In voluminous notebooks, Jefferson wrote down prodigious lists of the native plants, the wild game, the virgin forests, the succulent natural grasses, and the clean rivers and streams that abounded in his cherished native state of Virginia. At Monticello, his five-thousand-acre plantation, Jefferson successfully grew more than a dozen different crops with the labor of his 150 slaves—from tobacco and cotton to corn and beans, as well as eighty different varieties of vegetables and fruit. As agronomist and scientist, Jefferson experimented with native and imported plants, and he reported with great pride that his American land had the soil, aspect, and climate to make wines, "doubtless as good" as the finest ones produced in Europe.

As president of the United States in 1803, Jefferson dispatched Meriwether Lewis and William Clark to explore what natural riches might be found in the vast expanses that lay still unexamined beyond the Mississippi River. When Lewis and Clark reported back their findings in 1806, the dream of America's abundance took a quantum

"THE MIRACLE OF OUR BOUNTIFUL LAND AND TODAY'S INGENIOUS AND BOLD FAMILY FARMERS IS AN UNDER-APPRECIATED STORY, . . . FOR THE TRUTH IS THAT OUR LAND STILL IS OUR GREATEST RENEWABLE RESOURCE."

Daisies sprout alongside bales of hay on a farm in Michigan's Upper Peninsula, opposite. With much of the country well suited for agriculture, American farmers have produced a cornucopia of grains, cereals, and livestock. Their spiritual ancestor, Thomas Jefferson—a gentleman farmer from Monticello, below— envisioned a nation of yeoman farmers.

leap forward. The explorers described huge herds of buffalo and elk grazing on verdant prairie grasses, millions of acres of timber, and an amazing number of animals, birds, fishes, and plant species. From the tribes of Native Americans they encountered along their Journey of Discovery, Lewis and Clark learned how well people could feed and clothe themselves off this great land—and profit from it. As word of their discoveries spread to the eastern United States and then to Europe, the promise of America expanded still further, stirring millions of people who longed to be free and to seek a better life.

Thomas Jefferson's dream of an agrarian, land-based democracy soon sparked the imagination of wave after wave of immigrants who came to the United States seeking freedom and an opportunity to farm their own land. The serfs and indentured servants of the Old World, even those who came hoping for riches in gold and silver, soon discovered something better—rich, fertile land that could support their families for generations. The eighteenth century brought English farmers to New England; Dutch, German, Scotch-Irish, and English farmers to the Middle Colonies; and French farmers to plantations in the Virginia Tidewater. Great fortunes were built from the bountiful land and the forced toil of tens of thousands of African slaves. The potato famine in Ireland of 1848–55 and the German revolution of 1848 brought further waves of hopeful newcomers who broke the virgin sod and raised cattle and sheep from the Middle West all the way to South Texas. After the Civil War and liberation of the slaves, other Europeans came, stimulated in part by the Homestead Act of 1862, which granted 160 acres to settlers who would work the land for five years. Americans pushed west, lured by cheap or free land. Scandinavian farmers came to the upper Middle West from 1865 to 1890. The nineteenth century saw the country enriched by vast deposits of coal, copper, iron ore, and other valuable minerals, followed in the twentieth century by riches of oil and natural gas. The early twentieth century brought the Sooners and Boomers, who literally raced each other to claim land in the new state of Oklahoma. At the same time, Chinese and Japanese came as laborers on the railroads and farms, and then became successful farmers themselves. After the Vietnam War, the nation took to its bosom Vietnamese refugees, who skillfully netted shrimp off the Gulf Coast, and Hmong mountain people, who found new hope growing vegetables in the Central Valley of California. The West was conquered long ago, but the story keeps repeating itself, even into the twenty-first century—men and women seeking freedom in a land whose natural resources continue to reward the industrious and the daring.

Bison find winter browse in Yellowstone National Park. Once hunted nearly to extinction, today bison herds are thriving.

By horse and buggy—and even by bicycle—land-hungry settlers pour into the Cherokee Strip, a section of the Oklahoma Territory opened for settlement by the Dawes Act of 1887.

Underneath our spacious skies, America's lush waves of grain stretch for hundreds of miles, signifying the abundance that has fed our prosperity. Yet the miracle of our bountiful land and of today's ingenious and bold family farmers is an under-appreciated story, one that urbanites and suburbanites in a post-industrial age of communications mostly take for granted, if we think about it at all. For the truth is that our land still is our greatest renewable resource. We Americans feed ourselves on a smaller percentage of our income than any other people in the world. America remains the world's leader in agricultural exports and in food aid to hungry people throughout the world. We have the unused capacity to assist even more of our global community. We have the ingenuity and know-how to transform foreign lands enslaved by starvation into self-sufficient democracies. And our family farmers are as productive as any industry in America. Although the farm population continued to decline steadily as the nation became more urbanized, today the bulk of production comes from less than half a million American commercial farmers who innovate and risk huge investments in the face of all the uncertainties of weather and the marketplace. Unlike other American industries that have been gobbled up into larger and larger conglomerates, the family-owned

farm has not only survived but prevailed, growing wheat, corn, and soybeans more efficiently than any corporate giant.

The statistical measure of our productivity is almost mind-boggling. In 2001, American farmers produced nearly two billion bushels of wheat on 49 million acres of land; nearly three billion bushels of soybeans from 73 million acres of land; nine and a half billion bushels of corn from 69 million acres and nearly 39 million tons of vegetables from 3.8 million acres, as well as 97 million cows and calves, seven million lambs and sheep, and 60 million hogs and pigs.

Our federal government, with large-hearted popular support, has met emergency after emergency all over the world—in Asia, Europe, and Africa—contributing our agricultural riches to others less fortunate than ourselves. We came to the rescue of Europe after World War I, and again after World War II, with shiploads of American grain. In the 1960s, we came to the aid of India as it struggled through ten years of drought, further handicapped by antiquated farm practices that were doomed to failure. The story of U.S. agricultural aid to India is itself a remarkable one. First, we met the immediate emergency, shipping millions of tons of wheat to a starving people. Then, the federal government, in partnership with the Ford and Rockefeller Foundations, produced a

"Green Revolution" in India and other "Third World" countries. American scientists developed new breeds of hardy, drought-resistant seeds. American agronomists helped India build fertilizer plants and to focus its agricultural production on fewer areas with better climatic conditions for success. In less than twenty years, India evolved from a charity case to an exporter of grain.

At the height of the Cold War, we responded to the needs of our fiercest adversary, the Soviet Union, selling it millions of tons of wheat on favorable terms. In 1959, Soviet leader Nikita Khrushchev, on a trip to the United States, scoffed at most claims of American success, but he expressed only amazement and wonder to President Dwight D. Eisenhower about the productivity of American agriculture. After walking through the thick cornfields of Iowa, Khrushchev went home determined to produce there the rich harvest he had just seen. He bought and planted the finest American seed corn, but his experiment failed. His native land simply did not have those natural gifts—adequate rainfall, temperate weather, the rich black soil— that together yielded the rich crops of American corn.

Our land has sustained us and made us wealthy. Yet the story of our bountiful land is marked by setbacks and by chapters

Rows of corn in a Wisconsin field march toward the horizon, opposite. Most American farm products are produced by fewer than half a million farmers, but they are so efficient that their surpluses help to feed the world. A poster, left, advertising a cattleman's meeting in Illinois in 1940 features a winsome calf.

of shame, in which we have debased other human beings and abused the land itself. The first American agricultural success story was built on the back-breaking labor of African slaves and their descendants. In 1800, Jefferson's gracious living and freedom to pursue a life of the mind was sustained by the sweat of slaves, of which there were 367,000 in the state of Virginia alone. And the Emancipation Proclamation did not end the misery of the African Americans, whether in northern city or on southern land, where too many eked out survival in a new form of servitude, politely called the sharecropper system. As we were drawn irresistibly westward, we pushed out the Native Americans from their land, breaking solemn promises at every turn, and then plowed up the rich grasses that nourished the buffalo, replacing them with crops ill-suited to long-term sustainable agriculture. The infamous "Dust Bowl" of the 1930s wreaked its havoc partly because we didn't understand that areas of the magnificent Great Plains, so bountiful for grazing buffalo and cattle, lacked the consistent rainfall needed for intensive planting of crops. We have pressed the ecosystem too hard in creating vast gardens out of desert in the West, posing a water crisis of threatening dimensions. Today, our cornucopia of affordable fresh fruits and vegetables are subsidized for us by streams of migrant foreign laborers, to whom we do not pay

Secretary of Agriculture in the Eisenhower Administration, Ezra Taft Benson shields his eyes from a cloud of dust during a severe drought in 1955. The scene is reminiscent of the "Dust Bowl" days during the 1930s, when clouds of dust from farmland covered much of the country.

a living wage nor grant the most basic rights of our society. We have crippled millions of acres of once fertile land through flagrant misuse. We have wrecked our precious topsoil by failing to nurture it. Overplanting, misuse of fertilizers and pesticides, and failure to practice prudent conservation have not only ruined millions of acres of precious soil, but despoiled our rivers and streams with toxic runoff. We have needlessly clear-cut our forests and failed to replant them. And in the latest tragedy, we are devouring millions of acres of farmland as we feed the maw of endless urban sprawl. In one five-year period at the end of the twentieth century, three million acres of farm land were lost to urban development, including land of historic significance and pastoral beauty in Jefferson's own beloved Virginia Piedmont.

And yet, despite our mistakes, our greed, carelessness, and failure to plan for a sustainable future, our land has been amazingly forgiving, and our farmers have shown the capacity to learn from past mistakes. No-till planting and crop rotation have replaced much of the annual plowing that contributed to washing millions of tons of precious topsoil into rivers, streams, and oceans. The genius of American inventors and engineers has brought forth machinery that saves labor and is gentler with the land. Better management of forest land has placed new emphasis on replanting and conserving that valuable natural

Smiling with pride, a roadside vendor shows off his produce. In spite of mistakes—a heavy reliance on fertilizers and pesticides, overplanting, sacrificing farmland to suburban sprawl—America's agriculture remains a wonder of the world and the envy of its people.

resource. In recent decades, an alert American public, sharply divided on so many critical issues of national concern, has consistently supported the causes of conservation and environmental protection. There are even signs that we are awakening to the threat that endless sprawl poses to our agricultural production, and to our quality of life as a civilized people.

Through all kinds of adversity, and facing new threats such as global warming, American's bountiful land continues to be our most profoundly sustaining natural resource. Our farmers, though shrinking in numbers, still are capable of producing far more food than they can sell at even a modest profit to the American or foreign markets. The government pays billions of dollars to farmers to restrain their production, not because they are inefficient, but because they are so productive. The larger problem is our inability to match our splendid resources with unmet human needs. Our rich land and skilled farmers still have the capacity to feed not only ourselves but tens of millions of poor people at home and throughout the world. The next Green Revolution will be one in which we summon the will and find the means to unleash our agricultural power to help more people live the good life that we cherish.

CHAPTER TWO

THE STRENGTHS OF A FREE PEOPLE

★

"We were forewarned that [America] was too free, and her liberty has proved her security; too peaceable, and she has been found sufficient for her defence; too large, and her size has ensured her union. . . . A people who have bled together for liberty, who equally appreciate and equally enjoy that liberty which their own blood or that of their fathers has purchased, who feel, too, that the liberty which they love has found her last asylum on their shores—such a people are bound together by ties of amity and citizenship far beyond what is usual in national communities."

—Frances Wright, Scottish author and speaker relocated to America, in 1820

Confidence in Our Protections

by Anthony Lewis

THE EXTRAORDINARY WEALTH and power of the United States are the products of an open society as much as of fortunate geography or any other factor. From the beginning, freedom of the individual has been the fundamental theme in American life. No government, no hierarchy can tell us what we may believe, what we may say, what life we may seek. That credo, imperfectly realized though it has been from time to time, has liberated the spirit and the energy of Americans.

Historically, there were several elements in the development of the idea of freedom. One was freedom of religious belief. It took time to escape from the English and early American tradition of forced religious conformity. The symbol was Jefferson's Virginia Statute for Religious Freedom, enacted in 1786, which ended the taxation of citizens to support one established church. He put it on his tombstone, believing it to be one of the few works of his life worth noting there.

"THIS WAS THE DISTINCTIVE AMERICAN CONTRIBUTION TO POLITICAL THEORY: THE IDEA THAT LAW COULD PROTECT FREEDOM."

A second element was escape from social hierarchy. In English society everyone knew his or her place; the novels of Trollope or Jane Austen tell us how hard it was to move from the level assigned to one by birth. The American founders rejected the idea of inherited station. The Declaration of Independence said: "We hold these Truths to be self-evident, that all Men are created equal. . . ." The Constitution forbade titles of nobility, an important factor in inherited power.

Then, third, there was a pervasive suspicion of government power. The fear that power could lead to tyranny was so strong that when the Constitution was drafted in 1787, ratification was almost defeated by opponents who claimed that it would produce a centralized authority like that of King George III. Enough states were persuaded to

Drafters of the Declaration of Independence— opposite (from left), Benjamin Franklin, Thomas Jefferson, Robert Livingston, John Adams, and Roger Sherman— worked in Philadelphia. Jefferson, below, also wrote Virginia's Statute for Religious Freedom.

ratify it only when proponents promised to add a Bill of Rights limiting the powers of the new federal government.

The premise of the Bill of Rights, though not often stated, was that the courts would enforce the limits when a government failed to obey them—when the rhetorical force of the Constitution was not enough in itself. This was the distinctive American contribution to political theory: the idea that law could protect freedom.

The first ten amendments to the Constitution of the United States, right, make up the Bill of Rights, which was ratified in 1791.

The power of courts to hold acts of Congress unconstitutional was established by the Supreme Court under Chief Justice John Marshall in 1803, in the case of *Marbury v. Madison*. But state courts had exercised similar power before that. One case, in Massachusetts, is a dramatic example. It is the case of Quock Walker.

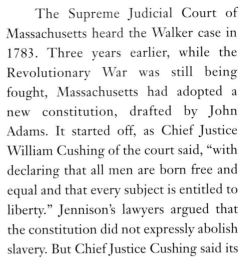

Walker was a slave, one of many in Massachusetts. (Slavery was not limited to the South.) He had been promised his freedom when he turned twenty-five. When he did not get it, he ran away. His owner, Nathaniel Jennison, found him, brought him back, and beat him. Jennison was prosecuted for assault and battery. His defense was that slavery was well established in Massachusetts law, and he had every right to seize and punish a runaway.

The Supreme Judicial Court of Massachusetts heard the Walker case in 1783. Three years earlier, while the Revolutionary War was still being fought, Massachusetts had adopted a new constitution, drafted by John Adams. It started off, as Chief Justice William Cushing of the court said, "with declaring that all men are born free and equal and that every subject is entitled to liberty." Jennison's lawyers argued that the constitution did not expressly abolish slavery. But Chief Justice Cushing said its language was "wholly incompatible" with "perpetual servitude."

With that, slavery was abolished in Massachusetts. It was another eighty-two years until the Thirteenth Amendment to the federal Constitution outlawed slavery in the nation. That required a Civil War first, and it still left black Americans subject to pervasive discrimination.

The guarantees of civil liberty that have come to be regarded as crucial played little part in the work of the Supreme Court through the nineteenth century. Indeed, it was not until well into the twentieth century that the now-familiar clauses of the First Amendment forbidding abridgement of "the freedom of speech, or of the press" were effectively enforced against official repression. Dissenters and radicals prosecuted for their speech lost in the Supreme Court because it said the First Amendment did not protect expression that had a "bad tendency"—a legal theory that was carte blanche for repression.

The first Supreme Court opinion that treated freedom of speech as a fundamental value was a dissent by Justice Oliver Wendell Holmes Jr., joined by Justice Louis D. Brandeis, in 1919. A group of radicals were convicted of "sedition," and sentenced to twenty years in prison, when they threw leaflets from the tops of buildings in New York protesting President Wilson's dispatch of American troops to Russia after the Bolshevik Revolution. Holmes said the "theory of our Constitution" was "free trade in ideas." He went on:

"It is an experiment, as all life is an experiment. . . . While that experiment is part of our system I think that we should be eternally vigilant against attempts to check the expression of opinions that we loathe and believe to be fraught with death. . . ."

That astonishing rhetoric was matched in a Brandeis opinion of 1927, in which he was joined by Justice Holmes. The California courts had convicted Anita Whitney of "criminal syndicalism" for her radical speech, and sentenced her to one to fourteen years in San Quentin prison. Brandeis wrote:

"Those who won our independence . . . believed liberty to be the secret of happiness and courage to be the secret of liberty. They believed that freedom to think as you will and to speak as you think are means indispensable to the discovery and spread of political truth; that without free speech and assembly discussion would be futile . . . that the greatest menace to freedom is an inert people. . . . They knew that order cannot be secured merely through fear of punishment for its infraction; that it is hazardous to discourage thought, hope, and imagination; that fear breeds repression; that repression breeds hate; that hate menaces stable government. . . ."

Holmes and Brandeis had no formal power beyond their two votes on a court of nine. But their rhetoric persuaded the country, and in time it persuaded the Supreme Court to enforce the freedom of speech as a fundamental American value.

Rhetoric and law have worked together to advance the ideals of American freedom. A striking example arose from the Civil Rights movement of the 1960s. Around the country, then,

Justices join forces: In Abrams v. United States *and* Whitney v. California, *Oliver Wendell Holmes Jr., top, and Louis D. Brandeis, bottom, collaborated to argue for freedom of speech in 1919 and 1927.*

Black teenager Elizabeth Eckford endures the vilification of white citizens as she tries to enter Central High School in Little Rock, Arkansas, in 1957. President Eisenhower soon ordered in paratroopers of the 101st Airborne to forcibly integrate the school.

few Americans were aware of the brutality of racism in the South— aware that in many areas blacks could not vote, nor could they attend "white" public universities, much less attend the desegregated schools declared by the Supreme Court in 1954, in *Brown v. Board of Education*, to be a constitutional requirement. Dr. Martin Luther King's strategy was to make Americans understand by showing them the savage racist response to his nonviolent protests against discrimination. He did show them, and Americans learned. Alexander M. Bickel, a constitutional scholar at the Yale Law School, wrote after confronta-

tions over school desegregation in Little Rock, Arkansas, and elsewhere:

"Compulsory segregation, like states' rights and like 'The Southern Way of Life,' is an abstraction and, to a good many people, a neutral or sympathetic one. These riots, which were brought instantly, dramatically, and literally home to the American people, showed what it means concretely. Here were grown men and women furiously confronting their enemy: two, three, a half dozen scrubbed, starched, scared, and incredibly brave colored children. The moral bankruptcy, the shame of the thing, was evident."

Southern segregationists found what they thought to be a shrewd way to counter Dr. King's strategy: to frighten the national press and broadcasters out of covering the civil rights story. A libel suit was brought against the *New York Times* over modest and inadvertent errors in an advertisement on behalf of Dr. King and the movement. The Alabama Supreme Court upheld huge damages against the *Times*. But the Supreme Court of the United States, in a landmark 1964 opinion by Justice William J. Brennan Jr., found the advertisement akin to political speech protected by the First Amendment. Justice Brennan relied on the opinions of Holmes and Brandeis. Their view of freedom was now the law of the Constitution.

The course of freedom in American history has hardly been an untroubled one. Repression has occurred again and again, especially in times of fear and war. Right at the beginning, just seven years after the adoption of the Bill of Rights in 1791, Congress passed a Sedition Act that made it a crime to criticize the president maliciously. The supposed reason was fear that French revolutionary terror would spread to America. James Madison, the author of the First Amendment, wrote a resolution of the Virginia Legislature protesting that the act was aimed at "the right of freely examining public characters and measures, and of free communication among the people thereon, which has even been justly deemed the only effectual guardian of every other right."

Madison's words defined what the Supreme Court in 1964 called "the central meaning of the First Amendment," the right of Americans to criticize their rulers. But there was also a minority report in the Virginia Legislature, defending the Sedition Act. It argued that a government had to be protected from criticism lest it "be deprived of the confidence and affection of the people." If that view had prevailed in American history, if governments had been able to punish dissent in order to protect their own power, this would be a different country—less free and less successful.

For 150 years the United States system of freedom has been enforced by judges. Now many other countries look to their courts as guarantors of rights, among them France, Germany, Israel, post-apartheid South Africa, and finally Britain. The president of the Israeli Supreme Court, Aharon Barak, spoke for many when he said that "democracy cannot exist without the protection of individual human rights." That was the very belief that animated the framers of the American Constitution.

James Madison, left, fourth president of the United States and author of the First Amendment, argued strongly for the right to speak freely, "the only effectual guardian of every other right."

The Challenge to State Sanctioned Racism

by Roger Wilkins

WHEN I STARTED SCHOOL in Kansas City, Missouri, in 1936, I was sent to a run-down, one-room schoolhouse in a small, isolated black neighborhood in that segregated city—not the brick school a few blocks away. When my little school was closed a few months later, we were put on a bus that went past that nice, bright school for white children to an old school in the main colored section of town. No matter what our parents and teachers told us, we knew that the white school nearer our house was a better school and that the white children got to go to it because they were smarter than we were. We knew that because the school arrangements mirrored everything else we knew about civic and personal life. Whites had all the power, all the best houses, all the nice places to go—and they had the right to do everything, including telling us what we couldn't do. Moreover, listening to our parents' conversations, we knew that whites could put limits on what black grown-ups could do and we knew that our parents bore deep hurts because of that. Our long ride to the old school mirrored and concentrated the omnipresent messages from the culture—we got America's leftovers because we were inferior and didn't really belong here. That made us tentative and uncertain in this highly competitive society. By the time we had reached the age of four or five, white culture had begun on us its relentless work of disabling each new generation of black Americans.

By the time I encountered it in the mid-1930s, the process of disabling blacks had been taking place on this continent for more than two centuries. Early in the eighteenth century, Robert "King" Carter, the largest slave owner in the Virginia colony, devised a brutal and efficient way of

> "IT IS HARD TO BELIEVE THAT THE FREEDOM RIDES, SIT-INS, AND WADE-INS THAT OCCURRED LATE IN THE 1950S AND INTO THE EARLY 1960S DURING THE GATHERING STORM OF THE CIVIL RIGHTS MOVEMENT WOULD HAVE OCCURRED HAD THERE NEVER BEEN A BROWN DECISION."

In a public school cafeteria in Alabama, opposite, white and black students share a meal in January 1967. Segregation in the schools was made official by the Supreme Court in Plessy v. Ferguson *in 1896, and the long and difficult battle for equality in the classroom has troubled Americans ever since.*

disabling newly arrived Africans. He would pick out the ones he deemed most likely to become rebellious and cut off a finger, a toe, or an ear. The message that blacks on this side of the Atlantic were to be submissive objects of the will and the fantasies of whites was thus delivered with brutal efficiency.

Systematic disabling of the black minority for the purposes of maintaining massive economic, psychic, and cultural advantages for American white people was vigorously and broadly employed in this country for the next two and a half centuries. The entire slave enterprise was disabling. After the Civil War, southern states enacted the Black Codes, which were designed to slam blacks back into a condition as close to slavery as possible. Then, after Reconstruction ended in 1877, the most serious forms of disabling were the denial of the vote, segregation, and terrorism highlighted by lynching. Any doubts that these measures grew out of the same intentions that motivated King Carter were dispelled by Senator Benjamin R. Tillman of South Carolina. Speaking roughly two hundred years after Carter began disabling his new slaves, Senator Tillman was moved to comment about one of President Theodore Roosevelt's dinner guests, Booker T. Washington:

"The action of President Roosevelt entertaining that nigger will necessitate our killing a thousand niggers in the South before they will learn their place again."

Segregation, elevated to constitutional status by the Supreme Court in its decision in the 1896 case *Plessy v. Ferguson*, was a way for white America to keep blacks "in their place" both literally and figuratively. The court decreed that the provision of separate but equal railroad accommodations satisfied the Fourteenth Amendment's requirement of equal protection of the laws. It also claimed that such separation did not connote the inferiority of either race: any suggestion to the contrary was simply the product of overwrought black imaginations. The fact is, however, that segregation was, in essence, a governmentally sanctioned and enforced form of national shunning of black America. Its powerful message was that blacks were inferior and unwanted here except in working and living as directed by whites. The practice soon infected virtually every aspect of human life. I was born in a segregated hospital in Kansas City in 1932 and my father was buried in a segregated cemetery there in 1941. Virtually everything in between was also segregated.

As they began developing more effective ways of attacking the racism so firmly planted at the core of American culture, blacks homed in on inferior education. In 1935, under the direction of Charles H. Houston, his former dean at Howard University Law School, Thurgood Marshall represented Donald Murray, a Marylander, who wanted to

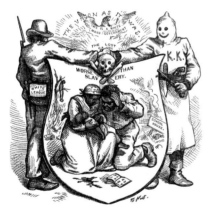

The White League and the Ku Klux Klan, nostalgic for "The Union As It Was," join hands over a terrorized black family in an 1874 cartoon.

study the law at his state university. As the law school was segregated, Murray was denied admission. Under the rule in the *Plessy* case, separate facilities were deemed to provide "equal protection under the law" as required by the Fourteenth Amendment to the Constitution if they were deemed equal to those provided for whites. The equality requirement was almost universally ignored by segregating governments. Since Maryland provided no law school whatsoever for blacks, the state supreme court ordered the University of Maryland to admit Murray. Over the next few years, Marshall, still under Houston's direction, branched out and began representing a series of black teachers in Maryland and Virginia who were seeking equal pay to that of their white counterparts.

From the time of slavery onward, blacks had come to see education as the key to freedom and equality, but as the nascent legal thrust for equal education was developing, a competing vision was being championed by Ralph Bunche, then a young political science professor at Howard University, and Roger Baldwin, the founder of the American Civil Liberties Union. They believed that economics was the key and argued that black and white workers should band together to seek more power, higher pay, and better conditions in the nation's workplaces. Even in the Depression-radicalized 1930s that proposition seemed a bridge too far for blacks, who were just emerging from their Lincoln-inspired loyalty to the Republican Party. Moreover, because opponents of racial equality were quick to label any effort to diminish the inequities visited upon by blacks as Communist or Communist-inspired, moderate strategies were adopted by most civil rights advocates. So Houston, now counsel to the NAACP, began investigations in the South that laid the foundations for the organization's assault on unequal education in America.

In 1934, Houston made a trip through Virginia, North and South Carolina, and Georgia to observe the educational conditions for black children. Notes he took for a film report he expected to make on the trip suggest the level of contempt southern government had for black people:

MT. ARAT SCHOOL BUILDING, CHESTER COUNTY (Reel I, Scene 25)

. . .

e. Road scene
For toilet facilities the boys have to cross the railroad and highway to get to the woods.

. . .

g. The student body. 68 pupils packed into one room, 20 x 16 feet on seven benches. No tables, no desks, no stove. One chair, one open fireplace. (Reel I, Scene 31)

. . .

Charles H. Houston, former dean of the Howard University Law School in Washington, D.C., addresses the city's school board. With Thurgood Marshall, Houston led the fight for equal schooling for blacks in the 1930s.

i. Richburg School, white about two miles from Mt. Arat School. Grades 1 through 11; six rooms, six teachers. Assembly hall, piano, individual desks. Three buses to transport children. Two Negro women janitresses clean entire building and make 6 fires daily for wages of $4.00 per month each. (Reel I, Scene 33).

As the litigation on educational inequalities progressed, two competing theories emerged. The first was to use the doctrine of the *Plessy* case to force southerners to make equal the separate educational opportunities made available to blacks and whites. Separate and nothing, as in the Murray case, would surely not do under this theory and neither would separate but awful, as in the Mt. Arat schools. Under this theory, NAACP lawsuits would press states to invest whatever it took to produce full equality in their segregated facilities. Such suits began to meet some success in education and public facilities litigation. This strategy had the advantage of preserving the jobs and the status of blacks who had achieved good positions in the segregated systems. Proponents of this view also noted that it would preserve the traditions and the expertise built up over generations of black educators, many of whom cared deeply about the youngsters they taught. This theory also held that ultimately the

Thurgood Marshall, a Baltimore lawyer and former head of the NAACP legal program, was appointed to the Supreme Court in 1967, the first African American to serve on the court.

requirement to equalize facilities would prove to be so expensive that the whole edifice of segregation would collapse.

Slowly but surely, however, pressures built on Thurgood Marshall, who succeeded his great mentor Houston as head of the NAACP legal program, to choose the strategy that attacked *Plessy* head-on and sought to destroy school segregation entirely. This view was based on the conviction that, given the histories of the United States, separate could never be equal because the dollars would always follow the white children.

Early on—while pursuing cases designed to ameliorate racism on all fronts, from housing to voting to criminal justice—Marshall was building an interracial staff of very able lawyers augmented by a brilliant interracial cadre of volunteers to help with his education docket. At first, the education cases were largely on the Murray case model, where the NAACP Legal Defense Fund (the Fund was legally separated from the NAACP in 1939 but remained intimately intertwined with it for many years afterward) would represent people who were seeking to enroll in graduate or professional programs at segregated southern state universities. After they had achieved some significant successes in these cases, Marshall and his staff began to represent plaintiffs—children and their parents—who were seeking to open up primary and secondary schools in segregated districts.

As the NAACP was scratching out its strategies on a case-by-case basis, the

With Old Glory unfurled, the 41st Corps of Engineers, an African-American Army battalion, stands in formation at Fort Bragg, North Carolina, around 1942. African-American soldiers still served in segregated units during World War II.

world was changing rapidly. The hypocrisy of fighting for freedom in World War II with a segregated army made many Americans, both black and white, rethink our national caste arrangements. In 1947, just after the war, Branch Rickey, president of the Brooklyn Dodgers, detonated a national cultural bombshell by hiring Jackie Robinson to play first base—the first acknowledged black to play in the major leagues in the twentieth century. Simultaneously, as the worldwide competition between the United States and the Soviet Union escalated, former colonies south of the equator began emerging as nation-states and segregation and unequal treatment of blacks began to be recognized as a serious embarrassment in America's presentation of itself to the colored populations of the emerging "Third World."

At home, black people pressed on—often at great peril to their physical and economic well-being—in their efforts to obtain better educational opportunities for their children. Finally, in 1952, a group of cases brought by black parents seeking integration of public schools arrived at the Supreme Court from South Carolina, Delaware, Kansas, Virginia, and the District of Columbia. They were argued before a bitterly fractured court headed by Chief Justice Fred Vinson, a Kentuckian. That court could reach no consensus during its 1952–53 term. The case was sent back to the parties with a request that they research a set of questions posed by the justices and was set for reargument in the 1953–54 term. Before the Court reconvened in the fall, Vinson died and President Dwight D. Eisenhower nominated Governor Earl Warren, a Republican from California, to replace him.

Warren, a career public official who had served as a county district attorney in northern California, as attorney general, and then governor, was a seasoned politician (he had been his party's vice presidential candidate in 1948) but not a legal philosopher. He had little confidence in the promises of the segregating jurisdictions to equalize services for blacks. At the reargument, he listened to the brilliant presentation of the distinguished lead counsel for the segregating jurisdictions, John W. Davis, who argued that separate but equal, having been the law of the land for fifty-seven years, was too embedded in the constitutional fabric of the country to be overturned. Davis had called the justices' attention to the fact that *Plessy* had been upheld seven times by the Supreme Court and concluded by claiming: "somewhere, some time, to every principle there comes a moment of repose when it has been so often announced, so confidently relied upon, so long continued that it passes the limits of judicial discretion and disturbance."

Marshall argued that to uphold segregation, the Court had "to find that for

Earl Warren, chief justice of the Supreme Court from 1953 to 1969, above, ruled that, "Separate educational facilities are inherently unequal." The ruling resulted from a Kansas case, Brown v. Topeka Board of Education. In the eye of the storm, little Linda Brown, opposite, sits in a classroom with her black classmates.

some reason Negroes are inferior to all other human beings." He charged the South with an "inherent determination that the people who were formerly in slavery, regardless of anything else, shall be kept as near that stage as possible, and now is the time, we submit, that this court should make it clear that is not what our Constitution stands for."

In light of what he later wrote, powerful testimony elicited at trial of the Kansas case from Louisa Holt, a young white sociology teacher at Kansas University, clearly caught the chief justice's attention. The testimony was contained in the record of the Kansas case, *Brown v. Topeka Board of Education.* Mrs. Holt had testified on the educational inequality inherent in segregation:

. . . The fact that it is enforced, that it is legal, I think, has more importance than the mere fact of segregation by itself does because this gives legal and official sanction to a policy which is inevitably interpreted both by white people and by Negroes as denoting the inferiority of the Negro group. . . .

Under questioning, Mrs. Holt expanded on the impact of a sense of inferiority on the learning process:

A sense of inferiority must always affect one's motivation for learning since it affects the feeling one has of oneself as a person . . . that sense of ego-identity is built up on the basis of attitudes that are

expressed toward a person by others who are important—first the parents and then teachers and then other people in the community, whether they are older or one's peers. It is other people's reactions to oneself that basically affects the conception of oneself. . . . If these attitudes that are reflected back and then internalized or projected, are unfavorable ones, then one develops a sense of oneself as an inferior being . . . and apathetic acceptance, fatalistic submission to the feeling others have expressed that one is inferior, and therefore any efforts to prove otherwise would be doomed to failure.

The case record also contained the opinion of the Kansas District Court, which had dutifully followed the dictates of the *Plessy* case by ruling against the black plaintiffs. Nevertheless, Chief Judge Walter Huxman, taking note of Mrs. Holt's testimony, found as fact that: "Segregation of white and colored children in public schools has a detrimental effect upon the colored children. The impact is greater when it has the sanction of the law; for the policy of separating the races is usually interpreted as denoting the inferiority of the Negro group. A sense of inferiority affects the motivation of a child to learn. . . ."

However the elements of his experience, his understanding of the nation and its political needs, and his sense of the Constitution mixed in his mind, Chief Justice Warren set out after the case was reargued to mold a unanimous court behind a judgment in favor of the black children. Warren not only had to persuade all of his colleagues (a few of whom had doubts about the wisdom or appropriateness of the Court's entering the public education thicket and at least one of whom—Stanley Reed—was flatly opposed to the outcome that Warren sought), he also sought a unanimous opinion. He wanted no dissents or concurrences that lower courts, legal scholars, the press, and other commentators could pick apart. After months of applying his finely honed, low-keyed, but firmly persistent political skills to this task, Warren achieved his goal. When the court convened on May 17, 1954, the chief justice read the opinion, which he had authored. It contained eerie echoes of a view expressed by Thomas Jefferson that is inscribed on a panel high on a wall of the Jefferson Memorial on the National Mall in Washington, D.C.

The eighteenth-century Virginia lawyer had written:

I am not an advocate for frequent changes in laws and Constitutions. But laws must and institutions must go hand in hand with the progress of the human mind. As that becomes more developed, more enlightened as new discoveries are made, new truths discovered and manners and opinions changed, with the change of circumstances, institutions

In the mid-1920s, blacks in the American South shopped at stores like this. Jim Crow laws, named for a comic minstrel character, mandated segregation.

must advance also to keep pace with the times. We might as well require a man to wear still the coat which fitted him when a boy as civilized society to remain ever under the regimen of their barbarous ancestors.

The twentieth-century chief justice wrote, in part:

In approaching this problem, we cannot turn the clock back to 1868 when the [Fourteenth] Amendment was written. We must consider public education in the light of its full development and its present place in American life throughout the Nation. Only in this way can it be determined if segregation in public schools deprives these plaintiffs of the equal protection of the laws. . . .

Whatever may have been the extent of psychological knowledge at the time of *Plessy v. Ferguson*, this finding [that segregation has a tendency to retard the educational and mental development of Negro children] is amply supported by modern authority. Any language in *Plessy v. Ferguson* contrary to this finding is rejected.

We conclude that in the field of public education the doctrine of 'separate but equal' has no place. Separate educational facilities are inherently unequal.

Black people all over the country could express jubilation in reading those words. Finally, the United States government had acknowledged the plain truth that we blacks had known all along.

Reading the opinion as a freshman at the University of Michigan Law School, I felt that we had just experienced a second Emancipation Day. Thurgood Marshall said that he thought that all the schools in the nation would be integrated by 1959 and that the race problem would be behind us by the hundredth anniversary of the Emancipation Proclamation in 1963. We were wrong about education and about a lot of white people. We thought that most people would obey the law. They didn't. We though that President Eisenhower would support the Court vigorously. He didn't. We thought that the dollars following white children into integrated classrooms would improve education for black children almost immediately. Black children, by and large, didn't flow into classes with white children, and most of the dollars went where they always had.

Troops of the 101st Airborne Division enforce integration at Central High School in Little Rock, Arkansas, in 1957. White students watch from a safe distance.

It all turned out to be far more complicated than we could possibly have imagined. Now, a half century after *Brown*, there is far more segregation in public schools in America than we could possibly have imagined fifty years ago, and the education of poor black children in large cities is far worse than anyone could have foreseen. Consequently, there are some people who argue that *Brown* didn't really matter all that much. That, I think, is a very mistaken conclusion, because *Brown* had both a substantial impact on American education and an enormous impact on American society beyond the classroom.

Blacks across the country felt energized, empowered, and emboldened by the decision. It is hard to imagine that the brave assault by Montgomery, Alabama, blacks against segregation in public transportation would have occurred the year after *Brown* was decided had it not been decided as it was. It is hard to believe that the Freedom Rides, sit-ins, and wade-ins that occurred late in the 1950s and into the early 1960s during the gathering storm of the Civil Rights movement would have occurred had there never been a *Brown* decision. Just as *Plessy*—a case about segregation on trains—came to form the platform for society-wide segregation, so, *Brown* radiated out from education and undermined the whole structure of that platform. The passage of the Civil Rights Act of 1964 completed the destruction of legalized segregation, and the Voting Rights Act of 1965 destroyed most of the barriers to vote. By the end of the 1960s, virtually every white institution in the North and many in the South were looking for some "qualified" Negro to come integrate it.

But what about education? How could Marshall and his brilliant interracial brain trust of lawyers and social scientists have walked so innocently into the wall of "Massive Resistance" thrown up by

Chicago burns following the assassination of Dr. Martin Luther King Jr. The death of the civil rights leader spawned riots and rage all over the United States in the late 1960s.

southern political, educational, and civic leaders? My answer is simply that I think that we overestimated the amount of goodness to be found in the hearts of American white people. We thought that they believed in American ideals as much as we did and that when the highest authority in the land told them what the ideals required, they would comply. It might take them time, but they were Americans, after all, and they would do it. Robert Carter, once Thurgood Marshall's deputy at the Legal Defense Fund, put it this way: "We thought segregation was the box we were in. We weren't thinking about white supremacy."

In large part, black optimism was based on a wishful analysis about the general white state of mind. We thought that anti-black feelings were relatively rational attachments—like preferences for GM cars over Chrysler, for example—which could be changed by altering people's perceptions of the facts. It turned out, however, that intensively in the South—and to a surprisingly large degree in the North as well—the privileges, both material and psychic, that accrued to whites from racism had "grown into the lives of the people," as one southern lawyer had put it in arguing against the desegregation case in South Carolina. Whiteness and its advantages had become emotional and deeply valued parts of the identities of many whites, not just the thugs on the front lines of racial skirmishes who used violence to beat off black challenges to the status quo. So, while the thugs tried to hold the line in the streets and around the schools, men in white shirts and suits in the Congress and in executive suites all over the South devised plans to undermine the *Brown* decision. They were all—in one way or another—engaged in an emotional defense of who they deemed themselves to be and of what they knew they were entitled to have.

For blacks it was a question of identity and deep emotionalism as well. We were clear that we were fully human and were profoundly offended by the continuing attempts to disable and diminish us by withholding aspects of our American birthright. Ultimately Martin Luther King's nonviolence in the South gave way to outbursts of rebellious violence in the North, which terrified many whites and sent them fleeing from the cities. With the noose of housing segregation somewhat loosened, many middle-class blacks fled the cities as well. Over the last decades of the twentieth century, many of the major American cities became blacker and poorer just as the effects of globalization hit. The industrial employment ladder, which had provided access to the middle class for generations of unskilled white immigrants from Europe and then in the mid-twentieth century to similar black immigrants from the South, began to disappear. Thus, the cities became less and less able to provide decent educational opportunities for poor black children or jobs for their parents. Opportunities to achieve urban school integration shriveled dramatically. Thus, a half century after *Brown*, the persistent educational achievement gap between black and white schoolchildren and our unwillingness to do what it takes to eliminate it stand as a stark reminder that for all the dramatic advances our country has made in race relations—and advances in both circumstances and in the emotional makeups of both whites and blacks—the disabling of many black Americans remains as a central feature of our national life.

Looking back over my seven completed decades, I am fairly sure that the damages inflicted on me by segregation during the first twelve years of my life left permanent scars. Though I have lived a fruitful middle-class American life, I know that my horizons were narrowed by the circumstances of my early life and that my cautious approach to competition and the wider world are products of my time. I have seen the same phenomena in the lives of many of my black contemporaries, which I happily do not observe in my three children, all middle-class beneficiaries of the richer and more diverse post-*Brown* world. But my children know, as I do, that the struggle will not be over as long as large numbers of our most vulnerable citizens, many of them poor black children, continue to be disabled by our deep cultural habits and our limited American commitment to social and economic justice.

Students take a break at the University of California, Berkeley. After proposition 209 banned affirmative action, enrollment of African-American students at Berkeley plunged.

The Right to Speak Freely

by John Seigenthaler

"SOMEWHERE I READ of the freedom of assembly! Somewhere I read of the freedom of speech! Somewhere I read of the freedom of the press! Somewhere I read that the greatness of America is the right to protest for right. . . ."

Martin Luther King Jr. spoke that night to a crowd of two thousand followers at the Mason Temple in Memphis—and before night fell again, his voice was stilled forever.

As he intoned the First Amendment liberties crafted by James Madison for the First Congress 180 years earlier, King was deriding the continuing contradiction between America's founding promise of equal justice for all and the nation's continuing denial of inalienable rights to African-American citizens. Even as he spoke that April night in 1968, a court injunction won by the city of Memphis sought to bar his protest march down famed Beale Street the next day.

"We aren't going to let any injunction turn us around," he told the crowd. "We are going on!" He was confident that the First Amendment again would trump any temporary government restraint on the people's right to protest.

It was his valedictory, delivered, as always, with the poetic resonance and melancholic cadence—but this time the religious symbolism in the rhetoric seemed almost to reflect a premonition of his death the next day.

"I have been to the mountaintop," he said. ". . . I have seen the promised land . . . I may not get there with you . . . But I want you to know that we as a people will get to the promised land . . . Mine eyes have seen the glory of the coming of the Lord."

> "FOR ALL HIS VISION, JAMES MADISON NEVER COULD HAVE IMAGINED THAT THE GREAT-GRANDCHILDREN OF THOSE HELD IN BONDAGE BY HIS GENERATION WOULD ONE DAY RELY ON THE WORDS OF THE AMENDMENT TO MAKE EQUALITY AND JUSTICE A REALITY FOR ALL AMERICANS."

With arms linked, leaders of the March on Washington—with Dr. Martin Luther King Jr. in the center—make their way down a Washington, D.C., avenue on August 28, 1963, opposite. Dr. King invoked the First Amendment to the Constitution, which guarantees freedom of speech, on the very eve of his death by assassination.

King left his listeners that night with his strong conviction that both God and the Bill of Rights were on the side of their movement; that his followers were empowered by the spiritual force of their religious faith and by the political force of the First Amendment. For a dozen years, from the Montgomery bus boycott through the Memphis sanitation workers' strike, the rights of protest, protected by the amendment, had sustained and energized the movement.

Absent religious liberty, the black church could not have been the venue where leaders most often met to plan, organize, and inculcate among followers the doctrine of nonviolence. It was from the pulpit that the faithful most often heard the clarion call to overcome.

Absent the freedom to speak and peaceably assemble—to parade in the streets and picket against Jim Crow injustice—the effort to transfer the fervor of the sanctuary to the fever of the street could not have occurred.

Absent the right to petition for redress of age-old wrongs, the string of court decisions that dismantled discrimination as the law of the land would not have come down.

Absent a free press, the horror of the story of demonstrators attacked by snarling police dogs, smashed to the ground by water hoses, and stunned by police cattle prods would not have shocked the conscience of an uninvolved and uncaring nation.

For all his vision, James Madison never could have imagined that the great-grandchildren of those held in bondage by his generation would one day rely on the words of the Amendment to make equality and justice a reality for all Americans. Madison was, after all, a slave-owner and had been part of the Constitutional Convention that valued the civic life of slaves at only three-fifths the worth of free men.

Nor, for that matter, could the "Father of the Bill of Rights" have envisioned that decades before the Civil Rights Movement, women would rely on the implied power of the Amendment to dramatize the nation's refusal to allow them to vote. To Madison and his colleagues in both the Convention and in the Congress, "all men created equal" meant only white men.

For all their egocentrism, racism, and chauvinism, the Founding Fathers who gave us the Bill of Rights understood a salient truth: Embedded in the nature of all government was the impulse to resist public censure, curb criticism, put down dissent, and punish protest that had been the American colonies' troubled experience with the British Crown. They could hope that the Bill of Rights would assure that their sons and grandsons never would be denied the natural right to protest the abusive power of government.

With George Washington presiding, delegates from every state but Rhode Island convene in Philadelphia in 1787 to draft a constitution for the United States.

"Neither the original Constitution nor the Bill of Rights bestows any rights on individuals," Ruth Bader Ginsburg, the associate justice of the Supreme Court, has reminded us. "To the Framers, no document could perform that task. . . . The Bill of Rights assumes the existence of fundamental human rights—for example, freedom of speech, press, and assembly—and simply instructs the State not to interfere with those rights." And what if the state ignored or misinterpreted the amendment?

Madison, thinking through how the government he helped create would operate, foresaw the judiciary assuming the role of protector. "Independent tribunals of justice," he predicted, "will consider themselves in a peculiar manner the guardians of those rights; they (the courts) will be an impenetrable bulwark . . . to resist every encroachment upon rights."

Madison was far-sighted—and at the same time myopic. His effort to bar state governments from "encroaching upon rights" of citizens failed to pass Congress, and for much of the nation's history Justice Ginsburg's antecedents on the Court failed to become Madison's "impenetrable bulwark."

In 1833, with the Bill of Rights less than a half-century old, Chief Justice John Marshall, speaking for a unanimous court, found that the first ten amendments restrained the federal government, but not state governments, from interfering with the natural right of citizen protest. As a general rule, any meeting that local officials guessed might disturb community tranquility could be prohibited—and the courts would approve.

In 1868, the Fourteenth Amendment and its equal protection clause finally provided that states were bound by the federal constitution—but well into the twentieth century the right to protest still was given short shrift by both state and federal courts. In 1897, the Reverend William Davis of Boston contended that he had a citizen's right to speak in the fifty-acre Boston Commons without a City Hall permit. The Massachusetts Supreme Court rebuffed him:

The Supreme Court of 1904: Famed jurist Oliver Wendell Holmes (in center, with mustache) became more liberal with age and retired in 1932 at age ninety.

"For the legislature absolutely or conditionally to forbid public speaking in a street or public park is no more infringement of the rights of a member of the public than for the owner of a private house to forbid it. . . ."

The author of that opinion was Oliver Wendell Holmes, who later would reverse himself as a U.S. Supreme Court justice and come to champion the right of dissent.

Negative judicial rulings did not deter many dissidents from assuming that speech, assembly, and petition were rights of birth; nor were many of them discouraged from exercising those rights, even when their actions offended state and local government statutes and ordinances.

Abolitionists, war protesters, anti-war demonstrators, those opposed to the draft, those seeking to change child labor laws, those favoring shorter work hours, those favoring temperance, those who marched for veterans' bonuses, those on strike—and those who stood opposed to all of those issues—participated in various public demonstrations, even though they were "legally" unprotected by countless court interpretations of the amendment.

Both the suffragist and the civil rights movements often were inhibited by local government ordinances and court injunctions as demonstrators campaigned to effect the two most dynamic societal reforms of the twentieth century. Both crusades helped broaden the freedom to dissent.

The heroic story of the civil rights revolution, tragically visited by terrorist merchants of death, has been told over the last quarter century in a series of illuminating books and gripping documentaries. That narrative stretches from the bus boycott, to school desegregation, to the sit-ins, to the Freedom Rides, to the police riot at Edmund Pettus bridge in Selma, to King's murder in Memphis.

The story of the suffragist revolution is far less well known. The long trek to win the vote by women, not nearly so threatening to human life as the Civil Rights struggle, was miles and difficult decades longer.

Susan B. Anthony, Elizabeth Cady Stanton, and Alice Paul, like Martin Luther King, "somewhere" had read of the constitutional right to criticize government. In 1848 Stanton and Mott called the first women's rights convention at Seneca Falls, New York—an initiative antithetical to the accepted norm of conduct for women. They were there to listen, learn, and act.

This was a time when the society considered it unseemly, unsightly, and uncouth for women to publicly take to the soapbox, much less band together in marches for their rights. When suffragists began to rally on sidewalks and parade in streets, they were reviled—shouted at, cursed, gossiped about, spat upon, often pelted, and sometimes threatened with violence. It took women of courage to challenge the iron barrier of custom that stood in their path and stunted the growth of their struggle.

Two decades after the Seneca Falls meeting Anthony and Stanton organized the National Women Suffrage Association (later to become the League of Women Voters), and their petitions to Congress produced the first proposed federal suffrage amendment. For another half century, the amendment, regularly introduced, went nowhere.

The women, however, went to the streets. Parades, pageants, rallies, more conventions, and more petitions gradually gained national attention and slowly

Foes of slavery rally on Boston Common in 1835. Free blacks also attend. The right to peaceably assemble is another First Amendment guarantee.

built public support. Everywhere along the way the demonstrators were met with harassment. Linda Lumsden's excellent book *Rampant Women—Suffragists and the Right of Assembly* includes this account:

"Hecklers turned an 1853 woman's rights convention into a riot." Those who attempted to speak were interrupted by "shouts, hisses, stamping, cheers, rude remarks and all manner of noisy demonstrations." The uproar closed down the meeting.

The *New York Herald* ridiculed the idea of women exercising First Amendment rights in such a gathering and identified it as the "Women's Wrong Convention." It was, the paper editorialized, "an interesting phase in the comic history of the nineteenth century." The paper described the meeting as "a gathering of 'unsexed' women." Most of the nation's free press, ironically protected by the same First Amendment, echoed similar critical comments about the suffragists.

Leaders of National Association Opposed to Woman Suffrage complained to the *New York Times* that "sex appeal was flagrant and the dominant note" in the Suffragist Movement.

Looking back more than eighty years to ratification of the amendment in 1920, it is difficult to conceive that this effort to win justice for what would become a majority of the population, conceived before the Civil War, still had not given birth to the vote by the end of World War I.

State governments, initially opposed to women protestors, turned out to be far less intransigent than Congress. Beginning in 1869, through 1914, twelve states heard the protesting female voices and gave women state voting rights.

In 1915, the largest pro-suffragist march in history brought out half a million spectators along New York's Fifth Avenue, many supportive, many curious, and many others vocally opposed to the amendment. Two years later the state assembly finally allowed women to vote in New York elections. Still, Congress held the line.

The failure to move federal legislators in a positive direction inevitably led to disagreements over tactics among leaders inside the movement. The organization held rigidly to a policy of non-partisanship.

With the 1916 presidential election approaching, Alice Paul broke away from the National American Women Suffrage Association. She first formed the Congressional Union for Woman Suffrage and later the National Woman's Party. Paul's strategy was to put direct political pressure on President Wilson to push Democrats in the House and Senate to back the amendment. Paul and her followers targeted the White House with what they called "perpetual pickets"—a strategy the *New York Times* called "silly."

For a time the president reacted personably, tipping his hat to the suffragists as he passed through the White House gates. As time passed and the Paul wing of the movement grew more militant, Wilson's patience wore thin. In 1917, as the United States was entering World War I, Paul intensified the pressure. On designated days, hundreds of banner-bearing women picketed the executive mansion.

On other occasions, the demonstrators burned Wilson's speeches at ceremonies they termed "Freedom Watch Fires." When the president traveled to public functions, he often would be welcomed in the street outside the theater by women bearing banners emblazoned with his words on freedom and democracy. On one occasion they burned the president in effigy.

Continuing confrontations with police and the Secret Service resulted in arrests and jail time for some protestors. Before the suffrage amendment finally was ratified, more than five hundred women had been arrested, 160 of them sentenced to terms ranging from a few days up to seven months. Alice Paul endured three separate periods of incarceration.

Some two dozen suffragists who had been jailed decided, on their release, to

Suffragette Alice Paul, top, was imprisoned three times by age twenty-three. After efforts including marching, bottom, women won Wilson's support and won suffrage in 1920.

take their story across the land. They boarded a train called the "Prison Special" and donned their jailhouse garb as they paraded in cities on their tour.

Finally, in 1919, with another presidential election approaching, the president, fearful that the growing popularity of the suffragists was hurting the Democratic Party, capitulated and endorsed the amendment.

It was passed by the House and Senate in the spring of 1919. In August 1920, after the Tennessee General Assembly approved the amendment, providing the necessary two-thirds majority of states approving, women finally could vote in every federal and state election. At least white women could. Jim Crow still barred black women the right to vote in much of the South.

Still, the Supreme Court had not formally put its stamp of approval on a citizen's right to publicly protest against government wrong. That ruling came in 1937 after Dirk Dejonge, a Communist, was convicted for violating Oregon's statute against "criminal syndicalism." Dejonge had spoken at a rally condemning police brutality against striking longshoremen. The court found "peaceable assembly for lawful discussion cannot be made a crime." Then it added:

"The greater the importance of safeguarding the community from incitements to overthrow our . . . institutions by force and violence, the more imperative is the need to preserve inviolate the constitutional rights of free speech, free press, and free assembly."

Two years later the Court held:

"Streets and parks . . . have immemorially been held in trust for the use of the public and, time out of mind, have been used for purposes of assembly."

Subsequently the Court found that while communities may reasonably regulate the time, place, and manner of protest demonstrations, the government may not arbitrarily ban peaceful protests or prevent unpopular points of view from being aired.

James Madison had no way to comprehend that the forty-five word amendment he wrote 215 years ago would continue to generate heat and light—from the Sedition Act of 1798 to the Patriot Act of 2001; from the aftermath of the Boston Massacre in 1770 to the aftermath of Kent State in 1970; from suffrage to civil rights. At times those words of the amendment spawned fractious disagreements, partisan debates, and truculent discord that seemed to endanger comity and undermine the common good. In fact, those forty-five words would construct an indestructible bridge of shared values over which the nation could walk in search of an ultimate definition of a free and just society.

Firmly protected by the United States Constitution, protesters march down Beacon Street in Boston in 2003 to oppose the upcoming war with Iraq.

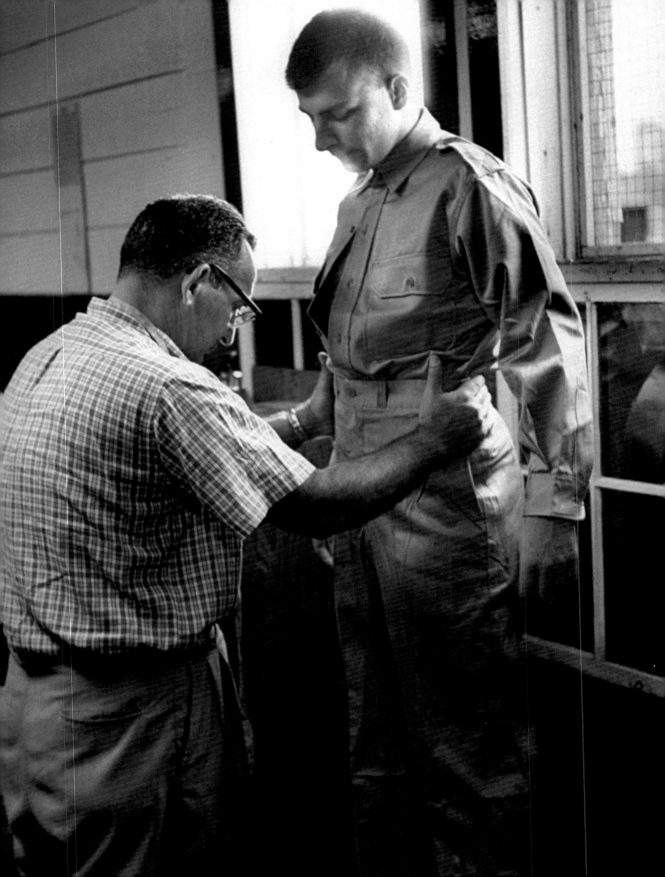

Making Citizens into Soldiers

by Harold G. Moore

LET ME BEGIN in the Ia Drang Valley in the Central Highlands of Vietnam in November 1965, when I commanded an undersized infantry battalion that landed on top of a reinforced regiment of North Vietnamese regulars— 450 of our men against roughly 2,000 of their very best troops, fierce, well armed, well trained soldiers. The battle, which marked the first time in the war that elite main force units of North Vietnam and the United States had fought each other, lasted three days and we finally prevailed, but it was a victory that, again and again, seemed to hang in the balance. The North Vietnamese Army (NVA) regulars came at us time and time again with vastly superior numbers in wave after wave of brutal fighting. On the first day of battle, with only 150 of our troops on the ground, we had been hit by about 1,000 enemy soldiers. Our situation was desperate. What probably saved us was the action of Specialist 4 Bill Beck, a twenty-two-year-old assistant gunner on an M-60, who was positioned on my left flank.

At first Bill was the spotter for Russell Adams, his best buddy and the machine gunner, but when Adams was hit in the head, Beck had immediately taken over the machine gun. He had from the start prevented the enemy from sweeping around the flank. At one critical point, with Adams severely wounded and enemy soldiers getting ever closer, his M-60 jammed. The enemy was only twenty-five yards away at that point and any prolonged silence from the M-60 was like a death warrant. "It's surprising how fast you think and act in a situation like that," he later told me. "Lying prone, I opened the feed cover, flipped the gun over, and hit it on the ground. It jarred the shells loose. Debris from the ground had caught in the ammo belt when Adams was hit. I flipped it right side up, slapped the ammo belt back in,

> "A SURPRISING NUMBER OF OUR GREATEST ACTS OF COURAGE — FOR WHICH OUR HIGHEST MEDALS ARE GIVEN — ARE DRIVEN BY RARE ACTS OF INDIVIDUALISM, OF SOLDIERS THINKING FOR THEMSELVES."

In a long American tradition of citizen-soldiers prepared to defend their country, a recruit gets fitted for his uniform at Fort Dix in 1961.

slammed the feed cover closed, and began firing again. It seemed like a lifetime, but wasn't more than five or ten seconds."

For a very long time Beck was out there, virtually alone, holding off the enemy. "Fear, real fear hit me. Fear like that I had never known before. Fear comes and once you recognize it and accept it, it passes just as fast as it comes, and you don't really think about it anymore. You just do what you have to do, but you learn the real meaning of fear and life and death. For the next two hours I was alone on that gun, shooting at the enemy." Bullets, he told me, were "hitting the ground beside me, and cracking above my head. They were attacking me all the time. I fired as fast as I could in long bursts. My M-60 was cooking."

Years later, when I was doing my research for my book, *We Were Soldiers Once . . . And Young,* I realized what Bill Beck had meant to our battalion—he had done nothing less than save it. He *was* our left flank. Without him, without his steadfast gallantry, when we were still so short on men, with only a third of our unit on the ground, the enemy would have overrun the left flank, and the battle would have been over. And he was seemingly the most ordinary of young Americans, twenty-two years old, a draftee from Steelton, Pennsylvania, a very good high school athlete in three sports, a young man who wanted to be a commercial artist. Yet somehow on that day he had ended up in the most critical place, doing something

Sobering images from the war in Vietnam came into American living rooms via television. Airborne soldiers, opposite, load their wounded into a Huey helicopter for evacuation, and a weary soldier, above, shows the strain of combat.

so remarkable that it helped carry the day for his battalion.

And when I think of that battle, I also think of Sergeant John Setelin, during the worst of the assault of the NVA on the second night. In the middle of the fight that night Sergeant Setelin, who was regular army, was hit in the arm with white phosphorus. Using the light from different flares, he used the point of his bayonet to dig the glowing phosphorous fragments out of his own flesh. Then, because the enemy kept attacking, he went back to firing his rifle, despite the excruciating pain from his burning arm. Finally, an hour later, the NVA assault defeated, Setelin was sent to the aid station. There they bandaged him up and told him he would be medical-evacuated out. So he sat there waiting for the chopper to take him out. "The longer I sat there, the more I realized I could not in good faith get on a chopper, fly out, and leave those six guys in my squad behind. So I took the sling off my arm and went back out. Somebody asked me where I was going and I said, "back to my foxhole."

Sometimes now I find it hard to believe how privileged I was to command men like these, and to be able to carry out so sacred an obligation for my country, one which entrusted me with the lives of the sons and now the daughters of my fellow citizens. And I ponder as well a question that I first heard posed, ironically enough, by a military man in a movie, the *Bridges of Toko-Ri,* but could have been uttered by any American officer who commands in

battle. Referring to the uncommon valor of ordinary citizens in difficult and dangerous times, he asked, "Where do we get such men?" Now having seen the bravery of our nurses and the sacrifices they made when I commanded in Vietnam and the role of women in the contemporary military, I would change it slightly to, "Where do we get such men and women?"

Where do we get them indeed? And what inspires them to take such extraordinary risks for their country, often in difficult, dangerous circumstances that they had no hand in shaping, but that duty and honor required them to deal with. Again and again they have performed at crucial moments with levels of couage they themselves did not know they possessed. Their courage, their loyalty, and their strength still manage to amaze me.

Who can entirely solve the great mystery of individual courage and bravery that takes young men and women from a democratic society where there is so much opportunity to do things that surely pay more and pose less danger and transforms them into truly admirable soldiers? And what makes them so good at being soldiers? What allows them to respond so well under the always unpredictable, quickly changing circumstances of combat?

I am all too aware, from my own years in the military going back to the early days of World War II, that there were all kinds of serious, highly intelligent people of all political backgrounds who worried about what would happen when our soldiers—products of so wonderfully disorganized a democracy, a society where so much is left to individual choice—went to war. How would they do against these new supersoldiers from the new super-states, Nazi Germany and Imperial Japan? Their soldiers, after all, seemed early on in that war like the prototype of the new invincible warrior of the twentieth century: men who had not only destroyed all those who had stood in their way, but also represented the perfectly trained, almost robotically fearless superwarrior of an authoritarian state. There was a certain undercurrent of fear, before the American troops were actively engaged, that the modern new dictatorship might be able to demand more of its men than our seemingly softer democratic society could—and that this would be our undoing.

But of course, our men did just fine against them. They proved to be just as tough, just as resilient, just as willing to make the ultimate sacrifice. Perhaps they had one additional quality, like Specialist 4 Beck: they were very good at responding to changing situations on the battlefield whenever innovative thinking was required. They were still very much citizens of a democratic society. They still had that wonderful edgy humor of Willie and Joe that Bill Mauldin passed on to us, and they could raise their eyebrows a bit when a junior officer did not quite come up to expectations (and managed to be quite officious about it). But when it mattered they were very good fighting men.

Their war over, wounded GIs are tended by medics and nurses as they ride a hospital train back from the Anzio front in Italy during World War II.

And during the Cold War, when some people feared the ability of the totalitarian society to put formidable armies in the field and worried that Americans had become too soft to fight, our military fought with great valor under miserable conditions in Korea and, as I was so fortunate to witness, with great honor in a difficult war in Vietnam.

I think now I've come to understand a good deal of what is at work in the somewhat mysterious process that transforms these men and women from citizens to soldiers. It's something not merely unique to a democratic society, but uniquely American as well. Every nation, I suspect, in some way or another puts the stamp of its national character, a reflection of its own special social texture and culture on its military. In America we are a nation of individualists. In so many homes our forefathers came here specifically because they were tired of people telling them what to do. As a nation we place a very high value on individualism and personal independence. We do not like people ordering us around and telling us what we have to do. Yet the military experience can seem at first glance like an all-out assault upon individualism. In the military you are taught to obey and to respond almost without hesitation to the commands of superior authority—the military depends on the almost un-American quality of obedience.

Somehow, though, we've managed to do something unusual in this country. It strikes me that the American military culture is an unusual hybrid of a highly individualistic culture blended with the traditional needs of discipline and order that the military requires. Thus the American soldier obeys orders when he needs to and thinks for himself when he needs to. There's just the right amount of elasticity in the way we do it, and a surprising number of our greatest acts of courage—for which our highest medals are given—are driven by rare acts of individualism, of soldiers thinking for themselves.

Growing doubts about the war in Vietnam in 1967 bring crowds of protesters to the Washington Monument grounds in Washington, D.C.

Two things help create that special American character of our soldiers. The first is the quality—and the special role, the absolute glue of the system—of our noncommissioned officers (NCOs). They are good, they are tough, they are instinctively democratic, and above all else, the best of them are born leaders; they are men and women who, when you are young, you do not want to fail and who, when you are an officer, you fail to listen to at your own risk. They are the very core of our Army—any good officer understands that what makes the Army run and run well is our sergeants. Occasionally there are a few who may be almost too tough for their own good, but mostly they are a marvelous blend of toughness when needed, and humanity when needed, a genuine reflection of both the occasionally cruel needs of their job, mixed with other, more tender requirements of dealing with valuable human beings in a democracy. By contrast all too often, I discovered as I studied other countries, many NCOs in other armies felt their only need was to be tough and pass on orders often as harshly as possible.

The raw recruits who meet them on the first day of training respect them for several reasons: first, they clearly know something that you don't know; second, more often than not they've done something you haven't done—served in combat and survived; and third, and most important, your life may depend on the quality of your listening.

I can still remember my first encounter with my first NCO, sixty-one years ago. When I arrived at West Point in July 1942, fresh and scared and green from Bardstown, Kentucky, I was met, along with a bunch of other equally raw appointees (soon to be sworn in as cadets on that first afternoon) at the train station by Sergeant Bonebrake. Sergeant Bone-

Civilian solidier trainees take a lesson in machine gun operation in 1940.

brake was wearing cavalry boots and riding breeches, a reminder that the old horse cavalry still existed in those days and that he had been in the horsedrawn artillery. I remember distinctly his pencil-thin moustache. His look implied that he had measured us, as he had measured hundreds of those before us, and we did not for an instant impress him. He thereupon marched us up the hill to the Cadet Barracks area.

In some ways Sergeant Bonebrake is with me to this day, and I was fortunate enough to have many men who could have been his lineal descendants serve with me

at the Ia Drang. Was there ever a more imposing figure in the eyes of a would-be cadet? Not just all those stripes, but his demeanor. Everything about him said that he was very good at what he did, and everything about him demanded respect. It was not just his special field—teaching cadets how to adjust artillery fire—it was the sum of his being, his absolute professionalism. My respect for NCOs and my belief in the great truth of the Army—that good officers listen to their NCOs—was born that day with Sergeant Bonebrake.

The other thing that I think is critical in shaping our army is something born in basic training. For years we have taken citizens of all shapes, colors, and backgrounds—some privileged, some as unprivileged as you can get—and somehow shaped them into soldiers. The fat ones get slimmer, and slim ones put on some weight. The ones who've gone to college learn respect for their fellow citizens who haven't been as fortunate, realizing that there are things their contemporaries who only went to the tenth grade can do better than they can. We teach our recruits not just how to be soldiers, how to assemble and disassemble a rifle while blindfolded, but how to respect, care for, and depend on each other. As important to learn as any single technical skill like how to crawl under live machine-gun fire is how to respect and depend on your buddies. As you go on to your units you inevitably become very close to the men in them—much closer than you would ever have imagined before joining

the Army—because you learn the importance of dependence, that one day you will surely need these men and there will be no one else there for you. They become your new family. Your old family is still your family and it still loves you as you love it, but it can't do you much good twelve thousand miles away from a killing zone. I was very lucky when I commanded my battalion in battle. More than half of the men had done basic infantry and then advanced to infantry together. They were already bonded and were family.

And so they were willing to risk their lives for each other. Out of this is a new and special kind of loyalty—a loyalty almost incomprehensible to outsiders, the loyalty of free citizens working together in a time of absolute danger—is forged. If you are going to share danger then you will also share love. And that produces the remarkable heroism that I described earlier, the willingness to make the ultimate sacrifice for buddies, friendship turned into love and strength. You do not let each other down. When Bill Beck looked down and saw Russell Adams lying next to him seriously wounded it was like his brother had been hit. You love the other soldiers in your unit and you would do for them what they would do for you. It's a powerful unwritten covenant. It's what I learned in the Korean War and what was reinforced in November 1965 in the Ia Drang Valley, and I think it answers why and where we get men and women like this.

The Bell Rings
2 MINUTES
BEFORE THE
TRAIN STARTS

CHAPTER THREE

AMERICA COMES OF AGE

★

"Such growth in wealth, in population, and in power, as a nation has seen during the century and a quarter of its national life, is inevitably accompanied by a like growth in the problems which are ever before every nation that rises to greatness.... Our forefathers faced certain perils which we have outgrown. We now face other perils the very existence of which it was impossible that they should foresee.... Upon the success of our experiment much depends—not only as regards our own welfare, but as regards the welfare of mankind."

—Theodore Roosevelt, from his 1905 inaugural address

Providing Opportunity to All

by Lee Bollinger

HIGHER EDUCATION in the United States is one of our greatest national successes. It is, by any measure, the best in the world. Many of the brightest, most energetic young people around the globe seek to come to the United States to finish their education. (Over 500,000 students from abroad were studying here at any one time in the first years of the twenty-first century.) Higher education offers an extraordinary range of benefits to the broader society: it has nurtured the creativity that has made our economy flourish and has prepared generations for various roles in society, including citizenship in a democracy.

A system of higher education that is affordable and accessible is the result of the vision and efforts of many people, but none played a more central role than two people—Thomas Jefferson, advocate for public education and founder of the first state university, and Justin Smith Morrill, the United States senator from Vermont who sponsored the federal law creating land-grant colleges in 1862.

As early as 1778, Jefferson advocated for a comprehensive plan for public education, including primary schools, secondary schools, and state universities. When Jefferson outlined his "Goals for Public Education" in 1818, higher education served a minuscule number in the United States, and colleges offered essentially the classical curriculum, with the purpose of educating future clergymen, gentlemen, and other members of the social elite. Free thinker, democrat, and scientist-farmer-inventor Jefferson argued for public higher education because his faith in democracy presupposed an educated populace. In 1786, he articulated six goals for public higher education:

> "IT HAS LONG BEEN RECOGNIZED THAT HIGHER EDUCATION IS A GOOD INVESTMENT. WHAT PIONEERS SUCH AS JEFFERSON AND MORRILL REALIZED IS THAT IT IS A GOOD INVESTMENT FOR SOCIETY AS WELL AS FOR STUDENTS."

Post-war students lounge on the campus of Cornell University, New York, in 1947, opposite. Inspired by the ideals of Thomas Jefferson, Senator Justin Smith Morrill, below, authored the Land Grants of Colleges Act of 1862, authorizing the sale of public lands to finance "at least one college" in every state.

To form the statesmen, legislators and judges, on whom public prosperity and individual happiness are so much to depend;

To expound the principles and structure of government;

To harmonize and promote the interests of agriculture, manufactures and commerce, and by well informed views of political economy to give a free scope to the public industry;

To develop the reasoning faculties of our youth, enlarge their minds, cultivate their morals, and instill into them the precepts of virtue and order;

To enlighten them with mathematical and physical sciences, which advance the arts, and administer to the health, subsistence, and comforts of human life;

And, generally, to form them to habits of reflection and correct action, rendering them examples of virtue to others, and of happiness within themselves.

The oldest institution of higher learning in the United States, Harvard University was founded in 1636. This peaceful scene shows it as it appeared around 1770.

Jefferson wrote, "Preach, my dear Sir, a crusade against ignorance; establish & improve the law for educating the common people . . . the tax which will be paid for this purpose is not more than the thousandth part of what will be paid . . . if we leave people in ignorance."

Inspired by fundamentally American ideals that flow directly from Jefferson, the land-grant college is a uniquely American idea. The Morrill Act provided that funds raised by the sale of public lands be used for the creation in each state of "at least one college where the leading object shall be, without excluding other scientific and classical studies, and including military tactics, to teach such branches of learning as are related to agriculture and the mechanic arts, . . . in order to promote the liberal and practical education of the industrial classes in the several pursuits and professions in life. . . ." The emphasis was on access and opportunity for all the people, including those in rural areas, and the addition of practical learning to the liberal education then offered by private colleges. Justin Morrill was the son of a blacksmith, and he was an experimental farmer and self-taught, well-educated man. Presumably his personal background fueled his interest in providing better educational opportunities for the children of farmers and artisans.

The purpose of the land-grant colleges was, then, explicitly utilitarian. The schools were to be closely engaged with the life and work of the people, to discover, teach, and disseminate knowledge useful to a growing nation, furthering its economic well-being and the well-being of its people. At the centennial anniversary of the Morrill Act's enactment, Harvard professor W. K. Jordan said it "was responsible for the democratization of education and for the establishment of a healthy diversity in our whole structure of higher education."

African Americans were not permitted to attend land-grant colleges in the

African-American students work in a science laboratory at the Tuskegee Institute in Alabama in 1884. A second Morrill Act in 1890 had included African-American colleges in the land-grant system. By 1997 they had awarded more than 700,000 degrees to African-American men and women.

South, and only Mississippi and Kentucky established "separate but equal" institutions for African-American students. This situation was rectified in 1890 with the passage of the Second Morrill Act, which expanded the 1862 system to include historically African-American colleges. These 1890 institutions have played a key role in providing access to higher education for African-American men and women. By 1997, seventeen predominantly African-American land-grant colleges and universities had awarded over 700,000 degrees.

In 1994, twenty-nine tribal colleges joined the land-grant system. Today there are a total of 105 land-grant colleges and universities, including institutions in every state and the U.S. territories. In 1997, three million students attended land-grant colleges and universities, including about 150,000 at the nine campuses of the University of California, the largest university, and fewer than 2,500 at Kentucky State University, the smallest. Over the years they have produced eleven American presidents and granted twenty million degrees (including one-third of all master's degrees and more than half of all doctorates) to millions of Americans who might otherwise not have been able to afford a college education. It took forty to fifty years for that investment to pay off, but pay off it did.

The Morrill Act not only provided for the creation of land-grant colleges, it also indirectly benefited public colleges that did not receive funds under the law. By the beginning of World War I, a public university dominated higher education in virtually every state outside the Northeast.

Additional federal support followed in succeeding decades, as did additional state support. The Morrill Act showed the way for the Hatch Act of 1887, which enabled agricultural research by funding state agricultural experiment stations; the Land Grant Act of 1890; the Smith-Lever Act of 1914, which created the cooperative extension program between land-grant institutions and the Department of Agriculture; the GI Bill; and the Higher Education Act of 1965, which committed the nation to the goal of equal opportunity for higher education for all Americans without regard to race or economic status. In that way, the Morrill Act helped effect—and inspire—the public higher education that Jefferson had envisioned.

In other words, the impact of the Morrill Act was not limited to the funds it provided, the institutions it enhanced or founded, the students it allowed to be taught and trained, and the learning advanced. It had at least as much to do with the stimulus it gave to states' support for public education and the validation of the idea that many can—and should—benefit from a college education. It has long been recognized that higher education is a good investment. What pioneers such as Jefferson and Morrill realized is that it is a good investment for society as well as for students. Frederick Jackson Turner, author of the seminal work *The Significance of the Frontier in American History*, concluded that the development of the state university system supplanted the frontier as the path to opportunity and guarantor that America's would not be a hierarchical society without prospects for upward mobility.

Higher education continues to play such a role. The proportion of high school graduates who enroll in college immediately after high school reflects both the accessibility of higher education and the value they place on college. That proportion has increased from 49 to 63 percent between 1972 and 2000.

It should be acknowledged that the bold idea that the Morrill Act embodied was not, however, paid for by taxes, but rather by a young nation selling a fraction of its vast public lands. Nations that were older than America was a year before the Gettysburg Address—nations that had "long endured," but that had not been "conceived in liberty and dedicated to the proposition that all men were created equal"—did not have such vast domestic lands to sell in order to fund broad-based higher education, even if they had been so inclined. (France had sold 828,000 square miles of Louisiana territories in 1803 to fund military ventures, and in 1867 Russia would sell 586,000 square miles of land in Alaska—both to the United States.)

Girls in Hawaii, above, and boys in Wisconsin, opposite, take advantage of land-grant opportunities. The girls are at the University of Hawaii Agriculture and Home Gardening School, and the boys at the University of Wisconsin Agricultural College.

A larger percentage of the population ages twenty-five to thirty-four in the United States has completed undergraduate or advanced research programs than in any of the other G-8 countries. A greater proportion of the American population that is older than thirty-four have also completed post-secondary education programs.

Public universities in the United States have not only brought practical knowledge and opportunity to many, they also have brought numerous values to the table of higher education generally. Perhaps five are of particular importance: access, diversity, secularism, constitutionally protected rights, and coeducation.

First is the value of openness or access. Public universities were founded upon the idea that the broader public should have the opportunities for education that were available through private institutions for people of wealth and status in the society. Representative of that sense is one of the most celebrated phrases in University of Michigan lore: "an uncommon education for the common man." The notion of a place where ordinary people could obtain the knowledge and intellectual capacities to succeed in the world resonates through the history of American public education. The sense that privilege has no place in deciding a young person's chances of improving his or her

lot in life through education is deeply embedded in the emergence and growth of public universities. They embody the egalitarian notion that a student's merit—his or her promise, not wealth or connections—should be the determining factor in that student's gaining access to higher education and its benefits, particularly an education at public institutions. That value has been embraced by private higher education as well. Indeed some of the most prestigious private universities, which admit students on a need-blind basis, may, in fact, be able to be more responsive to students' financial need than even the wealthiest public universities.

From this idea, a second value grows: that in educating youth for the world they will inhabit, and in particular for a democracy, it is necessary to bring people together from diverse parts of the society and to educate them in that context. Bringing people together to learn in a common setting results in a more diverse society, one committed to building an overarching national identity on top of a vast multiplicity of crosscutting groupings of citizens. This is the opposite of the view, so prominent in the nineteenth century, that the society needs a singular class of people educated and prepared to provide leadership over the masses, who cannot be expected to know their best interests. Indeed George Washington envisioned establishing a national university that would, among other things, have a similar result. He wrote to Alexander Hamilton in 1796 that a national univer-

Washington Bullets basketball player Juwan Howard (center) earns a degree from the University of Michigan in April 1995. He had left school a year early but completed his coursework during his rookie season and graduated on time.

sity should draw students in the "period of life, when friendships are being formed, & habits established that will stick by one; the Youth . . . from different parts of the United States would be assembled together, & would by degrees discover that there was not that cause for those jealousies & prejudices which one part of the union had imbibed against another part." It is this idea, of course, that causes higher education to seek diversity of all kinds—not only based on geography, which Washington saw as the principal source of "jealousies & prejudices" in his day.

A third defining characteristic of public higher education is the notion of nonreligious or secular education. David Riesman and Christopher Jencks have noted that the Morrill Act "symbolized the decline of sectarian veto groups to a point where Congress could vote with impunity for 'godless' non-sectarian colleges." Although many public universities, including the University of Michigan, had their origins in religious orders, as private institutions shed their religious undertones under social and constitutional pressure, especially in the twentieth century, public universities did so as well. Today, and for some time now, there simply has been no choice about the matter: public universities are forbidden from propagating or fostering religious beliefs.

Fourth, public institutions are subject to the Constitution of the United States and to laws applicable to governmental institutions, such as open meeting

and freedom-of-information laws. In the same way that private colleges and universities are not legally required to be secular but have nevertheless moved in that direction, most have chosen to embrace voluntarily many of the same constitutional guidelines and constraints.

Fifth, land-grant colleges—and typically, state universities—were coeducational from the outset, or from very early on in their history (although in some southern states, separate colleges existed for men and women). Now virtually all private higher-educational institutions have become coeducational.

It is a credit to the public higher-educational system that these values—access, diversity, secularism, respect for key constitutional and legal protections, and coeducation—have also gradually been embraced by most private higher-educational institutions. While it is difficult to say whether or when private universities would have acquired these qualities had there been no public universities in the United States, it is reasonable to suppose that the development was helped by their being nurtured in public institutions.

In these and other important ways, public higher education, which had its roots in Jeffersonian democracy and its greatest impetus in the Morrill Act, has now largely melded into a single educational system that is both public and private, and that has enriched the nation and its people immeasurably.

Students at Ohio State University enjoy a lakeside picnic. Since 1862, land-grant colleges have awarded some twenty million degrees.

The Freedom to Breathe Free

by Michael T. Kaufman

THE PROBLEM WITH TRYING to say something meaningful about how the experience and myths of immigration continue to shape and invigorate contemporary America is that it can easily degenerate into something resembling an essay in praise of sunlight. Surely by now everybody knows the details and comprehends the glory of the national influx during which over a mere four centuries—a span of only about twenty generations—more people traveled greater distances from more places to establish and shape the United States than was the case with any state or nation in history. Usually when these facts are cited and celebrated, the emphasis is on how the immigrant experience shaped the nation and its political and social institutions, but what I am concerned with here is how the experience and legacy of immigration transformed immigrants and continues to impact on their descendents.

With the exception of pure-blooded Native Americans, all us know in our

> "FOR ALL MY LIFE I HAVE BEEN OBSESSED BY THAT JOURNEY, STUDYING ITS DETAILS AND SEVERAL TIMES RETRACING THE ROUTE OF OUR ESCAPE."

bones that we must have come to America from elsewhere. That understanding is so widespread, so implicit, so intuitive, that Oscar Handlin, the retired Harvard historian who devoted his career to studying immigration, once wrote about giving up his long-cherished dream of writing a comprehensive "history of the immigrants in America," once he discovered "that the immigrants were American history."

Indeed it is the pervasive extent of immigrant mythology that makes it so distinctively compelling, allowing almost any American to link private or family experiences and dramas to the overarching narrative of the nation's growth and development. Not all of us can trace our personal stories to the Pilgrims or pioneers, or to struggles in the nation's wars, but even if we no longer know the full details of our particular forebearers' original crossings we are still aware that the

Fresh-off-the-boat immigrants, opposite, wait with their possessions at Ellis Island, portal to the New World, in 1907. Among their first tasks: learning a new language. The 1895 poster, below, offers English lessons in Hebrew.

peopling of America has involved our own flesh and blood, our real kith and kin, and thus it continues to be our own story. So we look backward for solace and inspiration as we head into our own unpredictable futures.

And since immigration is personal and pervasive, I feel justified in offering my own testimony about how experience has fused with national myth, not because my case is so unusual but rather the opposite, because I am certain accounts of similar magnitude are quite common. In addition, my thoughts about the benefits of immigration are obviously subjective extrapolations from my own story. Some fifty-five years ago, when I was an elementary school pupil in New York City, one of our civics teachers took our class to a museum where we were shown silver tea sets of English settlers who, the teacher seemed to suggest, were among America's most important immigrants. There was obviously little to link me and my parents to the owners of the tea sets, but I remember being struck by the notion that just like those settlers, I and my parents had also sailed across the Atlantic, in our case arriving in New York on October 13, 1940, aboard the *Nea Hellas* along with some six hundred anxious Europeans fleeing the furnaces of war.

Giant American flags fly above 1925 immigrants at Ellis Island as they wait to be interviewed by immigrant inspectors. They have already passed medical exams.

I was only two and a half years old when we made the crossing, and by the time I was in school I no longer had any true memory of the journey. And yet, now as I approach the end of a lifetime in which I pursued and cherished adventure, drama, and experience, I have come to the surprising realization that nothing has ever matched the emotional weight and importance of that wartime passage. In one sense this seems ridiculous, since besides having no recollections of our flight from Nazi-occupied Paris, as a toddler I played no active role in the story, nor was I aware of what was happening or what was at stake. And yet, for all my life I have been obsessed by that journey, studying its details and several times retracing the route of our escape. I searched for people who helped us and interviewed them, and I have pored over old records, trying to comprehend how in the face of such bitter odds the three of us managed to find an escape that eluded so many. I would use words like "miraculous" to describe how my parents, stateless Jews from Poland, ended up with emergency visas for America. As an adolescent I questioned what the Nazis and the Petainists would have done to us had we not been rescued. I can remember feeling that I had been anointed or singled out for some kind of success, and such thoughts were sometimes coupled with irrational presumptions of superiority and heroism, though there were also times when I knew I should be humble, realizing that so many others did not share my fate.

The act of coming here turned into a matter of great pride. It became a major foundation block of my identity and personality, and I can only assume that similar feelings were aroused in many of those who preceded and followed me on their own life-changing crossings so full of real perils and unavoidable anxiety. So often poor, bedraggled, and fearful, they must have nonetheless felt themselves each their own Columbus at some point, staking so much on their chance of finding a new world. And once they gained a foothold in the new land it seems likely they would convey the drama of their passage to their children and their children's children, just as I have done and am doing. This, then, is one transforming and beneficial aspect of the immigrant legacy: it sets standards for courage and initiative and expands family pride. I assume that along with fears of what awaited them, immigrants in every age must have encouraged themselves with notions that risks as great as the one they were taking deserved huge payoffs. Like the Calvinists who made sure to amass fortunes they believed would signal their predestined salvation, the immigrants must have been inspired to intensify their sacrifices and devote even greater energies to prove to themselves—as well as to those they left behind—that they had made the right choice. In the process they were transformed, and the country's emerging

spirit of creative dynamism was further
enriched.

Another consequence of the immigration myth that I consider beneficial lies
in its not always fully appreciated sense of
tragedy. Often the popular accounts of the
saga seem banal, appearing as immigration
fables in which the "huddled masses" and
"wretched refuse" of Emma Lazarus's great
sonnet, having long contended with failed
crops, vicious landlords, hunger, pogroms,
persecution, and chronic humiliation, leave
their respective old countries to thrive happily in this land of opportunity where they
and their descendents rather quickly create
the most diverse, free, and powerful nation
on the planet. Such panoramas, painted in
broad strokes, are clearly not wholly inac-

curate. Moreover, as morality tales of
transformation and legends of deliverance
they have served to propagate and per-
petuate useful values of tolerance and
melting-pot multiculturalism in an
America that still attracts and needs immigrants. But looking at our migrations with
so much emphasis on the happy ending
does tend to diminish an essential component of the story—the ennobling tragedy
inherent in the immigrant's experience of
dislocation, fear, loss, and sacrifice.

In the 1940s, as I was growing up
an American, my pride in my immigrant
story was tempered by my awareness of
my parents' sense of loss and dislocation.
As the letters with the Nazi postage
stamps from the Lodz ghetto stopped

coming, I often saw my mother cry. She kept telling me stories of her brothers and sisters, probably recognizing that I would never have the chance to meet them or their children. Of course, my parents were grateful for their rescue and they came to admire the country that had offered us sanctuary, but they remained separated from people they loved, removed from familiar settings, values, and issues and even enemies that had so long engaged and defined them. Though they certainly understood what had threatened them in Europe, they had arrived with apprehensions about life in a country whose language they did not know and where they had no family. Gradually, most of the doubts and fears eased. Starting as a presser, my father would retire two decades later as an economist. Both my parents grew appreciative of the security and opportunities that America offered to them and, more particularly, to their son and grandchildren. But at home we kept speaking Polish, and I was aware that their joys never fully cancelled out their losses. This was true for many, perhaps even most, immigrants. While 35 million had made arduous crossings in the nineteenth century, another 10 percent died on the way. Of those who arrived, many moved from steerage at sea to the squalor of slums, while others kept on moving, facing the dangers of various frontiers. "America," Handlin has written, "was the land of separated men."

Why should such tragic recollections now be counted as a benefit? Pain, suffering, and sacrifice are intrinsically significant elements of myth, and tragedy is invaluable in establishing virtue and seriousness. The evocation of loss and sacrifice have served to bind the citizenry of many nations in common yearnings. It may be said that some countries have suffered from too much suffering. But in America, where there has been so much opportunity and so many triumphs to celebrate, optimism and pragmatism have long overshadowed tragedy, leaving an entrenched notion that all problems, once identified, can be overcome. Tragedy ought to be valued as a relatively rare resource. It is also useful in confronting hubris, chauvinism, and the fevers of overenthusiastic boosterism. In America's relatively short history, the experience of slavery—itself a particular aspect of immigration that is seldom included in general discussions of the subject, though it should be—provides a major vein of tragedy. The Civil War is another important source. And the third arises from the experience of America's immigrants, more willingly transplanted than the slaves, but isolated and separated from the familiar, their eventual progress in the aggregate paid for with the considerable pain of individuals. One way to calculate the value of what has been accomplished is by weighing the costs of what has been endured.

Proud of their Irish heritage but eager to participate in American rituals, a father and daughter watch a St. Patrick's Day parade in New York City.

Rights for Those Who Fought for Them

by Richard Reeves

ON THE FIRST July 4th of the twenty-first century, July 4, 2000, a group of writers and historians on public television's nightly *NewsHour* were asked about the most important law of the last century. They began talking all over each other about the Servicemen's Readjustment Act of 1944, usually called the GI Bill of Rights.

"Listen," said Stephen Ambrose, a professor of history and best-selling author whose specialty was World War II, "that GI Bill was the best piece of legislation ever passed by the U.S. Congress. . . . It transformed our country. . . ."

"I was on the GI Bill," said Haynes Johnson, a *Washington Post* correspondent, ". . . that's how I got my graduate degree. . . ."

"Haynes and I went to the University of Wisconsin . . ." said Ambrose. "The American educational establishment of today, which is the envy of the world, was made by the GI Bill. . . . Thousands and thousands of small businesses were started in this country and are still there thanks to loans from the GI Bill."

"I bought my first house on the GI Bill," interjected the show's host, Jim Lehrer.

A lot of Americans did. The GI generation—the letters stand for "Government Issue," the words stamped on military equipment—fell in love with Public Law 346, the classification of the act after it was signed by President Franklin D. Roosevelt on June 22, 1944. And the romance continued for their children and grandchildren. It was, in the title of a prize-winning television documentary produced in 1997, "The Law That Changed America."

Let's start with some numbers:

About sixteen million American men and 350,000 American women—out of a 1940 population of 132 million—served in World War II from 1941 to 1945; more than nine million of them became members

> "IT WAS A NEW COUNTRY. AMERICAN LIFE WAS DEMOCRATIZED BEYOND PRE-WAR IMAGINATION. PEOPLE WHO HAD NEVER HEARD OF PRINCETON WERE GRADUATING FROM IT."

Exuberant Chicagoans celebrate VJ Day—the day victory over Japan was declared—with a bonfire, opposite. More than sixteen million American men and women served during World War II. Many would come home yearning for college, and the GI Bill, passed in 1944, would pave their way.

of the "52-20 Club," shorthand for a GI Bill clause that made all World War II veterans eligible to receive $20 a week for fifty-two weeks if they were unemployed during the first year after discharge. The average time taken was seventeen weeks.

About 2,172,000 men and sixty thousand women went to college on the GI Bill, receiving up to $500 a year for tuition and books, along with monthly shelter and food allotments of $50 for unmarried students and $75 for married students. Half of the recipients were married, and half of those married students had at least one child before they graduated.

About 3,500,000 men and women received the same kind of GI Bill aid for shorter training programs in vocational schools and ordinary high schools, at a time when fewer than 25 percent of Americans finished high school.

Some 1.1 million housing loans were approved in 1947 alone, thirteen million new homes were built in the United States during the 1950s, and eleven million of the new owners received GI Bill loans, called "VA Loans" because they were administered by the Veterans Administration.

More than 1,400,000 veterans received GI Bill business loans and on-the-job training subsidies, and 700,000 got farm loans, usually to buy equipment and supplies.

In 1940, 1.08 percent of college graduates were black; in 1950 that number reached almost 5 percent because of the GI Bill.

Approximately 450,000 engineers, 233,000 teachers, and 79,000 doctors and dentists were produced by the GI Bill classes.

A friend of mine named William Norris graduated from high school in a steel town, Turtle Creek, Pennsylvania—a town that usually sent one or two of its children to college each year before the war—and served in the U.S. Navy. He was the fifth of six children and no one in the family had ever gone to college—or even thought about it. When he was discharged in California, he bumped into a high school classmate, another sailor, a guy named Layman Allen, who told him about the college part of the GI Bill and said he knew of a college called Princeton.

"Where's Princeton?" said Norris.

"In Jersey."

The two of them headed back East to New Jersey, and they got in. Thirty of the 103 boys in the Turtle Creek High class of 1944 went to college, twenty-eight of them on the GI Bill. Norris went on to Stanford Law School, took a clerkship with Supreme Court Justice William O. Douglas, and became a Federal Appeals Court judge in California. Allen went to

GI BILL OF RIGHTS for SERVICE MEN & WOMEN WIVES, MOTHERS, FAMILIES 15¢

Warning! DON'T MISS OUT ON THE REWARDS A GRATEFUL NATION MAY GIVE YOU!

Read and Know Your Rights to:
- JOBS . LOANS . TRAINING
- HOMES . EDUCATION WITH PAY
- A YEAR'S SALARY
- MEDICAL CARE

ANSWERS TO 33 QUESTIONS VITAL TO EVERY VETERAN

Yale Law School and became a professor of law at the University of Michigan.

There are a lot of stories like that, partly because GI Bill payments went directly to individuals, giving men and women the chance to fulfill their own dreams. An orphan who became a marine, Art Buchwald, went to the University of Southern California and then used some of his GI Bill money to study in Paris, where he began writing a humor column and became one of America's favorite pundits. Harry Belafonte, Walter Matthau, and Rod Steiger were vets who met each other studying drama at the New School in New York. William Styron, the writer, went to Duke. A young lieutenant from Russell, Kansas, named Robert Dole was badly wounded on his first day in combat, in 1943 in Italy, but when he recovered he went on to Washburn Municipal University. Then he went to Washburn Law School, finishing up in 1952. Sixteen years later he became a United States senator and then the Republican candidate for president. Leo Lederman, a Signal Corps lieutenant for three years, did graduate work at Columbia University on the GI Bill and, in 1988, won a Nobel Prize in physics—one of ten Nobels won by GI Bill vets. When the National Aeronautics and Space Agency was created in the 1960s, more than half its engineers had gone to college on the GI Bill.

Cookie-cutter houses of Levittown, New York, right, were home sweet home to returning veterans. The Cape Cod model in Levittown was 800 square feet on a 60-by-100-foot lot, with two bedrooms, one bath, a living room, a kitchen, and an unfinished second floor. It sold for about $7,000. In the 1950s, eleven million GIs bought new homes with financial assistance from the Veterans Administration.

Although some of the vets would have gone on to college and there was a degree deficit after four years of war, the educational provisions of the GI Bill changed almost everything in the United States. Like the war itself, the college experience took millions of young men and women to places they never expected to see, enabling them to meet people they never would have met in the years before the war. Until then, most Americans married the girl or boy next door, someone they went to school or church with, someone like themselves. Suddenly, Catholic boys from Pennsylvania were marrying Protestant girls from California and going to Washington to work. Before the war, Americans lived in cities, towns, or on the farm. Suddenly, the couples eligible for VA housing loans were buying $7,500 houses on Long Island, built at a rate of thirty-five a day by an ex-Navy Seabee named William Levitt—with forty-year mortgages backed by the Veterans Administration. There were new words for the old farmland growing houses: "developments" and "suburbs." One of the buyers, Jerry Naples, an army medical corpsman who became a physician at the University of South Florida, went to Long Island with instructions from his new wife to buy one with a yellow kitchen. He did just that, not knowing all the kitchens in Levittown were yellow.

It was a new country. American life was democratized beyond pre-war imagination. People who had never heard of Princeton were graduating from it. The number of Americans in college went from fewer than 1.5 million in 1940, most of them from upper-class or ambitious middle-class families, to more than 2.5 million in 1947. There were 2.3 million marriages that year, a jump of 50 percent from 1945, and then came the children—the baby boom. "Fertile Valley" replaced "Vetsville" as the common name for the crowded and often muddy camps of trailers and old barracks where married veterans lived on and near their campuses. In 1946, more than 1.5 million vets were living in other people's homes.

At the University of Wisconsin, as enrollment went from 11,286 in 1940 to 18,693 (including 10,792 veterans) in 1948, those veterans living in tents put up signs like this one:

People of Madison!
VETS IN TENTS
NEED ROOMS TO RENT
Offer Your Spare Room!
Give a Vet the Chance to Use
The GI Bill.

They were serious men and women, most of them great students, more mature and motivated than their teenage competitors at schools around the country. At Stanford they were called the "DARs," for "Damn Average Raisers." Writing in November of 1947, the education editor of the *New York Times*, Benjamin Fine, confirmed that, "Here is the most astonishing fact in the history of American higher education . . . the GI's are hogging the honor rolls and the Dean's lists; they are walking away with the highest marks in all of their courses."

They were bigger and stronger, too. A nine-year-old growing up in Jersey City could feel the energy, even if all I understood was that college football touched a peak in those few years of the late 1940s. The star of the University of Michigan team that won the Rose Bowl that year was Bob Chappius, a twenty-four-year-old halfback who had been a B-25 radioman and gunner. He was shot down over Italy on his twenty-first mission and saved for the Rose Bowl by partisans moving him from one house to another, hiding him from the Nazis. And he was just one of a crowd of heroes that included Johnny Lujack of Notre Dame, Doak Walker of Southern Methodist, and Bobby Layne of Texas—all vets on the GI Bill.

It was a love story with a happy ending. Well, that was the way it was meant to be, wasn't it? No, not exactly.

The GI Bill came into being because the folks back home were terrified of what

Home from the war, Southern Methodist University football players, including Doak Walker (second from right), appear for practice, left. Older, stronger, and more mature than most of their classmates, many veterans on the GI Bill excelled at sports.

The Bonus Army—a ragtag crowd of World War I veterans—stages a massed vigil on the steps of the U.S. Capitol in 1932, right. The men are protesting the government's failure to advance them a promised $500 bonus. General Douglas MacArthur, opposite top, arrives with federal troops to evict them. The GI Bill, after the Second World War, would prevent similar hardships.

might happen when millions of young men and women came marching home to a country that still had 14.6 percent unemployment in 1940. The memory of what happened when five million Americans came home from World War I was still fresh when President Roosevelt, in a fireside radio chat on July 28, 1943, said, "Veterans must not be demobilized into an environment of inflation and unemployment, to a place on a breadline or on a corner selling apples." His wife, Eleanor Roosevelt, was even more direct, warning in April of 1942, only four months after Pearl Harbor:

"Veterans may well create a dangerous pressure group in our midst. . . . [We must] adjust our economic system so that opportunity is open to them on their return, or we may reap the whirlwind."

There had indeed been a whirlwind after World War I. Demobilized veterans of that war were given $60 and a free railroad ticket when they marched home. They were also promised a $500 bonus financed by bonds that would not come due until 1945. As the Great Depression set in, with unemployment rates that reached 23.6 percent, veterans began to demand earlier payment of the bonus. But Congress and President Hoover would not change the schedule and, in early 1932, a "bonus army" of fifteen thousand men gathered in Washington and set up a shantytown along the Anacostia River. When those old doughboys, now middle-aged family men without jobs, refused to leave town, Hoover called in the army. Troops and tanks, under the command of General Douglas MacArthur, burned their campgrounds and drove them out of the capital. Meanwhile, veterans in other countries were in the vanguards of revolutionary movements, particularly in Russia, Germany, and France. All that was part of the reason Roosevelt defeated Hoover. Ten years later, FDR began thinking about what to do when the war was over.

The president called on the country's largest veterans organization, the American Legion, to come up with post-war plans, and they did, pretty much writing the legislation. They called their suggestions and demands "A Bill of Rights for GI Joe and GI Jane." But the cleverness of the name did not prevent a good deal of controversy: conservatives considered the bill a welfare program—handouts for slackers; southern congressmen objected to equal payments for black veterans; and the education establishment anticipated the toppling of ivy walls and ivory towers. The president

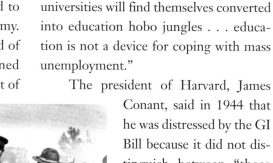

of the University of Chicago, Robert M. Hutchins, put it this way: "Colleges and universities will find themselves converted into education hobo jungles . . . education is not a device for coping with mass unemployment."

The president of Harvard, James Conant, said in 1944 that he was distressed by the GI Bill because it did not distinguish between "those who could profit from advanced education and those who cannot." Two years later, in June of 1946, Conant took it back, saying, "The veterans are the most mature and promising students Harvard has ever had."

The final endorsement of mass higher education came with the landslide passage of the Veteran's Readjusment Act of 1952, Public Law 550, the Korean War's GI Bill. It helped marine Jim Lehrer buy his first home and soldier Haynes Johnson get a graduate degree. The Senate vote was unanimous, and the House of Representatives vote was 361-to-1. In the debate over the bill, there was no mention of breadlines or disgruntled veterans, just lyrical talk about the wonders the World War II vets had done for themselves and their country.

Veterans and coeds take an exam at the University of Iowa, bottom. In 1947, some six thousand veterans on the GI Bill comprised 60 percent of the school's enrollment. Such figures told of a transformation of education in America.

Ribbons Across the Land

by Martin F. Nolan

THE WAR WAS OVER and the twenty-eight-year-old captain faced boredom and an uncertain future. "No human enterprise goes flat so instantly as an Army training camp," Dwight D. Eisenhower recalled years later. "As for my professional career, the prospects were none too bright," he wrote. "If not depressed, I was mad, disappointed and resented the fact that the war had passed me by." In World War I, he had trained other soldiers, but now the West Point graduate who would lead Allied forces in World War II was tempted "to try my luck as a civilian again."

Instead, he heeded the call of the open road. In 1919, the U.S. Army sought volunteers to survey the condition of American roads. Ike quickly signed up. From the White House in Washington to San Francisco's City Hall, a convoy of cars and trucks took sixty-two days to travel 3,251 miles. "Most of the time we hardly exceeded a

"IT IS CHARAC-
TERISTICALLY
AMERICAN THAT
THE GREATEST
PUBLIC WORKS
PROJECT
IN THE HISTORY
OF THE PLANET
WOULD BE
DEVOTED TO A
JOURNEY, NOT
A DESTINATION."

good bicyclist's speed," Eisenhower recalled. In the first three days, the column "spent twenty-nine hours on the road and moved 165 miles," an average speed of less than six miles an hour.

The saga stuck in the soldier's memory for decades until, as president in 1955, he proposed a "grand plan," an interstate highway system with no stoplights and no intersections, a matrix of limited-access pavement that would crisscross the nation. The system would run 46,000 miles by the end of the century, and, Ike wrote, would pour enough concrete "to build eighty Hoover Dams or six sidewalks to the moon." It would also fuel the largest mass migration in history, as millions of Americans moved from cities and small towns to a new nation within a nation, suburbia.

Ribbons of concrete point toward a Los Angeles sunset, opposite. The National System of Interstate and Defense Highways, begun in 1956, would eventually stretch for 46,000 miles across the country, and its roadsides would sprout the familiar red, white, and blue Interstate signs, below.

The concept, like so many other grand plans, stalled in Congress on the issue of how to pay for it. The roadblock was Harry Byrd of Virginia, chairman of the Senate Finance Committee. Elected to the Senate in 1932, the year of Franklin D. Roosevelt's landslide, Byrd was a Democrat in name only. He abhorred taxes and deficit financing. "Neither a borrower nor a lender be," the Polonius of the Shenandoah firmly believed. In his memoirs, Eisenhower wrote, "I grew restless with the quibbling over methods of financing. I wanted the job done." In 1956, House Democrats devised a plan with no long-term borrowing. By placing new taxes on oil, gasoline, and tires into an Interstate Highway Trust Fund, construction would be "pay-as-you-go," Harry Byrd's favorite way to travel.

Dwight David Eisenhower, right, a graduate of West Point, served as a surveyor for the first national road system in 1919. Later, as president, he lobbied for the interstate highways. They helped make possible the migration of citizens from the cities to the emerging suburban communities.

Congress quickly approved what was called the "National System of Interstate and Defense Highways" in 1956, when Cold War tensions were still vivid. That year the Soviet Union's Nikita Khrushchev warned the West, "History is on our side. We will bury you." In 1940, President Roosevelt sought new highways to serve navy yards in Brooklyn and Philadelphia, resulting in the Defense Highway Act of 1941. National security was a political ploy long after the Cold War. In 2003, during the war in Iraq, the president of a road-building lobby said, "Having the ability to move quickly and safely in the event of a national emergency—it's just common sense that it's good policy."

It is characteristically American that the greatest public works project in the history of the planet would be devoted to a journey, not a destination. The Interstate changed the landscape, the economy, and leisure habits. Even the names of the cars that took these journeys reflected developments. Earlier automobiles were named for tycoons and designers: Chrysler, Ford, Olds, Packard. In the 1930s, when motoring meant a leisurely Sunday drive, cars carried historic names of explorers: DeSoto, Hudson, LaSalle. But after limited-access straightaways, and after Ford's success with the Thunderbird in the 1950s, cars of the 1960s evoked creatures of the wild: Cougar, Stingray, and the popular Mustang.

"Pay-as-you-go" highways were politically painless and financed with 90 percent federal funding, which made them politically popular. In the mid-1950s, motorists could buy reliable, comfortable cars for less than $2,000. Gasoline had always been cheaper in the United States than in other countries. New oil fields and advances in technol-

A mid-1950s suburban family welcomes Mom home from a trip. As quick access to highways made it convenient to live outside central cities, many families relocated to suburban neighborhoods within easy commute of the city. They also began to use their vacation time to discover regions of the country previously too far away to visit. Another factor: Between 1950 and 2000, the real price of gasoline declined by a third.

ogy helped gasoline defy inflation in the second half of the twentieth century, even while taxed for the Highway Trust Fund. In *Suburbia*, his 1958 book popularizing the phrase, Robert C. Wood wrote "the suburbanite frequently finds that the automobile is not only the most convenient way to travel; it can be the cheapest." From 1950 to 2000, the adjusted-for-inflation price of gasoline fell 33 percent. Commuter railroads and other forms of public transit could not compete.

In 1956, two best-selling novels in America were autopsies of the old order. *The Last Hurrah* by Edwin O'Connor detailed the decline of big-city machine politics. *Peyton Place* by Grace Metalious uncovered the sordid secrets of small-town society. Social changes evident in politics and sex accelerated with the growth of the Interstate. Its highways drew wealth and population out of big cities, while taking large swaths of urban land, demolishing housing and businesses in the process. For small towns, the Interstate had the opposite effect. Many villages, bypassed by its bustle, shriveled up and died. On many an old road made obsolete by the Interstate, business was as grim as the trade in the Bates Motel, scene of Alfred Hitchcock's *Psycho*, filmed in 1959.

Traffic maneuvers through Ohio's worst intersection—the only stoplight in 180 miles between Detroit and Louisville. Eisenhower and his engineers modeled their highway system on Germany's autobahns.

Combined with millions of low-cost mortgages, the Interstate subsidized suburbia with federal money. Veterans' programs and other housing loans further undermined cities through the practice of "redlining," denying mortgages to poor urban neighborhoods. By the time the system reached the edge of cities in the late 1960s, "freeway revolts" halted construction in Boston, San Francisco, Washington, and other cities.

The Interstate's safety features clearly saved lives, particularly in rural areas. Its benefits for the farm economy were obvious, but for cities and suburbs, the imbalance in transportation funding was also obvious. Subway and bus lines

were constantly "in deficit." Interstate highways never were. In 1960, Daniel Patrick Moynihan wrote in *The Reporter* magazine, "To undertake a vast program of urban highway construction with no thought for other forms of transportation seemed lunatic." In the Senate, in 1991, Moynihan helped redress the balance with legislation allowing states and cities more access to Highway Trust Fund money for mass transit.

But American suspicion of cities is deeply rooted. "The American urban place is an 'anti-city' because we like it that way," Moynihan, then director of the Joint Center for Urban Studies at MIT and Harvard, said in 1966. "It may be said without great distortion that it is not the technology of the automobile that produced the embodiment in miniature of the agrarian ideal which our suburbs seem so intent upon, but rather the ideal that produced the technology." Testifying before Congress, Moynihan said, "The agrarian tradition has never died in America; it has simply found outlets in new forms."

An "anti-city" Interstate disappointed Eisenhower because he had hoped it would proceed on the European model and avoid central cities. "The matter of running Interstate routes through the congested parts of the cities was entirely against his original concept and wishes," his biographer, Stephen Ambrose, wrote. "He never anticipated that the program would turn out this way."

The Interstate system, later named for Eisenhower, helped create a wealthy America. The automobile was already an engine of growth in 1955, when Mamie Eisenhower was hostess for the wives of five thousand automobile dealers convening in the capital. She told her husband, as he recorded in his diary, "that is one crowd that is prospering! She never saw so many furs and diamonds." In retirement, Ike became a philosopher, writing folksy memoirs as stories for his grandchildren. In *At Ease: Stories I Tell to Friends* in 1969, he reminisced about his 1919 adventure:

"The trip had been difficult, tiring, and fun. I think that every officer on the convoy had recommended in his report that efforts should be made to get our people interested in producing better roads. A third of a century later, after seeing the autobahns of modern Germany and knowing the assets those highways were to the Germans, I decided, as president, to put an emphasis on this kind of road building. When we finally secured the necessary congressional approval, we started the 41,000 miles of super highways that are already proving their worth. This was one of the things that I felt deeply about, and I made a personal and absolute decision to see that the nation would benefit by it. The old convoy had started me thinking about good, two-lane highways, but Germany had made me see the wisdom of broader ribbons across the land."

Eisenhower grew up in Kansas in a farm community far from the urban, industrialized world he would know as general and president. He heard railroad whistles in his youth, but "as far as passenger travel was concerned," he wrote, "the automobile and the airplane did to the railroads what the locomotive had done to the waterways." The twentieth century was, in many ways, Dwight Eisenhower's century. The Interstate highway system remains a big, busy, and enduring monument to his vision.

Roadside advertising, which popped up as paved roads made auto travel convenient and inexpensive, here beckons travelers to "next time try the train."

Examining the American Dream

by Kenneth T. Jackson

THE UNITED STATES is a suburban nation. As early as 1950, a quarter of the national population lived on the metropolitan periphery. By 1960, that proportion reached one-third, and by 1990, it exceeded one-half. By 2000, more than 140 million people lived on the edges, usually in single-family homes. No other country on earth, with the possible exception of Australia, has deconcentrated so relentlessly, so overwhelmingly, so ubiquitously. Why did this happen in the United States? Why did it not happen in most other countries?

The term "suburb" is of course imprecise. As even casual reflection reveals, American suburbs come in all shapes and sizes, so much so that some suburbs, like Hoboken, New Jersey, are more like cities than the spacious enclaves for the comfortable that fit the stereotype. And some neighborhoods in cities, like River Oaks in Houston, Fieldston in the Bronx, and Bel-Air in Los Angeles, are closer to the suburban image than most suburbs themselves.

However defined, though, suburbs clearly exist in the United States, and they project an image of success and affluence. For example, a popular topic of conversation across the nation in recent decades has been suburban real estate, and especially its rapidly escalating cost. Who among us, it is often alleged, could afford to live in our own homes if we were required to pay the current price? And such anecdotal evidence is reinforced by television and newspaper reports, most of which trumpet the same message—if you already own shelter, count your blessings. If you have yet to enter the housing market, curse the stars.

The simple fact, however, is that American real estate prices are low and

> "WHY HAVE AMERICANS FLOCKED TO THE SUBURBS IN SUCH OVERWHELMING NUMBERS? . . . AND WHY HAVE CITIES SO OFTEN BECOME DISPIRITING COLLECTIONS OF WEED-FILLED LOTS, LITTERED STREETS, AND FADING CENTRAL BUSINESS DISTRICTS?"

Suburban sprawl, opposite—a dense development of similar homes and gently curving streets—distinguishes the edges of American cities from those in other industrialized countries. Americans' rush to the suburbs has had far-reaching consequences. Of 100 million dwellings in use in 2000, some two-thirds were single-family homes.

homeownership rates are high by international standards. In the United States, for example, about two-thirds of all households live in a domicile that they own. Among persons between forty-five and sixty-four years of age, the proportion of owners rises to about three-fourths, a rate about double that of other advanced industrial nations, such as Great Britain, Germany, France, Switzerland, Sweden, and Norway, and many times higher than that of

Housing crowds the base of the Eiffel Tower in Paris, a city where people tend to live not in suburbs but in town.

such former communist nations as Russia, Poland, or Bulgaria, where private ownership was technically illegal for many decades. Only Australia, Canada, Ireland, and New Zealand, all with small populations and a British-induced cultural dislike of dense cities, can also be described as home-owning societies.

The unusual character of the American residential pattern becomes clear when viewed from an international perspective. The United States has been thus far unusual in four important respects that can be summed up in the following sentence: Affluent and middle-class Americans live in suburban areas that are far from their workplaces, in homes that they own, and in the center of yards that by urban standards elsewhere are enormous. Thus, in addition to homeownership, this circumstance involves population density, residential status, and journey-to-work.

More than any other people, Americans are scattered over the landscape with an absence of sharp distinctions between city and country. Indeed, with broad streets and expansive lawns, entire metropolitan regions feature residential densities of fewer than five persons per acre, and in the distant suburbs less than one person per acre. The situation in the Memphis area is instructive. This growing metropolis, which included more than one million residents in 2000, stretched over many hundreds of square miles and had absorbed such distant communities as Arlington, Cordova, Collierville, and Lakeland. The central business district was depopulated and forlorn, and Main Street was not even a shadow of its former self. Such sprawl results from the privatization of American life and from the tendency to live in fully detached homes. For example, of the more than 100 million dwelling units in the United States in 2000, about two-thirds consisted of a single family living in a single dwelling surrounded by an ornamental yard.

By contrast, European and Asian megacities are more crowded and less suburban than those of the United States. For example, the outer boundaries of Copenhagen, Moscow, Cologne, and Vienna abruptly terminate with apartment buildings, and a twenty-minute train ride will take one well into the countryside. Similarly, open fields surround the narrow streets and crowded houses of Siena and Florence. Metropolitan Tokyo has swallowed up tens of thousands of tiny farms since World War II, but private building lots rarely exceed one-twentieth of an acre and are often less.

A third distinguishing characteristic of suburban living in the United States is the length of the average journey-to-work, whether measured in minutes or in miles. No other people, not even the Australians and the Canadians, travel so far to employment. According to the 2000 census, the typical American worker traveled ten miles and expended a half hour in each direction, and in larger metropolitan areas such as New York and Los Angeles the figures were higher. Precise figures are unavailable for Europe, Asia, and South America, but one need only think of the widespread practice in Italy and Spain of going home for lunch, often for a siesta as well, to realize that an easier connection between work and residence is more valued in other societies.

The fourth and final distinguishing characteristic of the American metropolitan pattern is the socioeconomic difference between the center and the periphery. Even elementary-school students know that "inner city" is a synonym for a range of pathologies, from crime to public housing to poverty to troubled schools to minority concentrations. Meanwhile, the suburbs provide the bedrooms for an overwhelming proportion of those with college educations, of those engaged in professional pursuits, and of those in the upper-income brackets. And despite hopes and claims of a revival of American cities in the 1990s, the 2000 census revealed a widening disparity between residents of cities and of suburbs. In fact, because low-income areas, public housing projects, and minority groups are so concentrated in city centers, economist Richard R. Muth calculated a third of a century ago that median income in American cities tended to rise at about 8 percent per mile as one moved away from the central business district, and that it doubled in ten miles.

The situation in other nations provides a striking contrast. In Cairo, the prestigious area lies almost at the center of the metropolis. In Calcutta and Bombay, the only neighborhoods with a passable water supply are those in the middle, where the wealthy live. In Brazil, the exclusion of slum dwellers from the urban cores is so deeply rooted in the culture that the Portuguese word used to describe them is "marginais," and the word used to describe their arrival is "invasao." Similarly in Mexico City, Lima, Buenos Aires, and Santiago, the most degrading poverty exists on the outskirts, where flush toilets, sewers, and running water,

Middle-class flight to the suburbs creates complex problems: time-consuming traffic congestion in Atlanta, top, and inner-city decay in Philadelphia, bottom.

Mom and the kids enjoy their suburban pool in the 1950s. Unlike in many European countries, where land is scarce, suburban land in the United States is both available and relatively cheap.

as well as police and fire protection, are almost unknown.

In sum, the suburbs of the United States differ from those of both advanced and developing nations. In fact, in all the world, only Australia and Canada can be said to exhibit an American-style residential pattern.

Why have Americans flocked to the suburbs in such overwhelming numbers? Why have they concentrated so much of their energy, their vitality, and their creativity on the metropolitan periphery? And why have cities so often become dispiriting collections of weed-filled lots, littered streets, and fading central business districts?

Clearly, no single answer can account for such an important phenomenon, but seven causes are fundamental: racial prejudice, inexpensive land, balloon-frame construction, efficient transportation, federal subsidies, the balkanization of local government, and weak land use controls.

No analysis of the suburbs of the United States can ignore the overriding significance of race. Quite simply, the American people have for more than four centuries been obsessed with the question of skin color. And in comparison with the relatively homogeneous character of Germany, Britain, Japan, or Denmark, the cities of this nation have long been extraordinarily diverse. In residential terms, this has provided an incentive for persons to move away from their urban domiciles: fear. Unlike the locked doors and grated windows of the city, the single-family settlements in the outskirts seem to promise relief from racial integration and its two presumed fellow travelers, interracial violence and interracial sex.

Citizens are prejudiced in other societies, however, and still do not move to the suburbs. Why is the suburban option so common in America? Essentially, the answer is economic. One difference between the United States and its industrial rivals is that American real estate is affordable and available, whereas in Europe it is expensive and scarce. Over the past century, for example, building lots in North America have typically been priced from one-fourth to one-half comparably sized and located parcels in Europe and Japan. This is because forests and farms have never been in short supply in the fifty states, and large tracts of land within commuting distance can typically be purchased at bargain prices, encouraging large-scale investment.

A second component of affordable price is inexpensive transport, which has brought home sites within the daily journey-to-work zone. Americans did not invent the omnibus, the railroad, the subway, or the automobile, but it was in the United States that they were most enthusiastically adopted and where they most immediately affected the lives of ordinary citizens. Before World War I, the nation had the world's best public transportation systems. Since that time, the mass production of motor vehicles and various government subsidies to the automobile have meant that Americans are a people on wheels.

The third component of affordable suburbs is the balloon-frame house. The development of an inexpensive and peculiarly American method of building houses with two-by-four wooden studs, beginning in the middle of the nineteenth century and continuing through today, has simplified construction and brought the price of a private dwelling within the reach of most citizens. Each region of the United States has a favored exterior material for new single-family houses—wood clapboard in the Northeast and the North Central states, brick in the South, and stucco in the West. But the majority of American houses have an essentially wood or balloon-frame core, regardless of exterior sheathing. Such structures are uncommon in other countries because their citizens regard the balloon frame as flimsy and because they lack the timber resources of the heavily forested United States.

The fourth component of suburban affordability has been the role of government, particularly at the federal level. The prevailing myth in the United

A brick home goes up in Lincolnshire, England. A building style developed in America, the balloon-frame house utilizes two-by-four wooden studs, a technique that simplifies construction and makes houses more affordable. Today's relatively huge American homes average nearly 700 square feet of living space per person.

States is that the post-war suburb blossomed because of the preference of consumers who made free choices in an open environment. Actually, public policies favored deconcentration. The Federal Housing Administration, the interstate highway system, the financing of sewers, and the placement of public housing at the center of ghetto neighborhoods, among many policies, encouraged scattered development in the open countryside. Thus, suburbanization is not a historical inevitability created by geography, technology, and culture, but has instead been the product of government policies.

The most important government inducement to single-family suburban residence is contained in the Internal Revenue Code, which allows taxpayers to deduct mortgage interest and property taxes from their total taxable income. Moreover, because persons with the largest houses typically have the highest interest payments and property taxes, it is they who receive the largest subsidies. These benefits make it increasingly likely, as taxable income rises, that homeownership will be preferred to renting.

The fifth inducement to suburbanization is political balkanization. In the United States, metropolitan regions stretch over hundreds and sometimes thousands of square miles, dwarfing the geographical spread of even the largest

As fractured as a cubist's image, the Stuyvesant Town housing projects, built for middle-income families, clutters several blocks on the east side of Manhattan in New York City. Urban renewal, intended to improve conditions for inner-city residents, instead resulted in a new form of urban bleakness.

agglomerations elsewhere. And because municipal annexation has not kept up with the outward movement of the American people, the number of local governments has multiplied; the New York metropolitan region alone is dotted with more than 1,700 separate taxing authorities. Such political balkanization is important because education, sanitation, public health, and fire and police protection are local responsibilities in the United States; they are national or regional responsibilities in other advanced nations. Thus, when middle-class families move from cities to suburbs, they take with them needed tax revenues. In Europe, Japan, and Australia, by contrast, outward population movements have little effect on schools, crime, or fire protection.

Finally, land use controls in the United States are weak. In Europe, land is regarded as a scarce resource to be controlled in the public interest rather than exploited for private gain. Thus, the national and municipal governments of the Old World have traditionally exercised stringent controls over land development, and they have operated on the theory that the preservation of farms and open space is an appropriate national goal and that suburban sprawl is undesirable. The English have been so effective in this regard that the rate of farmland conversion to residential use has actually been lower since World War II than it was in the 1930s. Similarly, in Sweden, the 1947 Building

and Planning Act effectively eliminated private land use decisions in metropolitan areas and abolished the free right to build in urbanized sections. In the United States, by contrast, the suburbs have been unregulated in the European sense of that term, and municipalities, counties, and states have traditionally imposed as few restrictions as possible on developers.

Suburbs represent the crowning physical achievement of the United States. They are more representative of our national culture than big cars, tall buildings, or professional football. The single-family house symbolizes the fullest, most unadulterated embodi-ment of who we are as a people. It is a manifestation of such fundamental characteristics of the American economy as conspicuous consumption, a reliance upon the private automobile, upward mobility, the separation of the family into nuclear units, the widening division between work and leisure, and the tendency toward economic disparity. And the aspiration to homeownership, the belief that somehow, someday one can purchase a detached dwelling on an individual lot with a two-car garage, has been as important in drawing newcomers to these shores as freedom of religion or freedom of speech and assembly.

Opening America

by James Fallows

ADVANCES IN TRANSPORTATION don't end up saving time. Mainly they let people go farther in the same amount of time they spent before. The steady increase in each person's possible radius of travel has had profound effects on the man-made landscape, especially in the United States.

When people traveled to and from work on foot, they had to live either at the workplace—the farm, the mill, the manor house—or in nearby villages. As they became able to commute by trolley, by bus, by subway, and eventually by freeway, cities went in size from Boston, with its compact downtown, to Oklahoma City or Albuquerque, spread out for dozens of miles. When the Spanish friar Junipero Serra laid out the twenty-one missions along the California coast in the 1700s, he separated them by one day's travel—or twenty-five-mile intervals, since the travel was on foot. When the American gangsters Bugsy Siegel and Meyer Lanksy laid out plans for the resort city of Las Vegas in the 1940s, its success depended on being within one day's travel of customers in Los Angeles—or three hundred miles, since the travel was by car.

> "BUT IT WAS WITH THE 727 THAT AIR TRAVEL BECAME FULLY MODERN— WHICH IS TO SAY, SO CHEAP AND RELIABLE THAT IT IS TAKEN FOR GRANTED. . . ."

One airplane changed America by altering the definition of one day's travel. With the coming of the Boeing 727, virtually any point in the continental United States was within one day's travel of any other. Technically this feat had been possible even before the 727 entered commercial service in 1964. With enough stops for fuel and enough patience for low-altitude turbulence, the propeller-driven airliners of the 1930s could go from coast to coast in eighteen hours or less. The first commercially successful American jet airliner, the Boeing 707, made transcontinental flights at speeds much like those of today's big jets. But while the 727 was neither the first, nor the fastest, nor

Sleek and elegant, a Boeing 727 climbs toward its cruising altitude, opposite. The 727s, introduced commercially in 1964, made air travel routine. They could fly coast to coast in five hours, a trip that had taken earlier propeller driven planes— like Pan American's DC-3s—as much as eighteen hours.

the safest, nor the highest-flying, nor the longest-range jet airliner of the twentieth century, it was the one with the most historic impact. It was the first to be simultaneously fast enough, affordable enough, safe enough, and convenient enough to make air travel a routine rather than exceptional part of American life.

The 727 repeated, in intensified form, the social impact of an earlier "revolutionary" airplane. That was the DC-3, from Douglas Aircraft of Los Angeles, which made its first flight in 1935 and which over the next few years significantly broadened the appeal of air travel. No single aspect in the DC's construction was a radical innovation, but in combination a number of elements made it look modern and work well. These included an aluminum "monocoque" design, which surrounded the entire fuselage in one smooth shell, rather than the boxy construction of most previous models; a single low wing; cowlings to enclose the engines; retractable landing gear to improve cruising speed; and an adjustable-pitch propeller, which made the plane more efficient. In the five years

About to be replaced, a DC-3 revs its engines for takeoff, top. Within a few years, jet engines will replace its propellers. A German Messerschmitt, bottom, capable of flying 530 miles an hour, sits on an Ohio airfield in August 1945.

between the DC-3's commercial debut, with American Airlines in 1936, and the United States' entry into World War II, U.S. air passenger traffic increased fivefold, nearly all because of the DC-3.

Although Douglas built ten thousand DC-3s as military transports during World War II, the clear lesson of wartime aviation was the coming importance of jet propulsion. For instance, in 1944 the aviation writer S. Paul Johnston published a book called *Wings After War*. It pointed out that propeller planes were nearing their limits, since they became less efficient the faster they went. If air travel were to become faster and safer, it would need to be by jet, based on technical advances during the war. The German *Luftwaffe* fielded the first jet fighter, the Messerschmitt 262, in 1944. The British test-flew the jet airliner, the DeHaviland Comet, in 1949, and introduced it to commercial service in 1952. In 1958, a Comet was the first airliner to cross the Atlantic nonstop. The first important American-built jets were the Douglas DC-9 and the Boeing 707. By the late 1950s, they took the world market from the Comet, which had suffered several well-publicized crashes.

Through these early post-war years, the market for air travel constantly grew. In 1940, fifteen Americans took railroad trips for every one who boarded an airplane. By the mid-1950s, airlines had become the dominant means of travel for trips of more than two hundred miles. In 1958, trans-

atlantic trips by air surpassed sea passages for the first time. But it was with the 727 that air travel became fully modern—which is to say, so cheap and reliable that it is taken for granted, and becomes notable less in itself than for its effects.

Like the DC-3, the 727 was remarkable because it combined so many preexisting innovations in one new package. To begin with, it was a jet, which improved its speed but, even more, improved its safety and comfort. Jet-powered airplanes were safer than propeller planes not just because the engines failed so rarely but also because they let the planes fly above rather than

through most turbulent or threatening weather. Higher-altitude travel was also more comfortable for passengers. The 727 had three jet engines, all mounted at its tail. The design had been introduced with the French Caravelle, and the extra engine was thought to be a margin of safety for long trips across the Rockies. (Today's jets are so reliable that two-engine planes cross the Pacific.) The 727's cabin was as wide around as the 707's, but the plane used far less fuel, especially on short hauls, and could land at smaller airports.

In the 727, the world's airlines saw a plane that was safer and more economical than anything previously on the market—and far more adaptable. It could be used, profitably, on a New York–Boston flight, or New York–Chicago, or New York–Dallas, and even, in a pinch, New York to Los Angeles.

The airlines rushed to buy. The first 727 off Boeing's line went to United Airlines in 1964, but by the end of that year American, Eastern, and TWA had also introduced them. Boeing's internal forecasts called for total sales of 250 727s. By 1984, it had sold 1831 of them and became the best-selling airliner ever, until the Boeing 737, designed to be even more efficient for short-haul travel, surpassed its total in the 1990s.

The first sign of the impact of cheap, reliable airline travel was a change in the "airport experience." Bruce Holmes, head of an aeronautics program of NASA, has pointed out that the conversion of the U.S. airline fleet from propellers to jets reduced the fatal accident rate by nearly 90 percent. From the 1930s through the 1990s, the real cost per mile of air travel fell nearly as much. As fares went down, the crowds increased. Through the 1950s, trips to the airport had been special occasions. In the 1960s the bitter jokes about airliners as cattle cars and "flying buses" began.

Passenger aircraft line up for a sunset takeoff. By 1984, Boeing had sold nearly two thousand of its 727s, making it the best-selling airliner until the 737 came along.

Of course, the nonspecialness of airline travel was a sign of its economic importance and success. In certain ways, cheap air travel made the United States one country as it had never been before. Its continental expanse was still huge, with the Plains and Mountain states underpopulated, but all of it was now within a day's reach. Salespeople could reach their clients, relatives could reach their loved ones, performers could get to an audience, politicians could get to a crowd, wherever it might be. The dominant colleges of the east coast began to recruit a truly national student body. People from the east coast could ski in Utah; people from Texas could go to Cape Cod on vacation. Student groups from everywhere could come to Washington, D.C. When my parents moved from Philadelphia to southern California in the early 1950s, the trip in their station wagon took five days, with a baby and two cranky toddlers in the back seat. When I was sent, for my tenth birthday, on a trip back to visit the relatives, the jet flight from Los Angeles to Philadelphia took five hours. In 1948, when Harry Truman made his whistle-stop campaign tour across America by train, it took him a week to go from Washington to San Francisco and another week to get back. In 1976, aboard a leased United Airlines 727 nicknamed "Peanut One," Jimmy Carter could go from Pennsylvania to Texas to Oregon to Michigan and home to Georgia in a single, if exhausting, campaign day.

National politics, national markets and business operations, and national sports competition all increased in the jet age. "For decades, the pro-baseball network had been circumscribed by the schedules of the overnight Pullman travel, which tied clubs to cities up and down the Atlantic seaboard and east of the Mississippi," wrote Roger Bilstein in his history *Flight in America*. "Airborne conveyance of teams made the migration of old clubs possible and lead to the expansion of the leagues as well." The famous departures of the baseball Giants and Dodgers for California in the 1950s commanded New York's attention. But the real impact on sports was the creation of new, non–east coast teams. None of the following cities had major-league baseball teams before the jet age, and now all of them do: Anaheim, Dallas–Fort Worth, Denver, Houston, Kansas City, Miami, Oakland, Seattle, and Tampa, plus Montreal and Toronto in Canada. The proportion of new teams is even higher in other sports.

In areas other than sports, jet travel hastened the rise of the Sunbelt. It was easier to reach national markets, make deals, attract talent, and set up branch offices when the 727 made southern and western states less remote than they had been. In the Sunbelt and elsewhere, jets hastened the rise of the "airport city." The first notable one had been the western frontier of Chicago, surrounding O'Hare airport. Hotels, malls, and office centers developed for no reason other than proximity to the airport. The "Dulles corridor" outside Washington followed this pattern; the previously separate cities of Dallas and Fort Worth were joined by the enormous DFW airport complex between them. Orlando, which had been a swamp, became a metropolitan area of nearly two million people thanks to a Disney park and a major airport.

As it united the country, air travel also divided it. The concept of "flyover states" would not be possible without jet travel, and it highlighted the social and political division between the coasts, which were in closer and closer touch with each other, and the interior states, from which "bicoastal" culture was estranged. The historian Daniel Boorstin wrote that the rise of jet travel was creating an ersatz life devoid of culture of any kind. You got on a plane at one featureless modern airport, got off the plane at another, and in some sense you had not gone anywhere at all.

Like all other aspects of modernization, like American openness itself, the taken-for-granted mobility brought by the 727 could be disruptive. But how much it shaped the modern character of the nation became clear when air travel was constricted in response to terrorist attacks. Mobility of every sort is too important to American culture to remain suppressed for long.

Passengers make their way through Chicago's O'Hare airport. Urban centers including hotels, malls, and office parks frequently grow up around today's airports.

A Nation Within a Nation

by Jeremiah Tower

PERHAPS NOT SINCE the early Christian and later Catholic Church embrace of pagan rituals has the world seen such a collection of diversities brought together into a sense of unity and commonwealth as has happened in the formation of the United States and its uniquely American identity. And no engine was more powerful than California, that nation within a nation, in shaping America's character, especially as it has evolved its present, casually open, form.

America's religion was America's dream that anyone with enough talent, skill, and resilient character could and would make good in the new country, up to or beyond one's wildest dreams. This was a country where privileged birth, inherited wealth, and social standing were not the required tools for making the good life for one's family: anything was possible if you worked hard and intelligently enough, preferably on any of America's frontiers, where all structures, especially the social ones, were primitive and permeable. And no frontier was more open than the wild opportunities of the various "Rushes" in California—first for gold, then the movies, and then agriculture and cuisine. The successes in money, entertainment, and food became the legends of California and of America itself.

There is nothing like a blank (if, for a moment, you overlook the Spanish in California) slate upon which to make a statement that stands out. That is what California was: virgin territory, unclaimed and untamed, and a rich one at that. Here was no rigid social structure of the East, where if you were not white, Anglo-Saxon, and Protestant, you didn't go anywhere—unless it was down in the world. And no better example of the American dream existed than the making of Hollywood,

> "NO FRONTIER WAS MORE OPEN THAN THE WILD OPPORTUNITIES OF THE VARIOUS "RUSHES" IN CALIFORNIA—FIRST FOR GOLD, THEN THE MOVIES, AND THEN AGRICULTURE AND CUISINE. THE SUCCESSES . . . BECAME THE LEGENDS OF CALIFORNIA AND OF AMERICA ITSELF."

The gold rush that followed the discovery of gold in the foothills of California's Sierra Nevada mountains, opposite, was the first great influx of people into what is now the most populous state in America. Despite its large population, California still boasts large and diverse areas of unspoiled land.

especially if you compare it, as does the Broadway historian Ethan Mordden (as quoted in William J. Mann's *Behind the Screen*), with what it was like trying to get into the "culturally paramount, long-established and in part elitist world of the [New York] stage." The people starting to make their way in Hollywood in the first two decades of the nineteenth century were "former junk dealers, salesmen, and opportunists." This new land of opportunity was wide open. California was the social equivalent of the movies themselves, new, as yet unformed, but full of promised dreams.

Not to say that taking D. W. Griffith's Biograph Company into Los Angeles in 1910 was an easy task, or the independents setting up in neighboring new development of Hollywood were a pushover. It took true American grit to make truly American glamour. But it helped that the climate was gentle, and gentle all year. It definitely helped that when an idea popped up there was no one (yet) to say "don't do it" and nothing other than available money (or not) to stop anyone from giving it a go. That egalitarian and at first casual attitude was all about "why not," and then how to get it done.

Having, as an American, grown up in England and then in Eastern establishment schools and society, I had never taken my jacket off in public unless I was at

Still "Hollywoodland" in 1925, opposite—a name derived from a real estate development—the more familiar Hollywood will be born in 1949 when the Chamber of Commerce drops the superfluous "land." Plentiful sunshine, necessary for outdoor filming, brought the movie industry here, but the boom had begun earlier with the discovery of gold. It brought an influx of miners like these sluicing Fosters Bar in 1851, right.

a rugby match, mucking out stables, or swimsuited. When my Greenwich, Connecticut, grandparents retired to Carmel, California, the tradition continued, even at home, at lunch, and on the summer terrace. But the first time I was in California by myself, I was invited to lunch in the country and then invited to take off not only my tie and jacket, but everything else as well. "Shed it all" was the message. Hot tubs, drugs, and orgies flashed through my mind as I stood at the front door at what I realized was perhaps the most important personal tipping point in my life. Why not, I decided. What I found was indeed a room with a hot tub, but one filled with orchids, edible plants festooning the glass ceiling, and music coming from an organ modeled after the one Bach composed on. On the table was a bottle of vintage Krug, nearby a magnum of Volnay, and standing there to greet me were musicians, writers, sculptors, and food writers. This, I said to myself, trying to treat a newly found nudity as something casual and oddly elegant in that setting, must be the Promised Land. Certainly Nirvana, and at the end of the lunch of superbly cooked food I vowed to all that I would return—without my tie.

When I first started then to cook professionally, it was amusing to read the accounts of the endless complaints

of the early Gold Rush miners about the kind of food available to them, which they thought was garbage. And it was laughable to read an account of their culinary plight: ears of fresh corn grilled in their husks over camp charcoal fires and then sauced with nothing but local olive oil. Before reading that, I had figured that any of the gold rushers would have given a bag of nuggets for a plate of that corn, and I laughed that now, in my new Californian bars and grill, their gold-plated descendants were paying the equivalent.

My deciding to become a chef in the Bay Area in 1970 was an accident—an opportunity that picked me up and swept me away in what was, as one wag later called it, the California Food Rush. It was the kind of chance happening that could only have existed on a frontier unformed, primitive, and permeable; otherwise I could never have risen more or less overnight from obscurity to become what other wags, calling on the tradition of Hollywood, named "Star Chefs." Since the French were there in force and first (and often brilliantly), breaking into the California food establishment in the 1970s was accomplished as easily as someone right off the immigrant boat in New York in the 1920s getting an appointment with Ziegfeld.

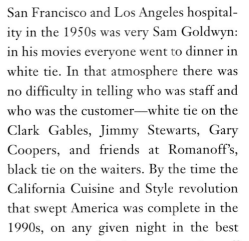

In November 1969, Time *magazine featured the artwork of Milton Glaser in its cover piece on California.*

San Francisco and Los Angeles hospitality in the 1950s was very Sam Goldwyn: in his movies everyone went to dinner in white tie. In that atmosphere there was no difficulty in telling who was staff and who was the customer—white tie on the Clark Gables, Jimmy Stewarts, Gary Coopers, and friends at Romanoff's, black tie on the waiters. By the time the California Cuisine and Style revolution that swept America was complete in the 1990s, on any given night in the best place in town, a waiter off duty could be sitting at a table near San Francisco's or Los Angeles's most dazzling socialite, and only the waiters had ties of any kind.

Just as the American public embraced with open arms the new, far more egalitarian (available cheaply to all) entertainment of the movies instead of the theater, so the same public gleefully accepted the change from the Establishment potted ferns and red plush of Old World–style restaurants and hotels to the new casual style born in California. Putting on the Ritz now meant dancing to piped-in music that everyone liked rather than a few tony customers on New York's Stork Club dance floor tangoing between courses, as they had learned to do at their proms on the "roof" of the Pierre Hotel. As for clothes, at a Beverly Hills restaurant, even on

Rodeo Drive or Melrose, fashion on the customers' backs was ready to wear: only the sauces were made to order. Ritzy décor gave way to a restaurant in Santa Monica where the owner's suit, the curtains, and the upholstery were all the same natural linen color. It was cool to have the décor be as stark as the color of the plain white walls, as long as the flowers were enormous and fresh and the lighting made the customers, now dressed in everything from black tie (on their way to a prom) to blue jeans (billionaire studio head), look better. And whereas sometimes "casual" meant that the service persons introduced themselves and then knelt down at the table so that they would not be in a more lofty position than the customers, it was generally known that it was just fine to say, "May I call you waiter?"

When restaurants and food brought the California lifestyle to America in the late 1980s the way had been paved by Hollywood, and it was clear to everyone that it was definitely more preferable in life to be able to take part in this throwaway elegance every day rather than a more rarefied grandeur only on occasions. The east coast was the first to embrace the new California food-lifestyle (New York saw the first California restaurant outside the home state). Easily approached, good-looking, healthy, and openly friendly were the qualities of California's food and manners that many young easterners welcomed with open arms (especially in those prep schools still insisting on a tie worn with lunch) and then took with them, via the press, on the rebound across the country into the rest of the states of America.

In the movie *Giant* the vast openness of Texas is relentlessly flat and endless, in all directions, to the horizon. But space in California, though just as huge, is more gentle, and more easily persuades one to be expansive in one's thoughts in an all-encompassing way rather than in a circling-the-wagons way against the harsh and threatening Texas void. When one drives down from the Rockies and Sierras westward into California it is the light and the open space, and the sheer strength of them both, that is the first impression. Then when you land in a southern California orange grove, it is not a great stretch to get into the frame of mind of being wide open to opportunities and suggestions. No easterner is immune to the light, or the lightening of style that is a result. It just happens. And it helped change America forever from the world of Cole Porter to "Anything Goes."

The casual elegance of the "California lifestyle" permeated American culture—especially its cuisine—in the late 1980s.

A Nation on Wheels

by Bill Geist

WE WON'T GET OUT of our cars. Not if we can help it.

Americans and our automobiles. Love at first sight. Most of us have two. Or more. During the early courtship we took them to dinner at drive-in restaurants and a show at drive-in theaters. Now we take them everywhere.

Cars are our freedom machines. We can go anywhere, anytime—and do, even when we really have no particular place to go. We feel good on the go. Free. Cars make everything convenient. Our entire country is built around them, from interstates to drive-through windows. We're safe in our cars. We're anonymous. We don't have to dress up. We can return videos, mail letters, and do serious banking in our pajamas.

Cars are our legs. At the mall, cars patrol the parking lot for ten minutes waiting for a better spot to open up twenty feet closer to the door.

> "AS AMERICANS, WE WANT IT, WE WANT IT NOW, AND WE DON'T WANT TO GET OUT OF OUR CARS TO GET IT. OURS IS A NATION OF DRIVE-THRU WINDOWS OF OPPORTUNITY."

Cars are our homes, our mobile homes. Go ahead, sell the house. You could live in some of the cavernous new SUVs, equipped with a dozen cup-holders, concert-hall sound systems, TVs (some now embedded in steering wheels!), plenty of room to lie down and stretch out for the evening there in the back, and electrical outlets for hair dryers and frying pans.

We won't get out of our cars even for nourishment. Don't want to stop the wheels turning to eat? New lines of car cookery (like the Port-a-Fry) are being introduced. Just plug 'em into your cigarette lighter, and you can fry bacon and eggs in the passenger seat (not on the dashboard, too much grease splatter on the windshield) while you drive to work. Make a pot of stew on the armrest on your way home. Or surprise your spouse or that special someone when you get

Rush hour grinds to a halt on a United States freeway, opposite. As the automobile and its culture conquer the world, walking is sometimes a better—though largely unpopular—option.

At a 1940s drive-in movie, a carhop offers window service. Her tray will hang from a partly opened window supported by a buttress-like leg. The nation's first drive-in movie theater opened in Camden, New Jersey, in 1933. The phenomenon flourished for a few years, then largely disappeared when television came along.

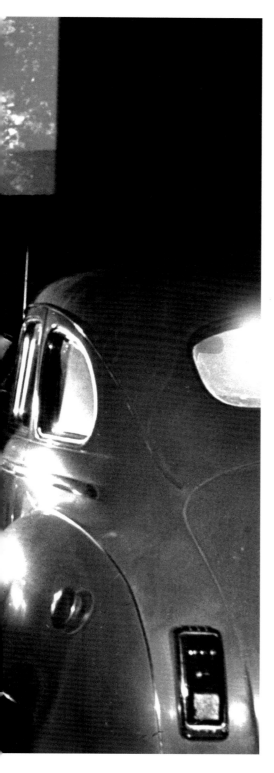

home: "Honey, let's go out for dinner tonight, just the two of us. The frying pan's in the back seat—can you reach it?—and there are some pork chops in the glove compartment."

Americans have long been eating in their cars, of course. I grew up eating in the car at one of those 1950s drive-in restaurants called Steak n' Shake, where you park and a carhop (usually a young woman in a paper hat) takes your order and then brings the food to your car on a tray that hangs precariously on the slightly rolled-up driver's window. At some places the carhops wore roller skates.

That was at the dawn of the explosion of our carborne culture: when the very word "motel" sounded salacious; when roadside attractions like Hillbilly Mini-Golf and Dinosaur World, featuring life-sized brontosauri, and Weekie Wachie's underwater mermaid shows (she's drinking a Coke, underwater!) lured us off major, but still two-lane, highways.

An early motel in Holbrook, Arizona, mimics the teepees of local Native Americans. Invented to serve increasing numbers of highway travelers, motels got their name from a blending of "motor" and "hotel."

Increasingly, people eat meals in their cars while the wheels just keep on turning. A woman in southern California, cradle of our car culture, eats cereal while driving to work every morning. (Almost 90 percent of Americans drive to work; three-fourths of those drive alone.) This woman steers with her knees—the road's fairly straight for the most part. Eating while driving is pretty common in California. So is Mexican food. The combination calls for a high degree of skill. You see drivers moving along briskly while hanging their burritos out the window and biting into them—hot sauce dripping down and streaking the side of the car and jalapeño peppers blowing off, then reentering the car through the open rear window. It's especially fun to watch if they're talking on the phone at the same time. Then, they have to go to the drive-through laundry and dry cleaners.

Invoking an outdoor blessing, the Reverend Robert White preaches to his parked flock, right. The first drive-in church was apparently opened in California in 1954.

People do still walk some in a few isolated locales. Like New York City, where there are still really odd, somewhat un-American people, without drivers' licenses, and lots of shoe repair shops and podiatrists offices.

But in the suburbs, where Americans are most likely to live these days, if you're walking in your residential neighborhood and not wearing a Walkman and a jogging suit, you're subject to suspicion. People call the cops.

You can live in the suburbs of our coldest northern cities and not need a winter coat. Hop in the car in a heated garage, park right in front of a store in a strip shopping center, or thirty feet from the mall entrance, and run in.

Better yet, drive through, or *thru*. America has drive-thru banking, of course, and drive-thru cleaners, and

drive-thru hamburgers and tacos and donuts (including a really cool place in California, where you drive into a giant donut to pick them up).

Need a loaf of bread? Drive thru the mini-mart. Headache? Hit the drive-thru pharmacy. Roses? There are drive-thru florists. Fellatio? Available in many major cities in the comfort and privacy of your own car. Curb service. Seeking salvation? There are drive-in churches. At the one I attended in suburban Chicago, parishioners honked their horns whenever the pastor said, "Amen."

In Michigan, you can get a drive-thru flu shot, which may be only the beginning. Can drive-thru liposuction be far behind?

"Welcome to Auto-Suc, may I take your order?"

"Yes, I'm here for my weekly appointment."

"Window 2. Swipe your credit card, it's $100 a minute, self-service. Insert the Fat-Vac 2000 into your pre-drilled portal. Don't forget to put your car in park. Would you like fries with that?"

In Salt Lake City, there's a drive-thru art gallery. High culture at five miles per hour. In Arkansas, a judge will come out of the courthouse to your car to provide curbside jurisprudence. In Florida, there are places to pay your taxes at drive-thrus.

In Las Vegas you can get married in your car at a drive-up window. By an Elvis impersonator. Watch out, it's legally binding. Some people don't take off their seat belts to do it. Some don't wash their cars. No blood test, no waiting period. "Honey, on our way back from picking up a bucket of chicken at KFC, you wanna get hitched?" Can these marriages possibly last? Well, if they don't, it's not like you have to shut off the engine. You can file for divorce with a real attorney at a drive-up window in Salem, Oregon.

A lot of people are conceived in cars, of course, and now you can check out of life at a drive-thru facility. At the Junior Funeral Home in Pensacola, Florida (among others), you can have a drive-thru funeral. The bereaved drive up, look through a big glass window at the loved one, pay their respects, sign the guest book, and drive away.

My favorite drive-thrus, and ones that a lot of people still have trouble believing, are the drive-thru cocktail lounges. Not the drive-thru Beer Barn, where you can pick up a sixer, or drive-thru liquor stores where you can get packaged liquor. We're talking drive-thru mixed drinks! In some jurisdictions in Louisiana, you can drive up to a window, order a martini with olives, and they hand it to you, the driver. Happy motoring. These places usually feature daiquiris, but you can get almost anything you can order from a bartender at the corner bar. My martini came in a Styrofoam cup, with the top taped on (so it's a "closed container") but with a straw through the top, for sippin' and drivin'. What a country!

Midnight at McDonald's. It's open, but completely empty. Two cashiers, no waiting. Outside, twelve cars are in line waiting twenty minutes or more at the drive-thru window.

As Americans, we want it, we want it now, and we don't want to get out of our cars to get it. Ours is a nation of drive-thru windows of opportunity.

Come what may, be it dire warnings of polluted air, global warming, wars for oil, gas shortages, rising traffic fatalities, or high gas prices, public transportation enthusiasts and environmentalists alike must surely know by now: we won't get out of our cars.

Drive-ins strive to satisfy every need: Brides and grooms can tie the knot without getting out of their cars in Las Vegas, top, and diners can stop for burgers and fries at McDonald's restaurants, bottom, all over the world.

CHAPTER FOUR

SOME STRUGGLES ALONG THE WAY

★

*"This freedom is not a celestial condition received once
and for all, and to be simply enjoyed.... [I]t is
perpetually threatened by new obstacles and perils
arising from new situations in the process of time; and
it must be perpetually defended and improved, it must
be a new conquest and creation for each generation.
It permits of no inertia, no passivity, no rest. It must
be unceasingly regenerated by the life-breath of a free
people, and so it is one with this very life-breath."*

— Jacques Maritain, in his 1956 *Reflections on America*

Democratizing the Workplace

by Sam Roberts

ON DECEMBER 30, 1936, a few hundred men in Flint, Michigan, stood up for what they believed in by sitting down. Those men, and the women who defended them on the frontlines, were illegally demanding only what federal legislation had just recently allowed: the legitimacy of organized labor. They achieved a lot more. Their victory in Flint that bitter winter represented a quantum leap for economic democracy. Millions of unskilled Americans who manned the assembly lines in mass-production industries surged into an emerging middle class—fulfilling the political vision of the New Deal. Financially strapped blue-collar workers who manufactured automobiles could finally afford to buy them, generating greater demand. The Flint sit-down strike cost Michigan's courageous governor, Frank Murphy, reelection but catapulted him onto the United States Supreme Court. And the strikers' radical strategy—rooted in Gandhi's nonviolent civil disobedience and traced to European coal miners earlier in the twentieth century, workers building the Rouen Cathedral in fifteenth-century France, and even masons constructing a chapel for a Pharaoh in ancient Egypt—would inspire America's civil rights movement a generation later.

"The GM sit-down strike of 1936–37," Professor Sidney Fine of the University of Michigan wrote, "was, all in all, the most significant American labor conflict in the twentieth century."

Flint, a gritty company town northwest of Detroit, was the industrial heart of General Motors, the world's largest manufacturing corporation. Flint was also where the fledgling United Auto Workers, founded in 1935 and a constituent of John L. Lewis's breakaway Congress of Industrial Organizations, decided to militate for the recognition that was guaranteed by the new National Labor Relations

> "FOR THE FIRST TIME, A UNION HAD WON COMPANY-WIDE RECOGNITION FROM THE CORPORATION THAT PRODUCED MORE THAN HALF OF AMERICA'S CARS."

United Auto Workers picket a General Motors plant in Flint, Michigan, in June 1998, opposite. This worker's union forebears staged a successful sit-down strike in 1936 at the General Motors plant in Flint that has been called "the most significant American labor conflict" of the twentieth century.

Act (but which corporate America was challenging in court). Driven by its own paternal version of welfare capitalism, the automobile industry paid its workers relatively well—when they were working. The problem was, they worked irregularly. In 1937, the average GM worker probably made less than the $1,400 that a federal study estimated was the subsistence budget for a family of four in urban Michigan. Plant foremen, armed with gossip gathered by company spies, were often capricious, sometimes corrupt, and oblivious to individual grievances. Job security was an oxymoron, especially as the Depression deepened and auto sales, and production, plummeted. Seniority and overtime were novelties. Even wearing an emblem proclaiming union membership was grounds for dismissal. Coupled with pay by piecework, the brutal, arbitrary pace of assembly-line speed-ups—captured, less grimly, in Charlie Chaplin's film *Modern Times*—imposed a punishing physical and emotional toll.

At the cavernous Fisher No. 1 plant, squatting in a valley by the Flint River, 7,300 workers produced 1,400 Buick bodies a day. Exactly why the storied strike started there is uncertain, but the impetus appeared to be that GM, to ensure uninterrupted production, had begun shipping dies for the 1937 model-year car bodies from Fisher No. 1 to other plants,

"Labor as wide as the earth has its summit in heaven," boasts a 1902 certificate of membership in the United Mine Workers of America.

where the union was weaker. The signal for the strike was unmistakable: a bare 200-watt red bulb blinked on in the window of the United Auto Workers headquarters across the street from the plant, announcing an emergency union meeting. At about 10 P.M. on December 30, 1936, after the lunch break on the night shift, several hundred workers returned to the assembly line but refused to work.

Logistically, the sit-down, or stay-in, was enormously appealing. It was cozier than manning a picket line in winter, safer from company goons, and, above all, it was effective. A relatively small number of striking workers could cripple production. Within weeks, sit-downs spread to other plants, idling about 135,000 GM workers nationwide. The world's biggest manufacturer, which had turned out 50,000 cars in December 1936 in its United States factories, managed during the first ten days of February 1937 to produce a mere 151 cars.

For all the sympathy that the plight of struggling working people generated during the Depression, for all the resonance of President Franklin D. Roosevelt's denunciations of "economic royalists," the sit-down strike struck a lot of Americans as alarmingly radical. That Communists were so supportive and even involved didn't help either (a New York merchants' association warned that John L. Lewis had "set out on a road the end of which—if traveled to the end—means that every plant in the United States will be Sovietized, a road that is the antithesis of industrial freedom"). Nor did the fact that the number of card-carrying union members, to say nothing of the striking workers, constituted only a minority of GM employees. What the workers had done, after all, was to seize the means of production from private owners. While their goals weren't revolutionary, their tactics arguably were (even if they were defying injunctions at the very same time that FDR was being accused of undermining the judiciary by maneuvering to pack the Supreme Court in his favor, and if one of the Michigan judges who issued an injunction against the strikers happened to hold more than $200,000 in General Motors stock). The owners were in a bind, though. They not only feared vandalism and destruction of crucial matrixes and machinery, but also the enduring impact of bad publicity if evicting striking workers by force resulted in bloodshed. The owners weren't the only ones who were worried. Governor Frank Murphy deployed the Michigan National Guard, but pointedly only to maintain order—not to evict the strikers. Murphy, a New Deal Democrat whose grandfather was hanged by the British in Ireland for Fenian militancy and whose father was imprisoned there, declared, "I will not go down in history as 'Bloody Murphy.'" By choosing to selectively enforce court mandates, demanding that outsiders—from either side—be barred from the struck plants, and indefatigably pressing for negotiations (for all its insistence that grievances could be resolved individually without the intervention of a union, GM executives refused to even meet with Lewis until Roosevelt personally intervened), Murphy was rewarded by being anointed a hero. Violence erupted nonetheless. On January 11, police officers halted food deliveries to one of the plants, precipitating a riot—dubbed the Battle of the Running Bulls—in which red-bereted members of the Emergency Women's Brigade boldly interposed themselves between the workers, who were their husbands, sons, and brothers, and the bulls, as the police were pejoratively known. Sixteen strikers and spectators and eleven officers were injured. On February 1, workers again clashed with the authorities when, after a diversionary strike, they seized control of Chevrolet No. 4, GM's giant engine factory, in a strategic coup that gave them a chokehold on production. Thanks largely to Governor Murphy's adroitness in reconciling the principles of labor and property rights, though, not a single life was lost.

At 2:40 A.M. on February 11, 1937, forty-four days after the sit-down began, Governor Murphy announced an agreement. That afternoon, at 5:42 P.M., as a "Victory Is Ours" banner was lowered

As the Great Depression nears its end, in 1938, a group of union members picket their employer. The roots of peaceful worker protest can be traced back to reluctant masons building a Pharaoh's chapel.

More effective than a picket line, a sit-down strike by even a few workers can cripple a plant's production. These strikers relax during the 1936 strike at the GM plant in Flint. Country music was piped to them over the PA system. The strike was finally settled in the union's favor in February 1937.

from the roof of Fisher No. 1, about four hundred bedraggled strikers marched out of the plant singing "Solidarity Forever" and sporting American flags. Two by two, they proceeded, appropriately enough, to join a flag-bedecked motorcade that snaked its way through Flint in a celebration of industrial democracy. About 125 strikers evacuated Fisher No. 2, and several hundred more ended their sit-down at Chevrolet No. 4. For the first time, the union had won full nationwide recognition as a bargaining agent from the corporation that produced more than half of America's cars. Stunned by the effectiveness of the sit-down and the sympathy for organized labor, other major industries capitulated. Less than three weeks after the Flint agreement was reached, United States Steel, the world's largest producer, shocked corporate America by signing an accord with a CIO affiliate.

Alfred P. Sloan Jr., president and chairman of the board of General Motors during the 1940s, controlled a giant firm that employed 250,000 workers in 110 plants in fourteen states and eighteen countries. He fought the unions fiercely but unsuccessfully.

Some businessmen considered the accords inevitable. But Alfred P. Sloan Jr., the GM president, warned that if unions ever succeeded in imposing a closed shop (one open only to union members), it would mean "the economic and political slavery of the worker, and an important step toward an economic political dictatorship." He described the Flint strike as an "unfortunate controversy, which like all industrial disputes which interfere with production, has resulted in a staggering loss to every one

Violence is only seconds away as members of the Ford Motors Service Department—who dealt with "troublemakers"—approach members of the fledgling United Auto Workers Union, including future president Walter Reuther (second from right) in May 1937. The union organizers were badly beaten and thrown down thirty-nine steps of an overpass. But a photographer from the Detroit News caught it all, and his photos helped convince courts that Ford was violating workers' rights.

concerned." In the short run, Sloan was right. GM's share of new car registrations in the United States, 44 percent in the first quarter of 1936, plunged to 34 percent in the first quarter of 1937. Workers lost some $30 million in wages. And the peace terms, which took up only one typewritten page, were short of what the union had demanded. GM agreed not to discriminate against employees because of their union membership, to establish an elaborate grievance procedure, and to grant the United Auto Workers exclusive bargaining rights—though only for its own members and only for six months. It would be long enough to gain a foothold. In 1940, after

the National Labor Relations Act was upheld as constitutional, the UAW won a majority at forty-eight GM plants with 120,000 workers. Within two more years the union, with about 600,000 members nationwide by then, vanquished Ford to capture the trifecta of Big Three auto giants. John L. Lewis, godfather of the United Auto Workers, had convincingly sold his "one shop, one union" credo to decisively establish the CIO as a credible alternative to the craft unions of the American Federation of Labor. And the Reuther brothers, who would dominate the auto workers union for decades, built on a victory that redefined labor relations in America and transformed workers into consumers who, benefiting from a higher standard of living, "eschewed the overthrow of capitalism," as the historian David M. Kennedy concluded, "to embrace bread-and-butter unionism." (The feared sit-down strike was ruled illegal by the Supreme Court in 1939, but not until, as Walter Lippman wrote, "the essential fact has been that certain rights of property were impaired and could not be repaired until the human right to representation had been established.") In a sense, Charles E. Wilson, the former president of General Motors, turned out to be right when he said famously in 1953: "What was good for our country was good for General Motors, vice versa." By then, more than one in three American workers were represented by unions.

After the Flint strike, a freight company executive told Congress that "two colossal forces are standing astride the stream of commerce." As a result of what happened in Flint, those forces begrudgingly joined hands. Almost overnight, corporate paternalism morphed into institutional hostility tempered by government regulation and, ultimately, mutual interest. "Capital gave up some of its prerogatives but won a measure of industrial peace," David Kennedy wrote. "Labor subjected itself to the sometimes meddlesome tutelage of the regulatory state but achieved a degree of parity with management at the bargaining table and, no less important, unprecedented prosperity and security as well."

Today, the United Automobile, Aerospace and Agricultural Implement Workers of America claims 700,000 active members. But America's unions now represent only about 13 percent of the total work force and even less—under 10 percent—among private-sector employees. State right-to-work laws and the paternalism of Japanese automakers discouraged union organizing in other states. The Big Three manufacturers, who, together, now account for fewer than half the cars sold in the United States, opened plants where labor was cheaper and bought more parts from private suppliers. In *Roger and Me*, the filmmaker Michael Moore chronicled his campaign to confront a General Motors executive about the plant closings that ravaged Moore's hometown of Flint. In 1987, Fisher Nos. 1 and 2 were shuttered by GM, displacing about three thousand workers. Protected by a contract much more elaborate than the historic one-page agreement that had been signed fifty years before, all but six hundred of those workers were guaranteed some other job with GM, early retirement, or pay until they retired.

President Ronald Reagan holds a meeting in the Cabinet Room on September 30, 1981, left. The month before, when thirteen thousand air traffic controllers walked off their jobs, Reagan gave them forty-eight hours to get back to work, then fired them all, virtually destroying PATCO, their union.

The Turning Point

by Ben Bradlee

BARELY FOUR MONTHS after the devastation that was Pearl Harbor, the Japanese were riding high. Their biggest naval loss had been a single destroyer.

But the Japanese high command was split between the army generals, who wanted to consolidate and develop their new land acquisitions, and the navy, under the powerful Admiral Yamamoto, who wanted to lure what was left of the U.S. Navy into battle and destroy it forever.

Yamamoto won. On April 16, the ambitious order to invade Midway Island and the Aleutians was given. Two days later all opposition to Yamamoto's plan disappeared with the brave but symbolic daylight raid on Tokyo, led by Colonel Jimmy Doolittle flying twenty-six B-25 bombers from the carrier *Hornet*.

U.S. forces were greatly outnumbered—all but fatally outnumbered had it not been for the skills of one William Friedman and a team of U.S. cryptanalysts who had managed to break the Japanese "Purple Code." But OP-20-G,

> "THE TIDE OF THE PACIFIC WAR HAD DEFINITELY TURNED. THE JAPANESE WOULD NEVER AGAIN BE ON THE OFFENSIVE."

the Navy Signals intelligence operation at Pearl Harbor, could decode only about 15 percent of Japanese Navy traffic by early 1942. The Purple Code consisted of some 45,000 five-digit numbers, further enciphered by a changing additive table. To break the code, the cryptanalysts first had to identify and remove the additives, then painstakingly try to make some sense of the thousands of number groups. In addition to all that, the Japanese had a separate code for times and dates.

The commander-in-chief of the Pacific fleet, Admiral Chester Nimitz, knew the Japanese were going to invade Port Moresby on May 3, and had assembled a carrier task force to look for trouble in the Coral Sea off New Guinea. They found it.

The day was May 7, 1942, the day after the surrender of American forces under General Wainwright in the Philippines.

Navy torpedo bombers, opposite, look for a target during the Battle of Midway in June 1942. One of World War II's decisive battles was fought here between June 4 and 7. Earlier, Lieutenant Colonel Jimmy Doolittle, below, here checking a bomb on the deck of the USS Hornet, led a symbolic bombing raid on Tokyo that took the Japanese by surprise.

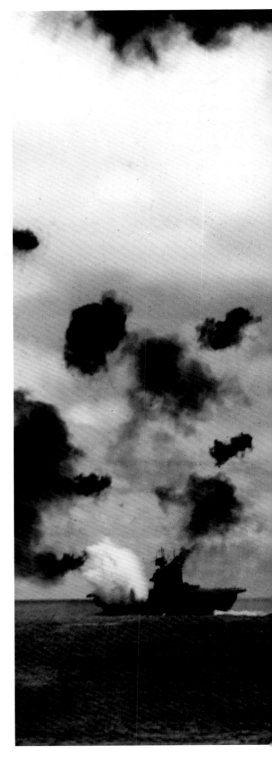

Smoke blossoms from the U.S. aircraft carrier Yorktown as it suffers a direct hit by a Japanese torpedo, right. Black clouds of anti-aircraft fire fill the sky. Damaged at the earlier Battle of Coral Sea, the Yorktown nonetheless was ready for duty after two days in dry dock.

The Battle of Coral Sea began with the loss of an American destroyer and the fleet oiler it was escorting. But at 10 A.M. ninety-three planes from the *Lexington* and the *Yorktown* jumped the Japanese light carrier *Shoho*, which sank in thirty-six minutes; it was the first Japanese ship bigger than a destroyer to disappear under the water. The next day, the Americans lost the *Lexington*, but without losing a single sailor, and the Battle of Coral Sea was over. It was a tactical victory for the Japanese because they sank another American carrier, but a strategic victory for the United States, because for the first time in the war, a Japanese invasion (of Port Moresby) had been called off. It was the first naval battle fought between carriers, and the first naval battle fought between ships that never saw, nor fired shots at, each other.

The scene was now set for the critical sea battle of World War II, the Battle of Midway.

On one side was the greatest sea force ever assembled—more than two hundred Japanese combat ships, including eight carriers, eleven battleships, twenty-two cruisers, sixty-five destroyers, twenty-one submarines, and more than seven hundred planes. The fearsome Admiral Yamamoto was in command. The size is no easier to grasp today than it was on June 3, 1942. This armada was divided into three groups: a four-carrier strike force approaching from the northwest; an invasion/occupation force approaching from the west; and a main battle force of the battleships between the other two.

On the other side, Admiral Nimitz had only three carriers, eight cruisers, and fifteen destroyers. One of the carriers, the *Yorktown*, had been so badly damaged at Coral Sea that experts said it would take three months to repair her, but 1,400 repairmen managed to patch it up in a Pearl Harbor dry dock in two days. Nimitz split this force into two groups— one commanded by Admiral Fletcher, the other by Admiral Raymond Spruance, a last-minute substitute for Admiral Bull Halsey, who had come down with a severe case of shingles. Many students of the Pacific war consider Spruance to have been its greatest American admiral.

The Americans started with a small problem: despite their ability to read Japanese messages, they didn't know exactly where the Japanese were going to attack. Decoded, the messages described the point of attack as only "AF." Most of the navy brass thought "AF" was Oahu. Nimitz thought it was Midway. Looking for that vital certainty, the navy sent a fake, uncoded message that described a breakdown in Midway's desalinization plant. And sure enough, two days later the navy cryptanalysts intercepted and decoded a Japanese message, reporting that "AF" was low on fresh water.

Bingo. Problem solved. Yet even after tricking the Japanese into confirming Midway as the target of the massive attack, the exact date was unknown until almost the last minute. On May 25, the navy's top

Fatally wounded, the Yorktown *lists steeply to port after being struck repeatedly by Japanese dive bombers and torpedoes.*

cryptanalyst, Commander Joseph J. Rochefort, succeeded in decoding the cable that gave June 4 as the day of the enemy attack. (Three days later the Japanese changed their code, leaving Nimitz without further information until after the battle.)

Once that was solved, "the meticulous intelligence on the Japanese movements seemed almost incredible," one of the carrier officers could only say to himself, adding, "that man of ours in Tokyo is worth every cent we pay him."

How good was the intelligence?

So good that the Americans never fell into the trap set for them by a diversionary attack on June 3 by the Japanese Second Strike Force on Dutch Harbor in the Aleutians with planes from two light carriers—*Ryujo* and *Junyo*.

So good that when the pilot of a navy PBY scout plane spotted what he thought was the Japanese carrier force and messaged Midway "main body . . . bearing 262 [almost due west of Midway], distance 700 [miles] . . ." Nimitz in Pearl Harbor immediately messaged the fleet, ". . . that is not repeat not the enemy striking force. That is the landing force. The striking force will hit from the northwest at daylight tomorrow."

Foes in the Pacific: Navy bomber pilots, top, pose prior to the Battle of Midway. All but one of this squadron will be killed, perhaps by Zeros like those, bottom, being prepared for launch from the Hiryu for the attack on Pearl Harbor.

June 4 began badly for the Yanks. Japanese fighter planes (Zeros) could out-maneuver and destroy anything the Americans were flying. Only two of the twenty-five fighters who rose from Midway Airfield to meet the Japanese air attacks returned to fly again. At Midway, the "poor F-2 Brewster Buffalo fighter was a dismal failure . . . a stationary target for the Zeros . . . never again deployed by U.S. air forces in WW II," according to one official history. B-17s from Midway scored no hits all day on enemy carriers. Same for the lumbering dauntless dive bombers: no hits.

The first U.S. carrier plane attacks didn't do much better. The *Hornet*'s legendary Torpedo 8 Squadron was led by Lieutenant Commander John Waldron. All of their planes, and all but one of their pilots, were destroyed. Torpedo 6, under Lieutenant Commander Gene Lindsey, was challenged by the same Zeros that hit Torpedo 8. Out of fourteen torpedo planes, only four got close enough to launch their torpedoes. No hits, once again. The *Yorktown*'s planes were the last planes airborne. Four of its dive bombers dropped their thousand-pound bombs into the sea—by mistake.

By 10:20 on the morning of June 4, eight U.S. carrier attacks had been turned back without inflicting any damage to the Japanese fleet.

But the U.S. luck was about to change. Big time.

In less than ten minutes time, the tide of the war would turn.

Lieutenant Commander Clarence Wade McCluskey and his squadron of ASBD dive bombers, on an expanding-square search for the Japanese carriers, were close to a decision to return to their ship or run out of fuel. At that moment they spotted the wake of a Japanese destroyer making high speed. And they followed that wake into the heart of the Japanese carrier fleet. Strangest of all, there was no anti-aircraft fire, and no fighter cover. Twenty-five of his dive bombers hurtled straight down at two carriers, taking dead aim before swinging their bombs at the targets from an altitude of 1,500 feet. At the same time, the *Yorktown*'s SBDs pounced on a similarly undefended third carrier. Japanese planes on all three carriers were warming up for take off. Gasoline lines snaked across all three decks. Ordnance was stacked everywhere to reload returning planes.

Within minutes, planes were exploding on all three carrier decks. Men and planes were going over the sides, and holes began to appear in the wooden flight decks. According to one historian, "The *Kaga*, the *Akagi*, and the *Soryu*, carriers that only moments before had been the pride and the heart of the Japanese Navy, were doomed."

But there was more bloody battle before night fell. A fourth Japanese carrier, the *Hiryu*, had become separated from the main Japanese force during the U.S. torpedo attacks. Only eighteen dive bombers and six fighters were airworthy, but they took off shortly before the *Soryu*

sank. Eight Japanese planes got through the *Yorktown*'s defense, scored three direct hits, and reduced her speed to six knots. A second attack from the *Hiryu* scored two more direct torpedo hits, and at 14:55 she was abandoned.

But Admiral Yamaguchi aboard the *Hiryu* had little time to gloat—or even to live. Lieutenant Wilmer Earl Gallaher from the *Enterprise* took off at three in the afternoon, gunning for his second carrier of the day. Gallaher's dive bombers joined up with sixteen planes from the *Hornet*.

Things were quiet aboard the *Hiryu*, not far away. The commanding officer had decided to give his exhausted pilots ninety minutes' rest. That delay was fatal. Shortly after 5 P.M., the Americans spotted her—unprotected by any air cover. The *Hiryu* dodged the first few attackers, but then three straight direct hits smashed through her flight deck. The damage was so dramatic that other U.S. planes switched to a new target, the battleship *Haruna*.

When the Japanese commanders finally learned the *Hiryu* was sunk, the fate of Operation MI was clear. The invasion of Midway was aborted. The tide of the Pacific war had definitively turned. The Japanese would never again be on the offensive.

Dead in the water, the Japanese heavy cruiser Mikuma is one of many casualties of Midway. The battle represented Japan's last offensive in World War II.

THE DESEGREGATION OF OLE MISS

Triumph of the Law

by Curtis Wilkie

To A DETACHED SPECTATOR watching the celebration at a college football game in the autumn of 2002, the scene may have looked like just another outburst by students bathed in delirium. But for those of us who attended the University of Mississippi when segregation fell during a bloody insurrection forty years earlier and a few hundred yards from the stadium, there was priceless irony to the commotion swirling on the field. Ole Miss had upset heavily favored Florida, and in the frenzy of falling goalposts, joyous white students raised the uniformed figure of Eddie Strong, a black linebacker and team captain, to their shoulders in a tableau of biracial jubilation my generation could not have imagined when we were in school. The moment was preserved in a photograph, displayed the next day across the front of the sports section of the *Clarion-Ledger*, the state's biggest newspaper.

> "THE LESSON FROM THE CONFLICT TURNED OUT TO BE ONE OF THE ENDURING ONES I LEARNED IN COLLEGE: . . . JUSTICE, IF IT COULD BE OBTAINED, WOULD COME THROUGH THE FEDERAL COURTS. "

Events were not always so happy in Oxford. When I was a senior at Ole Miss, a white southerner who had been taught that he would never share a classroom with a member of the black race, many of our society's myths and codes shattered on a single night in 1962 in a violent collision of states' rights and federal law. Two people died on our campus, hundreds were wounded, and thousands of troops had to be dispatched to restore order and ensure the enrollment of one black student in our school.

When the blinding cloak of tear gas laid down by federal forces on the night of the riot lifted at last from the Lyceum, the university's administration building, it began to become clear to us how foolish had been the resistance, how the leaders of our state had lied to us, how our elders had counseled us unwisely, and how law in

Federal marshals escort student James Meredith to class at Ole Miss—the University of Mississippi—in the autumn of 1962, opposite. That same year, Sports Illustrated featured the Ole Miss Flag Girls, who at the time carried the Confederate flag, on its cover, below. It took the full force of the federal government to topple the walls of segregation in the South.

America might take its time, but will ultimately prevail.

I was thirteen when the U.S. Supreme Court declared public school segregation unlawful. Although the 1954 *Brown v. Board of Education* decision was unanimous, the state of Mississippi officially scoffed. We dwelled then in the midst of a cult that said never, and we were nurtured in the belief that this new law could either be resisted through an endless series of stalling tactics that would wear down Washington or be defied with impunity by local leaders claiming protection under an interpretation of the U.S. Constitution that gave to the states any rights not specifically delegated to the federal government.

We heard bravado in the speeches of politicians who promised that our schools would never be integrated. The sentiment echoed in the state's newspapers,

Governor Ross Barnett, a fierce foe of integration, waves a Mississippi state flag at one of the school's football games, above. Local Mississippi women, opposite, make their views known outside a meeting of the NAACP in Mississippi.

controlled for the most part by leaders of the Citizens Council, a network founded in the days following the *Brown* decision and dedicated to the preservation of the southern way of life. In the fundamentalist churches, as dense on the Mississippi landscape as thickets of kudzu, segregationist sermons rained down from the pulpit messages invoking the biblical allegory of Ham and admonitions from the Book of Ezra against the mixing of a holy race. We were even assured in our classrooms that integration would never come to Mississippi.

Many of us felt privately that the system was cruel and unfair. Yet we were inhibited by a rigid, racist orthodoxy that ruled our state. The time period, it should be remembered, was already rich with hysteria. These were the grim days of the Cold War, and the country kept alert to the communist menace. In Mississippi, it became easy to equate the concept of racial integration with communism: both represented a foreign ideology designed to destroy our comfortable underpinnings.

The challenge to our society bred a silly sort of anti-Semitism, too. Since many of the northern lawyers conducting the legal struggle against segregation were Jewish, these troublemakers were branded as "outside agitators" and linked to the Bolsheviks. No one seemed quite sure who Marx had been, but we knew he was not a Southern Baptist.

My senior year in high school coincided with President Eisenhower's move to send paratroopers to enforce an integration order at Central High School in Little Rock. With neighboring Arkansas said to be under "occupation" by the U.S. Army, Mississippi's segregationist leaders vowed that we would never knuckle under. They compared themselves to the "freedom fighters" of the short-lived Hungarian revolution a year before, though their roots extended farther back, to the nineteenth-century Ku Klux Klan.

In 1959, the year that Mack Charles Parker, a black man accused of raping a white woman, was dragged from a jail in south Mississippi in the last known

lynching in America, a country lawyer named Ross Barnett was elected governor. Barnett was not an innately evil man, simply the son of a Confederate veteran who knew nothing other than segregation. But a cadre of evil men, associates of the Citizens Council, empowered him because he seemed pliable to their wishes and eager to carry their banner in the campaign. From the steps of courthouses, Barnett shouted that integration would never take place on his watch, and a hillbilly band that accompanied him on his rounds sang:

White students jeer as Meredith, protected by marshals, is registered at Ole Miss. A few years later he was shot and wounded while taking part in a civil rights march.

"He's for segregation, one hundred percent/He's not a moderate, like some other gent. . . ."

Under Barnett, the state of Mississippi remained the stronghold of resistance. There appeared to be no reason for concern in the state's councils of power when an obscure U.S. Air Force veteran, James Meredith, applied for admission to the University of Mississippi as "an American-Mississippi-Negro citizen" on the day after John F. Kennedy's inauguration in 1961. The last person who tried to breach the color barrier at Ole Miss, a Negro citizen named Clennon King, had instead been consigned by state authorities to a mental institution in 1958, my freshman year at the school.

Meredith's application was first rejected on the grounds that it had been submitted too late. Later, school officials told Meredith that his credits from an all-black college could not be transferred, that he lacked the requisite recommendations from five alumni, and that his application faced insurmountable bureaucratic problems. Though Meredith persevered, his case seemed almost frivolous to Mississippi's white leadership. While university officials threw up obstacles, a federal district judge in Mississippi obligingly dithered.

Few Mississippians took Meredith's lawsuit seriously until the U.S. Fifth Circuit Court of Appeals—which had a reputation for brooking no nonsense—ordered the judge to conduct a trial, observing wryly that the case had been stymied "in the eerie atmosphere of never-never land." When the trial produced the curious verdict that there was insufficient evidence that Ole Miss was racially segregated, those of us on the all-white campus thought the status quo had won. But the Fifth Circuit reversed the decision, setting off a bizarre summer of legal maneuvers, climaxed by an order from Justice Hugo Black, speaking for the entire Supreme Court, demanding that the university accept Meredith.

The endgame was played out in the fall of 1962, my last semester at Ole Miss. For a while we were lulled into thinking that Ross Barnett and the Citizens Council crowd could still circumvent the law. More than once, Meredith was turned back at the gates of the university. Even after the governor had been hit with a $10,000-a-day fine for contempt, he continued to rally the segregationists. Much later, we would learn that Barnett had been secretly negotiating surrender with the Kennedy administration. But no one in the mob—composed mostly of hard-bitten southern men who had never been to college—that began ransacking our campus on the eve of Meredith's registration knew of the governor's deals; nor were they yet ready to submit to any court order.

We saw the full power of the law that night in the form of thousands of soldiers sent by President Kennedy to put down the riot and uphold the court order. It took force, but the back of segregation in Mississippi was broken.

The lesson from the conflict turned out to be one of the enduring ones I learned in college: The gospel of states' rights I had heard throughout my youth represented a feeble war cry. Our local officials, deaf to the appeals of blacks who made up more than one-third of the state's population, could not be counted on. Justice, if it could be obtained, would come through the federal courts.

Eventually, passions ebbed and the catharsis at Ole Miss paid dividends. Other public schools were desegregated without incident across the state. The Citizens Council disintegrated. Barnett finished last in a field of five serious candidates the next time he ran for governor. With federal observers looking over our shoulders, the Civil Rights Act of 1964 and the Voting Rights Act of 1965 were implemented in Mississippi. Today, there are more black public officials in Mississippi than in any other state. Young black men have twice been elected president of the Ole Miss student body in recent years. The *Clarion-Ledger*, the Jackson newspaper that once served as a strident voice of the Citizens Council, has a black Ole Miss graduate as its editor.

The racial scene at Ole Miss is not perfect, but I suspect it is no better or worse than race relations, say, at the University of Michigan. On the fortieth anniversary of the integration of Ole Miss, a gray-bearded Meredith returned to the campus for an observance. It was the same week as that football game with Florida. He was joined by many of the student leaders from that era. Old soldiers and federal marshals who helped protect him were also honored. At twilight, hundreds of black and white citizens of Mississippi held a picnic together on the same spot of land where the bullets and tear gas were fired in 1962.

"We cannot undo the misdeeds of the past," the university's chancellor, Robert Khayat, told the gathering that night. But he added, "Out of the ashes and pain of fear, resistance, and intimidation, Ole Miss has risen to champion the values of respect, tolerance, and civility."

Two families achieve racial harmony in a backyard get-together.

LUNCHEONETTE

LUNCHEONETTE
CLOSED

IN INTREST OF

PUBLIC SAFETY

The Children of a Revolution

by David Halberstam

Now, FORTY-THREE YEARS LATER, the first thing I remember about them is their sense of purpose, which was so unshakable, and then their fearlessness. They were not really that fearless of course, no one ever is in the face of death, but they seemed fearless as they went off to be assaulted each time by raging mobs of white segregationists. Diane Nash, the beautiful young woman from Chicago whom all the rest of them so admired (and who half of the men were in love with), seemed utterly without fear, and that goaded many of the men to be a bit braver. But in fact, every day in her last class at Fisk, as she readied herself to go off to yet another sit-in, she was aware of her own mounting fear, her palms began to sweat, and she would notice a huge wet hand print—a fear print, really—on the desk in her English class. And then she would pull herself together and become the Diane Nash she was supposed to be, the Diane Nash who was always so cool and icy, afraid of nothing in the eyes of her male peers.

She herself thought at first that there was something almost innocent about their plan, and that it was doomed to failure—a group of black students ("Negro" was the word still being used at the time, and the word "black," in terms of this usage, was still a few years away) was going to challenge the most powerful merchants in the big city of Nashville. The merchants, she thought to herself, were rich and powerful and were connected to rich and powerful city officials, the mayor and city councilmen, who had the city's police force, not always warm and friendly to black people, under their command. What chance did a bunch of poor, powerless black children have to challenge so formidable a structure of white men who were each other's friends, took care of each other all the time, and were sworn to stop any challenge by blacks, even scared black children?

> "THOSE STUDENTS CHANGED THE COUNTRY WITH THEIR ACTS OF CONSCIENCE AND BRAVERY, TURNING AROUND IN THE PROCESS FIRST THE JUSTICE DEPARTMENT, THEN TWO SOMEWHAT WARY PRESIDENTS."

Protesting segregation, students stage a sit-in at a Nashville lunch counter on March 1, 1960, opposite. They learned their peaceful tactics from India's Mahatma Gandhi.

And that's finally what they were, she had thought, young black kids who weren't even from Nashville. They knew no one in the city—had no powerful friends or allies, had no money. They had even in most cases lied to their parents about what they were doing, fearing that their parents would forbid it, or would come up and pull them out of college, because they were putting at risk something so precious, in most cases the rare chance of a poor black family to produce its first college graduate.

But their teacher, Jim Lawson, dissented from that view, and they had come to trust him completely. Jim Lawson was a brilliant man, they all agreed, and for several months he had been teaching them about Gandhian nonviolence, which he learned during his three years as a missionary in India, walking in Gandhi's footsteps as best he could. He had also spent time in a federal prison as a conscientious objector and draft resistor during the Korean War. What Jim Lawson told them again and again was that their cause was just. And if they acted on their beliefs—if they demanded to be served just like anyone else at stores where they spent their money for goods (downtown stores that were absolutely dependent upon black customers)—a number of things would be true.

Jailed students are served a meal in prison. Nashville students later formed SNCC, the Student Nonviolent Coordinating Committee, to fight for justice.

First and foremost, that what they would be asking for was absolutely fair and just in the eyes of ordinary Americans. So the legitimacy of what they would do would be obvious, as would the injustice of those who might try and thwart them. That would leave the store owners, and in time the city fathers of Nashville, with two options. The first would be to serve them, which would be the right thing to do. But that, given the traditions and instincts of the leaders in a southern city, would be unlikely. The more likely course was that they would be arrested. But that tactic would fail if they were arrested for trying to do something so just and reasonable, so American, Lawson had said, and they would no longer be anonymous. Their deed would create their fame; soon everyone would know their names, others would soon take their place, and, if their successors were arrested, others would take *their* place.

Which in the end was exactly what happened.

The protests had begun in February 1960 in Nashville, a moderately liberal capital city in a border state with a moderately liberal mayor, blacks who could vote, one moderate newspaper that tried to report what happened with marginal prejudice, and one segregationist paper that sought to destroy the protestors.

The children themselves, for it really was a revolution run by students, seemed the most unlikely leaders of what became a revolution within a revolution, a student movement that drove a larger movement to ever more dangerous—indeed absolutely terrifying—levels of confrontation with recalcitrant forces in the most violent places in the South, and brought the movement in time to ever greater levels of success.

These students were not the children of the black middle class. Rather, most of them were Depression-era children, the sons and daughters of the poorest people in the poorest part of the country with the worst jobs. In most instances their parents had not gone beyond the sixth grade. In many cases, the parents made their living from jobs so menial that they were often paid off the books. Diane Nash, raised in Chicago and light skinned—that was important in the black student hierarchy of the day—was not like the other leaders. She had become politically active early in her freshman year at Fisk when a boyfriend took her to the Tennessee State Fair and she had been stunned by the signs over the restrooms: WHITE ONLY.

John Lewis, by contrast, was more typical of the group. He hoped to be a preacher (he ended up a congressman) and was a student at American Baptist Theological Seminary, a small black Baptist school in Nashville. It might have been the smallest, poorest school in America at the time: Tuition was $40 a semester, but you could pay it off in a work-study program. Lewis was a poor rural kid from Troy, Alabama, where his parents miraculously managed to own a parcel of land. As a boy he had hated the

days in picking season when he was supposed to work on the farm and miss school. On those days, he would hide until the moment the bus arrived. His siblings would try to warn his parents, "Momma and Daddy, he's got his school clothes on, he's plannin' to go to school." Then he would race for the bus. His boyhood hero was Martin Luther King Jr., and he had practiced for the ministry by preaching to the chickens on the farm, telling them to be good Christians and learn to love each other. He had hated the quality of segregated life in Troy, the ice-cream counters that blacks could not eat at, the libraries they could not borrow books from, and the movie theaters that they could attend only by sitting in a separate section upstairs.

They all were, it would turn out, more ready to act than they realized when Jim Lawson first reached them in the fall of 1959 and brought them into his workshops. It was almost six years after *Brown v. Board of Education*, the Supreme Court ruling that was supposed to change their lives, had been decided. And almost nothing had changed. So they were ready: they had the right teacher, Lawson, and they went to their workshops and acted out what might happen. Yelling "Nigger go home" at each other, they prepared for the moment when the local whites would put cigarettes out on their heads and pour coffee and ketchup on them, and the police would come and arrest them

Sign of the times, 1961: Waiting rooms—as well as most other public and private venues—then were still commonly segregated in the South.

Apprehensive but determined, David Dennis sits tight as a Freedom Rider. He and some twenty-five other riders are aboard an interstate bus heading from Montgomery, Alabama, to Jackson, Mississippi, in May 1961. Mississippi National Guardsmen, bayonets fixed, escort them.

instead of their attackers. All of this would happen.

Jim Lawson turned out to be not just a brilliant teacher, but something of a prophet. The leadership group, well trained in Gandhian display of nonviolence, was quickly arrested, and soon others took their place. And when they in turn were arrested, still others took their place. The parents of the leaders, fearful of losing a cherished college education, and even more terrified of having a child killed as well, gradually swung around. Back in Whiteville, in rural West Tennessee, Buck Murphy, the father of student leader Curtis Murphy, found himself taunted by a local white man. "How's

that jailbird son of yours doing?" the white man shouted.

"He's doing just fine," said Buck, who had at first argued passionately with his son against taking part.

"Is he still in that Nashville jail?"

"Wherever he is, I am, too," Buck answered, as if for a generation of parents.

In Nashville, a powerful black boycott squeezed the offending stores mercilessly. In time the black community was galvanized, and the stores surrendered.

But the students did not stop with so priceless, albeit so peripheral, a victory in a border state. There were many more battles still to be won, most of them in the

Deep South. "The valley of the shadow of death," Bernard Lafayette, one of the leaders, called Alabama and Mississippi. A year later, when in Alabama the Klan stopped what were called Freedom Rides and set fire to their buses, the Nashville young people—now known as Snick, or SNCC, the Student Nonviolent Coordinating Committee—took over the Freedom Rides. The Kennedy Justice Department, fearful of more deaths—and a greater wedge driven between southern and northern Democrats—asked John Seigenthaler, a former Nashville journalist working for Robert Kennedy, to talk Diane Nash out of it. "She's from your goddamned city," Burke Marshall, one of the assistant attorneys general, told Seigenthaler, "see what you can do to stop them."

So Seigenthaler called and hit a wall. He pleaded with Nash about the danger of what they were doing. She was unmoved. "You're going to get your people killed," Seigenthaler said. "Then others will follow them," she answered. And if they, too, were killed? Seigenthaler asked. "Then even more will follow," she said. As she spoke, the steel in her voice reminded him of the words from the old hymn that had come to be used as a protest song:

Just like a tree that's planted near the water/we will not be moved.

Seigenthaler then called his bosses in Washington, knowing they would be furious and knowing as well that they could not turn back this movement.

Even the more senior ministers from Martin Luther King's leadership group tried to slow the students down, fearing the deaths that would come in Alabama and Mississippi. "If not us, who, and if not now, when?" John Lewis had answered them. And so it continued, and in five years, from the first victories in the sit-ins to the passage of the Voter's Right Act of 1965, those students changed the country with their acts of conscience and bravery, turning around in the process first the Justice Department, then two somewhat wary presidents of the United States, Kennedy and Johnson, and then the Congress of the United States.

Somewhat to his own surprise, John Lewis, who had always intended to be a minister, found himself in politics, and some twenty-five years after he had first gone to Mississippi as a Freedom Rider he was elected to the Congress of the United States. There, at an early congressional function, he ran into a fellow congressman named Sonny Montgomery, who had commanded the Mississippi National Guard troops who had escorted—and not in a friendly way—the Freedom Riders into the state. They introduced themselves and talked of old times, finding to their surprise that in fact they had shared this extraordinary moment a quarter century earlier. "Isn't that something," said Montgomery. Then he congratulated Lewis on his election. "You've come a long way, Congressman," Montgomery said.

"So have you, Congressman," Lewis answered, "so have you."

U.S. Representative John Lewis, Democrat of Georgia, appears on Meet the Press *in December 2002. Lewis did not foresee his future in politics when he participated in the sit-ins and Freedom Rides.*

The Nation's Intractable Debate

by Cynthia Gorney

OF ALL THE LEGAL OPINIONS handed down throughout the two-century history of the United States Supreme Court, only one is commemorated by an annual citizens' march to assail it. The march occurs in the middle of January, in Washington, D.C., when even the indifferent winters of the Potomac region can turn harsh enough to require thick mufflers and overcoats. The chartered buses always begin converging on the nation's capital at dawn, having rolled through the darkness from cities many hours away; when the bus doors open, the people who step outside carry banners, signboards, baby strollers, megaphones. They made the first of these pilgrimages on January 22, 1974, the one-year anniversary of *Roe et al v. Wade, District Attorney of Dallas County,* and by the thirtieth anniversary they were still making them, still descending from the buses, their ranks reinforced by new generations of young women and men for whom no cause in America will ever matter as much as this.

There is supposed to be an irreproachable finality about the decisions of the highest court in the land, but *Roe v. Wade,* the ruling that declared abortion to be a constitutionally protected fundamental right of women, was delivered with a built-in advance apology. "We forthwith acknowledge our awareness of the sensitive and emotional nature of the abortion controversy, of the vigorous opposing views, even among physicians, and of the deep and seemingly absolute convictions that the subject inspires," read the justices' preface to *Roe v. Wade*—a warning, of sorts, about the volatile text that was to follow. "One's philosophy, one's experiences, one's exposure to the raw edges of human existence, one's religious training, one's attitude toward life and family and their values, are all likely to influence and to color

> "HISTORIANS AND LEGAL SCHOLARS, SEEKING TO UNDERSTAND WHY ABORTION CONFLICT CONSUMED THIS NATION . . . SOMETIMES POINT TO ROE ITSELF AS A CATALYST."

Dueling slogans summarize the American abortion dilemma, opposite, and its chief battleground—the U.S. Supreme Court—looms in the background. Since the Roe v. Wade ruling in 1973, which made abortion legal in the United States, Americans have marched, protested, and argued over this issue.

one's thinking and conclusions about abortion."

One of the many widespread misimpressions about *Roe*—the things people think they know about this most name-dropped of twentieth-century Supreme Court rulings but that aren't exactly true—is that Justice Harry Blackmun wrote it, all of it, the way a poet composes stanzas or an author writes a book. It is indeed Justice Blackmun's name that appears in capital letters atop the printed opinion; the fact that it was a majority opinion, negotiated over and agreed to by seven of the nine justices, was often overlooked during Blackmun's remaining years on the Court. Blackmun himself did little to dispel the idea that Roe had been his alone, the great triumph and burden of one judge's working life. When he spoke publicly about the abortion ruling, which he would do from time to time before select audiences, Blackmun always mentioned the hate mail, year after year, sixty thousand letters delivered personally to him at his chambers in court. These letters addressed him as Pontius Pilate, they called him a perpetrator of genocide, they wished harm to his family, they prayed for his misbegotten

soul. Blackmun was a small man, slender by nature and increasingly frail as he aged, and as he stood before audiences he would describe the content of the letters in a low voice that seemed to quaver less with anger than with despair. He would say this, finally, as he came to the end of his talks: "I believe Roe against Wade will stand as a watershed in the history of the emancipation of the American woman."

And this: "I will carry Roe against Wade to my grave."

In both predictions Harry Blackmun proved correct. When he died at ninety in 1999, five years after his retirement from the Supreme Court, every news account of Blackmun's passing commenced with the abortion ruling and included, somewhere in the text, the word "controversial." The controversy over legal abortion did not begin with *Roe v. Wade*—that is another common misimpression, especially for those too young to remember the pre-1973 years, when American abortion law was left to the discretion of the states. Throughout the late 1960s and early 1970s, as state legislatures began to consider making it legal for doctors to perform abortions, arguments had swelled and subsided in one statehouse after another; there were marches then, too, and nose-to-nose sidewalk debates, and letters-to-the-editor exchanges that had the heady, astonished tone of a first-time fight over a genuinely radical idea. The initial state to loosen its criminal abortion law was Colorado, in 1967; North Carolina and California followed shortly afterward, and by the early weeks of January 1973 the national map was a rough mosaic of Yes, No, and Depends: induced abortion was mostly unrestricted in some parts of the country; legal but closely restricted in others; and illegal under all but life-saving circumstances in the rest, including Texas, the state whose felony abortion law had been challenged in *Roe v. Wade*.

The public brawl over state abortion law was six years old, in other words, the morning the Supreme Court stepped in to end it. No one, not even the attorneys who brought the two abortion cases the Court decided as a single package that day, expected the breadth of the rulings the justices handed down. That state laws could no longer prohibit abortion or specify what reasons for abortion were and were not acceptable; that state legislatures could no longer require a woman to obtain abortion permission from a hospital committee; that electing to end a pregnancy was "a woman's decision" safeguarded by the United States Constitution—these were huge pronouncements in 1973, exhilarating to those who approved of them, incomprehensible to those who did not.

From what had been a haphazard agglomeration of state-by-state opposition groups, the volunteer and parish organizations that had labeled themselves "right to life," a national movement now coalesced in shared outrage and solidified within a week. The target: a constitutional amendment to protect fetal life, and in doing so, erase *Roe v. Wade*.

Did Harry Blackmun imagine—assuming it was he who wrote those somber lines about the "sensitive and emotional nature," the "vigorous opposing views," the "deep and seemingly absolute convictions"—how prescient the ruling's preface would prove to be? Historians and legal scholars, seeking to understand why the abortion conflict consumed this nation as it did no other during the closing years of the twentieth century, sometimes point to *Roe* itself as the catalyst: too much, too abrupt, too

A grisly reminder of a former abortion technique, a twisted wire coat hanger appears on the sign of a pro-choice marcher in New York in 1970, top. An anti-abortion protester at an American Medical Association annual convention, also in New York, states his view with a conundrum, bottom.

soon. Too great a conceptual leap, the critics have said, dissecting the *Roe* majority reasoning section by section; too unconvincing a set of assertions and arguments to justify shutting off the legislative voice of the people. "A very bad decision," read one influential critique, by Yale law professor John Hart Ely, in a 1973 issue of the *Yale Law Journal*. "Not because it conflicts with either my idea of progress or what the evidence suggests is society's—it doesn't. It is bad because it is bad constitutional law."

But the central question in *Roe v. Wade*, the role of the state in weighing fetal life against individual women's autonomy, also happened to be perfectly suited for inflaming American passions. We are among the most religious people on the planet, when commitment to faith is measured by attendance at places of worship, and at the same time the most vehement about separating religion from government power. We tend to become erratic and quarrelsome on the subjects of sexual behavior, sexual morality, and motherhood, all of which are instantly, perilously invoked when the topic of abortion comes up. We regard ourselves both as adamant protectors of the defenseless and adamant champions of individual liberty. We like adamance in general, in fact, in the public

James Kopp is escorted into Erie County Court, New York, after admitting to shooting Dr. Barnett Slepian, who performed abortions, in 1998.

advocacy of causes; as a rule we prefer our issues simple, condensable, and loud. The bumper sticker is an American invention, and no other other modern social controversy has been so readily and repeatedly distilled into the one-line shout: U.S. Out of My Uterus. Abortion Stops a Beating Heart. I'm Pro-Choice and I Vote. It's a Child, Not a Choice.

There was a time in the early 1970s, those first months after *Roe v. Wade*, when abortion partisans on both sides believed resolution was now close at hand—that the Supreme Court had settled the question boldly and for all time, or that the Supreme Court had acted so preposterously that surely a constitutional amendment would quickly put things right. It took a decade or so to see how wrong both suppositions were. By the thirtieth anniversary of *Roe*, the fight over legal abortion had spread into nearly every major venue in American public life: theology, medicine, law, culture, foreign policy, and electoral politics, from presidential campaigns to local assembly races to back-room party caucuses at which abortion-related platform language might be shouted over just one more time. So intractable had the issue become, so fiercely resistant to every familiar form of compromise, that at one point toward the end of the century an informal movement calling itself Common Ground started up in a few American cities, with the sole purpose of trying to arrange civil conversations about abortion—trying to place people

Thousands of pro-life activists rally to march down Constitution Avenue in Washington D.C., on January 22, 2003, the thirtieth anniversary of the Roe v. Wade *decision. Many people see no easy resolution to the abortion debate.*

from opposing camps in rooms together to search for areas of agreement and mutual respect.

The movement never made much headway. If he was aware of its existence at all before he died, Justice Blackmun must have felt a special sorrow in learning how hard it had become simply for Americans to talk to each other about this. Ethical questions in medicine mattered deeply to Harry Blackmun; he had once served as counsel to Minnesota's Mayo Clinic, and while gathering ideas for early drafts of *Roe*, the justice returned to Minnesota to spend scholarly time among the volumes of the clinic library. In such a setting a man might be expected to look away from the pages now and then, to think for a while about the consequences of the passages he is preparing to write. "Our task, of course, is to resolve the issue by constitutional measurement, free of emotion and predilection"—that line, too, would appear in *Roe*'s final text in January 1973, when no one saw yet what was coming: the clinic doctors strapping on bulletproof vests before work; the judiciary candidates facing question after question about their resolve to uphold or overturn this one particular Supreme Court ruling; the winter buses rolling toward Washington, their windows open wide enough to let passersby hear the full-throated singing of the people inside.

CHAPTER FIVE

OUR FELLOW AMERICANS

★

"It is not by wearing down into uniformity all that is individual in themselves, but by cultivating it and calling it forth, within the limits imposed by the rights and interests of others, that human beings become a noble and beautiful object of contemplation; and as the works partake the character of those who do them, by the same process human life also becomes rich, diversified, and animating, furnishing more abundant aliment to high thoughts and elevating feelings, and strengthening the tie which binds every individual to the race, by making the race infinitely better worth belonging to."

—John Stuart Mill, from his 1869 book On Liberty

FRANKLIN DELANO ROOSEVELT

Reinventing the Presidency

by Russell Baker

CLOSE STUDENTS OF Franklin Delano Roosevelt often say it was his heroic fight to survive polio that made him a great president. The theory is the stuff of legend, and may even be true, though who can do more than guess about such mysteries?

Poliomyelitis was a disease that commonly preyed on children—"infantile paralysis," most people called it—but it did not strike Roosevelt until he was thirty-nine years old, and then it struck with soul- and body-crushing ferocity. Within days after the first symptoms appeared, his legs were useless. They were to remain useless for the rest of his life, although he never abandoned the effort to make them work again.

Until that terrible August at his summer home in Campobello, he had seemed headed for a reasonably successful political career. He had served briefly in the New York legislature, had been

appointed assistant secretary of the U.S. Navy under President Wilson, had even been the vice presidential candidate on the doomed ticket the Democrats ran against Warren Harding in 1920.

Then, calamity. Suddenly he seemed destined to spin out his remaining years growing old and inconsequential in wheelchairs. That was in 1921.

Yet twelve years later, with metal braces helping him to stand upright on the Capitol steps in Washington, he was inaugurated president of the United States. His audience was an entire nation partially paralyzed by economic catastrophe, and he spoke as one who knew better than most what it meant to be catastrophically stricken: The only thing one had to fear, he said, was "fear itself."

The story invites mythic treatment: Whimsical fate mocks a rich young

> "IT WAS ROOSEVELT WHO STARTED THIS CONCENTRATION OF POWER IN THE PRESIDENCY. . . . PRESIDENTS EVER SINCE HAVE RISEN AND FALLEN ON THEIR PERFORMANCE SKILLS."

On the campaign trail in 1932, Franklin Roosevelt, opposite, flanked by his wife Eleanor and son, Elliott, waves to a crowd. (The foreground of the photo has apparently been altered.) Afflicted with poliomyelitis in 1921, Roosevelt's public life might have ended, but in 1933 he was inaugurated president. Earlier, in 1920, he had made a try for the vice presidency, below.

Play ball! In Griffin Stadium, Jacksonville, Florida, President Roosevelt throws out the first ball of the baseball season. Presidential Secretary Edwin M. Watson supports him. Roosevelt brought a buoyant and optimistic surge of confidence to a country emerging from the Great Depression.

dilettante's trivial ambitions and small accomplishments by striking him down with a child's disease. Is it punishing him for not aspiring to higher goals? Or is it confronting him with a supreme test of character? Whatever the gods may be up to, he refuses to surrender to self-pity, accepts the blow as a challenge, and fights a long, agonizing struggle to make his damaged body obey his will. He becomes one of the great men of his age, a giant of his century.

What a story! Books, plays, movies, and television have told it repeatedly, and only a hard, hard heart can fail to feel a thrill of pride in the human spirit when, at the end, he rises on those crutches and with a triumphant smile serves notice that he is back in the game.

Thereafter the résumé is the longest of any twentieth-century president: Elected president of the United States four times . . . Led the country through the worst economic collapse in history, preserving democratic capitalism while other desperate nations were turning to totalitarianism and planned economies . . . Built and commanded the huge war machine that made the country victorious in World War II . . . Developed the system of international alliances that made the United States the world's dominant leader through the end of the twentieth century.

The list goes on and on: Social Security begun. Beginning of public housing. Creation of the Tennessee Valley Authority. The Securities and Exchange Commission. Federal insurance for bank deposits. The atomic bomb. The United Nations . . .

And of course, the welfare state.

Applying humanitarian philosophy to government, the welfare state represented the "new deal" he had promised a down-and-out nation. For the first time, an American government assumed the country had an obligation to help people survive when they became unable to help themselves. The welfare state has been under political attack ever since, and is still modified to suit changing times, but it continues to thrive and seems likely to endure, barring revolution in Washington.

No less remarkable was Roosevelt's remaking of the presidency itself. Ten men followed him to the White House before the century ended, and all found themselves captives of the Roosevelt presidency. Thus every president was

expected to give a star performance in a new kind of popular entertainment: government as theater, or film, or television. It was Roosevelt who first used modern mass-communications technology to convert theatrical talent into massive political power.

This conversion of star quality into personal power is what is happening in the television competitions that comprise today's presidential elections. When the president becomes a star, other branches of government fall into minor roles— supporting actors, spear carriers—and power tilts more heavily to the White House. It was Roosevelt who started this concentration of power in the presidency, and the instrument he used was radio. At the microphone he was a master performer.

Presidents ever since have risen and fallen on their performance skills. Gerald Ford, without an ounce of ham anywhere on his bones, inevitably lost to Jimmy Carter of the gleaming show-biz teeth and country-boy persona. Carter projected the affable decency associated with heroes of down-home TV sitcoms. Richard Nixon, aware of his awkward

Differing personalities project disparate images: President Jimmy Carter, top, projected a folksy, down-home character that people trusted—but not enough for two terms. Richard Nixon, bottom, who didn't give good television "performances," never overcame a dark and sinister image.

stage presence, labored hard to master the theatrical graces, but could never work his stiffness out. Watching him on TV was like watching the smartest kid in the class playing the lead in the high school play.

Lyndon Johnson, who quit when all cheering had stopped, was famous for his lack of charisma, as was Harry Truman, who ended his term with a 25-percent public approval rating. In contrast, John Kennedy, Dwight Eisenhower, and Ronald Reagan, each in his distinctive way, may have been Roosevelt's equal at projecting star quality.

Taking office at the nadir of the Great Depression, Roosevelt's first goal was to get the country's chin up off the floor. He wanted to become an active, exciting presence to a public that seemed defeated, haggard, hopeless. In modern jargon, he wanted to "create a new image" of what a president was. Radio was the image-making machine of the era. With a sound man and a few actors at the microphone, radio could create warm, personal disembodied voices and listeners, and did so every day.

A child of the 1930s felt a personal relationship with Buck Rogers, Tonto, and the Singing Lady. The housewife bent over the afternoon ironing might feel that Bing Crosby was singing to her alone. Men brought home the evening papers but tuned in to hear Lowell Thomas or Boake Carter read the news because the voice sounded serious, trustworthy, exciting.

Radio was the nation's mass entertainment medium, and it was new, adventurous, and exciting, as Roosevelt wanted his presidency to be. The president as an old-fashioned, stern uncle of the Hoover-Coolidge-Wilson school, with those funny shirt collars and solemn bankers' eyes, was to become a man of the past.

Radio audiences made pictures in their own minds. Out of the sounds issuing from the box, each listener constructed his own personal vision of the people making them, and formed judgments about character and honesty.

Roosevelt's radio voice became one of the most distinctive sounds of the age. In schoolyards children did imitations of the big, confident voice that said "My friends" at the opening of his "fireside chats." They were not really chats by the fireside, but radio-side lectures that took him into millions of parlors and kitchens, shantytown shacks and penthouses. Families gathered to gaze at the radio as the president's words traveled from the faraway White House along incomprehensible

"My little dog Fala" became nearly as famous as the rest of the Roosevelt family during the White House years, right. Roosevelt perfected the use of a new invention, radio, to communicate directly with the American people. Fred Wilfang, opposite, at home in Black Hawk County, Iowa, in 1939, reads a rural newspaper while listening to his radio.

A pince-nez, a cigarette holder, a pinkie ring, a tuxedo, a cocktail— despite the trappings of the upper crust, Roosevelt and his administration's New Deal genuinely helped middle-class Americans. Here he revels in politics, listening to speeches during a Jackson Day dinner.

complexities of wire and vacuum tubes and filled the great national living room with that warm, confident, neighborly voice. It spoke of complicated matters in plain English. It sounded competent, trustworthy.

The new president was to be jaunty, confident, smiling, glad to see you. He would be a man who liked a good joke, and knew how to tell one, too. Naturally he would have a dog, "my little dog Fala," in Roosevelt's case. This new president would be the kind of man who could come into your kitchen, sit down with the family, and talk plain talk about his problems, and

your problems, the whole country's problems.

To fit himself into this role as the common man's friend in the White House, Roosevelt had to overcome handicaps. One was an upper-drawer accent that came with his upper-class background. Reporters trying to explain how thoroughly upper-class he was described him as a "patrician," to suggest that his family had been upper class so long that nobody could remember where the money came from.

He was not given to fretting about such problems. Polio had been a problem, an accent was only an accent. He went right on talking that way, and sounding upper class, and getting elected anyhow. He went right on wearing his pince-nez eyeglasses too, and smoking through a cigarette holder, which was not the way the common man took his smoke. Soon the cigarette holder became a part of his caricature and an instantly recognizable symbol of the cocky spirit he was trying to cultivate in the country.

Above all, the new president would be a man who did things, who acted instead of waiting for problems to solve themselves. The old-style president did not esteem action. Calvin Coolidge was praised because he "never wasted any time, never wasted any words, and never wasted any public money." Herbert Hoover, with the Depression in its third year and fifteen million people out of work, still held to the classic economic theory, believing that the market, left to its own dynamics, would inevitably bring the system back to prosperity. Under Hoover, "Prosperity is just around the corner" had become a national joke line.

Roosevelt saw a country desperate for somebody to do something, do anything—simply to act. He immedi-

ately deluged Congress with dozens of bills and insisted on swift passage. Congress was powerless to resist the whirlwind. It was filled with people swept into office by the force of Roosevelt's victory, and they swiftly passed anything he sent to the Capitol. Later, old-timers who had been there said they would have passed a laundry list if Roosevelt had sent them one.

The three months of frenzied legislating that began his administration became known as "the hundred days," and for the past seventy years every new president has lived with the dreadful knowledge that after three months and ten days on the job the country is going to pass judgment on how well he has done in his own "hundred days."

Yes, it is a silly moment at which to start judging a new administration of a robust and contented superpower, yet such is the power of the precedents Roosevelt created. Whether because of the polio or in spite of it, he created a presidency that still forces its Rooseveltian character on everyone who takes the oath of office, including those who would have disliked him most heartily.

A poster created by the WPA—the Work Projects Administration, an agency designed to give work to the unemployed during the Depression—raises funds for the fight against poliomyelitis, left.

The Birth of the Feminist Movement

by Anna Quindlen

THE AMERICAN FEMINIST MOVEMENT of the twentieth century was a movement built on autobiography. This is not to denigrate it, but to extol it. Many of the other great movements toward social justice were founded on the top-down principle, or noblesse oblige: the educated and well-to-do worked to liberate the underprivileged. In this way slaves were freed, children fed, and public housing created, but the progress toward those goals was often haphazard, built as it was on an intellectual construct, not a reading of real life. By contrast the women of the women's movement, who begot one of the greatest social revolutions in the history of the nation, most often acted out of the inequities, humiliations, deprivations, and needs of their own lives. That was the key to their success.

Of no one was this truer than of Margaret Sanger, the public health nurse who utterly changed the lives of American women. By the time her struggle ended with her death in 1966, she had seen the issue of family planning transformed from a shamefaced whisper to an open discussion. The organization she had founded in 1921, the American Birth Control League, had become Planned Parenthood, with chapters and clinics in nearly every American city. The questions she had raised about population control and sexual health were no longer considered radical, but increasingly mainstream. She had impressed on the public consciousness a simple notion that would reach its zenith in the decades after her death: that the ability of women to control their own fertility was the linchpin of liberation, and that women's liberation was the linchpin of human progress.

And it all began with her mother. Sanger was the daughter of the fecund Irish immigrant working class, prevented by ignorance, poverty,

> "SHE HAD IMPRESSED ON THE PUBLIC CONSCIOUSNESS . . . THAT WOMEN'S LIBERATION WAS THE LINCHPIN OF HUMAN PROGRESS."

A trio of prominent feminists—Kelli Conlin, Gloria Steinem, and actress Olympia Dukakis, opposite—lead a march on New York streets to protest the arrival of Pope John Paul II in October 1995. Many leaders of the women's movement disagree with the Catholic Church's position on birth control and abortion. Their forebear Margaret Sanger, below, pioneered family planning early in the twentieth century.

and the iron rule of the Catholic Church from curtailing the size of families they could ill afford. Her mother was pregnant eighteen times and gave birth to eleven children. She died by inches of tuberculosis, her health destroyed by deprivation and one pregnancy after another. When Margaret went to work in New York City as a nurse and midwife, she saw her mother everywhere, in one crowded tenement after another where women in poor health gave birth to children they knew they could not feed. She also sat at the deathbed of many a desperate woman who was bleeding to death in the aftermath of a botched illegal abortion, often leaving a roomful of little orphans.

The appropriate response to this seemed simple to Sanger. She knew that there were ways to prevent pregnancy; she knew that women with more money and education were using those methods, condoms and spermicides dispensed under the cover of disease prevention or hygiene. In 1914 she began publishing a feminist monthly, *The Woman Rebel*, that advocated the use of contraception. As a result, she was indicted for promoting obscenity. By 1916 she had gone a step further and opened a clinic in Brooklyn to teach poor women how to use pessaries. She was arrested and the clinic shut down after less than two weeks, but not before it had served several hundred women.

This was radical indeed. At the time of Sanger's work in the slums of New York,

A mother and her seven children crowd a New York tenement in 1910, opposite. With little or no reliable information about birth control, and no legal abortions, women of her generation often were condemned to a life of near-constant pregnancy. In Britain, above, a Miss Billington takes to the streets around 1912.

the notion that women sometimes might want to eschew motherhood was considered not only unnatural but also immoral. In many states women had no rights of inheritance and property ownership. Women of social stature were expected to concentrate on the running of their homes and the details of their clothing. Their children were cared for by servants. Divorce was rare for them and for the poorer women who were trying to eke out an existence for themselves and their rapidly growing families, in large part because both groups were dependent on their husbands for protection, status, and money.

This was considered the natural order of things, even by educated men. It was commonplace for sentiments like these to appear in learned journals: "No one can evade the fact that, in taking up a masculine calling, studying and working in a man's way, woman is doing something not wholly in agreement with, if not directly injurious to, her feminine nature." That was Carl Jung in a journal of psychology in 1928.

In response to these conditions various women's groups formed to clean up the slums, to increase educational opportunities, and above all to overturn the most basic inequities of gender. Some tried to overturn laws, others to have women admitted to schools and professions from which they had always been barred. The best known were the suffragettes, who worked in both England and the United States to guarantee women the right to vote. They believed that if women

American women mount a Planned Parenthood exhibit in 1941. Since its founding, the organization has worked to advocate for education and personal liberties in the areas of birth control, family planning, and reproductive health care.

could choose their leaders, they could change their laws and therefore their lives. "Suffrage is the pivotal right," argued Susan B. Anthony, one of the most influential of the nineteenth-century feminists.

At a time when these women argued that biology was not destiny, Margaret Sanger's nascent movement suggested that in critical ways it was, and that the pivotal right was not legislative but reproductive. Sanger believed that education, opportunity, and the franchise would not really change the lives of women unless they had the ability to decide when and how often they would become pregnant and give birth. Her own experience had taught her that one of the keys to poverty was the unconscionably large families that immigrant women had neither the means to support nor the means to prevent. And as

a political radical she believed that this was not accidental, that the enormous families of the underclass were convenient for the privileged, providing an endless supply of cheap household and factory labor.

In a 1928 book entitled *Motherhood in Bondage*, she did what would later become the most important work of consciousness-raising feminism: tear the pastel veil from the experiences of ordinary women. She quoted one woman working six days a week to support her four children: "I think I would rather die than ever have any more. Not that I don't love them but it is so hard." By then Sanger's motto was simple and direct: "Every child a wanted child."

This became the work of her life—in her writing, her political organizing, and the speeches she gave throughout the country—often accompanied by considerable opposition. In 1921 when she was scheduled to give a lecture at Town Hall in New York, she arrived to find the doors padlocked and one hundred police officers around the hall; when she tried to speak on the street, she was arrested for disorderly conduct. The Catholic Church mounted concerted opposition over many decades to her work, and even today she is accused of being a proponent of eugenics, and of supporting the extermination of the poor and the unfit in pursuit of a better society. Most of this is a distortion or outright misstatement of her positions, although like many other progressives of the early twentieth century she made the mistake of supporting sterilization for those with hereditary conditions and strict enforcement of immigration bans on the retarded and the disabled.

But real opposition to Sanger always has and always will coalesce around what her biographer, Ellen Chesler, called "the deceptively simple proposition" that the ability to control pregnancy is the bedrock of freedom for women. It is only in retrospect that it is possible to see how true this was. Much of the work Sanger had done came to fruition near the end of her life. The Supreme Court recognized a right to privacy in reproductive matters in 1965, around the same time that the birth control pill, for which Sanger had been an early proponent, came into widespread use, allowing millions of women to take for granted the reproductive freedom for which Sanger had struggled for so long.

Other women's stories would shape the triumph of feminism at the end of the twentieth century. Betty Friedan's torment as an intelligent woman sentenced to a life of domestic busywork would raise the consciousness of a nation with *The Feminine Mystique*. Gloria Steinem would be changed forever by caring as a young girl for her clinically depressed mother. Gloria Feldt, the president of the Planned Parenthood Federation of America at the end of the twentieth century, had been a fifteen-year-old first-time mother who had three children by the time she was twenty and who saw herself in the overwhelmed women Sanger described in her writings.

Suburban housewife and mother of three, author Betty Friedan helped found NOW, the National Organization of Women in the late 1960s and became its president in 1970.

Like most feminists, they were first radicalized by the facts of their own lives. So was Sanger, who built the bulwark for those others. Her legacy is contraception, but with her fight for the right to control fertility came a hugely symbolic change in attitude that set the stage for women judges and senators, women cadets at West Point, and women hockey players in the Olympics. Sanger's work was always about the right of women to be full citizens and free people, about the dangerous suggestion that if a woman had the right to her own person, she might well have a right to every human possibility. At the end of her life she summed it up. "No woman can call herself free," she said, "who does not own and control her body."

EDWARD R. MURROW

The Voice That Reached a Nation

by James T. Wooten

No DOUBT OTHER SONGS preceded it on the musical learning-curve of my childhood—probably "Happy Birthday" or "Jesus Loves Me"—but the first one I can remember committing to memory was "Filipino Baby."

That was in Detroit, during World War II, when my mother provided room-and-board for navy personnel learning to maintain and repair PT-boat engines built at the nearby Packard Motor Co. Most were southerners who enjoyed her cooking (Mom was a Kentucky girl) and after dinner they usually settled in our living room to play country music on our old windup Victrola, including records by Roy Acuff and Ernest Tubbs—and every evening, unfailingly, I listened at least once if not several times to:

She's my Filipino baby, she's my treasure and my pet . . . lovin' pet.

It was Tubbs's adenoidal account of a sailor's farewell to the girl he'd ardently courted while in port. For young men inevitably bound for the South Pacific, it was naturally their favorite and therefore mine as well.

As the warship left Manila, Sailing proudly through the sea . . . deep blue sea . . . All the sailors' hearts were filled with deep regret.

One of the men— I believe his name was Lex— sported a snazzy Bulova with a black dial and gold hands worn on the underside of his wrist and consulted by turning his palm upward in an odd gesture I copied the moment someone gave me a watch. When he tapped the face of it, as eventually he did every night, the music promptly ended, the big radio came on, and, after a bit of fiddling with the dials, Acuff and Tubbs were replaced by the CBS *World News Roundup*. There and then, in the nightly repetition of those moments, was born my

> "IT WAS HIS ROLE, HE THOUGHT, TO TELL [HIS LISTENERS] WHAT THEY NEEDED TO KNOW, TO PROVIDE INFORMATION THEY WERE IN NO POSITION TO HAVE ACQUIRED ON THEIR OWN, . . . TO ENLARGE THEIR WORLDS AND ENRICH THEIR LIVES."

With a voice that the entire world recognized, Edward R. Murrow, opposite, was the first journalist to employ radio to its fullest and most dramatic extent. During World War II he broadcast from Europe, keeping Americans informed about the war's progress. Over their new-fangled radios, below, Americans could hear the sounds of sirens, anti-aircraft fire, and real bombs falling.

lifelong passion for the news, a fascination with faraway places and an abiding interest in Edward R. Murrow.

Before long, with my pal Lex nodding a cue in my direction, I learned to speak his famous preamble in near perfect synchronization. "This . . . is London," I would say along with him, allowing just that millisecond of hesitation between the first word and the second, and all the southern sailors would chuckle at the contrast between my childish chirp and Murrow's mellifluous tones, which by then offered no trace of his own birth in North Carolina.

He'd grown up in the Northwest, studied drama at Washington State, then come to New York to work for CBS in 1935, and in 1937, the year I was born, he'd been posted to Europe, a continent on the edge of war. His first broadcast was from Vienna in 1938, reporting the Anschluss, Austria's capitulation to Germany. He was barely past thirty and about to become electronic journalism's first genuine star. By 1943, with America in the war, his was the principal voice describing it to millions of Americans in living rooms across the country—including ours.

These were memorable learning experiences for me. On most evenings, while my mother was tidying up in the kitchen, I was far from Detroit . . . all over the map: Manila and London, the Philippines and Great Britain, plus San Antonio to boot (as in "San Antonio Rose," another country clanker with geography potential), and Lex would often use my globe-shaped bank—the size of a softball with a coin slot at the North Pole—to locate such places for me, including his hometown in Mississippi, Pascagoula, even though its name wasn't really there where he was pointing. "It's right near N'awlins," he said, "and that's in Looziana, which is right next to Texas. And there, you see, is San Antonio."

I didn't realize it then, of course, but that young sailor and Murrow had transformed our parlor into a classroom; and no kid ever had better teachers. In fact, Murrow often used such terms—teacher and classroom—to define his responsibilities. Yes, he was a reporter and broadcaster, but he also saw himself as an educator and, without a hint of condescension, regarded his listeners as students. It was his role, he thought, to tell them what they needed to know, to provide information they were in no position to have acquired on their own, to explain what they might not have understood, to enlighten their minds, to enlarge their worlds and enrich their lives. Appropriately, after the war, when he was trying to hire a young American planning to teach high school French, Murrow asked, "How'd you like the biggest classroom in the world?"

The country was lucky to have him. I know I was—and so was radio and so, eventually, was television. Simply by talking to his audience (that was just about all Murrow ever really did: talk), he brought to their formative days an intelligence and

"This . . . is London," Murrow intoned. He was there for the German Blitz, in 1940, when much of the city was reduced to rubble.

a gravitas—a sense of worthy purpose—that allowed people to take seriously first radio, then TV, to embrace each in turn as a legitimate instrument of journalism, an essential tool for creating something akin to a national community. Traditionally a country of distinct regions with separate accents and customs, even cuisines, America would have its internal borders and boundaries blurred and many of its differences mitigated by the information and education available to everyone on radio and television, the country's twin towers of communication. And it was Murrow, always and ever the teacher, standing at the front of the classroom just talking to America, talking about London in the blitz, talking about the Nazis' con-centration camps, talking about migrant workers in America, talking about Joe McCarthy. It was, I eventually decided, exactly what I wanted to do as well—and so did two or three generations of reporters, both print and broadcast, who also recognized in Murrow the emblematic ideal of a worthy career.

The fact that we inevitably discovered that he was also a man with warts and flaws did not diminish his stature for us or our esteem for what he had accomplished . . . just by talking to America.

As a tribe, we Americans have always been grand talkers. We wrote a Constitution that guaranteed we could freely speak, but we also held as a self-evident truth the equal importance of being heard.

From the very start of us—whether seated on straight-backed pews in frontier churches or hard benches in town halls or squatting on the dirt floors of log cabins—we not only insisted on talking, we by God demanded that someone listen. We were always determined to stay in touch with each other, to communicate. Even the old mountain men, the grizzled trappers surviving alone in the wilderness of the West, probably talked as much to their pack mules as to themselves.

It was no random rotation of fortune's wheel that so many of the most seminal inventions and innovations in communications, from Ben Franklin's postal service to the Internet—with the notable exception of Herr Gutenberg's press and movable type—have roots of one kind or another in America. It was a classic case of invention mothered by necessity, for even now we remain a country populated by nomadic souls, eager or at least willing to seek their fortunes in some new place (Murrow reversed the prevailing direction and, as a young man, went east), following their noses or their families or their herds or, like Daniel Boone, in the market for a little elbow room. Friends and relatives, home offices and headquarters, backyard fences and familiar faces soon disappeared, which complicated but did not eliminate the country's need and its compulsion to stay in touch. If not ingrained or instinctive, it was at least portable.

Information moved at a slower pace when it was up to the Pony Express to carry it. The trip from St. Joseph, Missouri, to Sacramento, California, took about ten days in 1860 and 1861, when the Pony Express was in service.

Consider the Pony Express, that rowdy relay of men and mounts carrying mail over vast prairies and rugged mountains simply to satisfy the great American urge to communicate at a greater speed and distance today than yesterday. How different, really, were Murrow's dramatic descriptions of the war or words or pictures from such faraway places as the moon or Earth's orbit or the Iraqi desert? Or, for that matter, e-mail?

Admittedly, it's a bit of a stretch to argue that Americans are unique, that only we are built this way (Israelis and Russians are clearly competitive in the talking business); moreover, as our indigenous techniques and technologies have been adopted or adapted, our distinctiveness has been inevitably diminished. From Kosovo to Kenya, from the Gaza Strip to Guatemala, in wretched rural villages and desperate urban slums all over the world, satellite dishes can be found attached to the rudest of residences. Yet it's no exaggeration to suggest that only in America have communications become something akin to a national religion, an inherent component of every aspect of the culture, from commerce and entertainment to politics and government to sports and scholarship. Not staying in touch—with the country, with the world, with each other—is nearly un-American. In fact, communication has become an industry unto itself and hundreds of college and graduate students now earn degrees in communications, although I must admit that I've never been sure exactly what such diplomas qualify them to do.

Perhaps it enables a few of them to understand the technology. That is, maybe they've figured out how it works and what makes it work. I say, more power to them. I've been in the television business a long time now and I don't have the slightest idea—but that doesn't make me feel inferior. In fact, once again, I can take my cue from Murrow, who was also technologically challenged and who once said that unless it were used in remarkable ways, television would always be just a box with a bunch of wires. He was right, of course. When it is used in such unremarkable ways as sometime seems the rage these days, it is only technology. Technology that amazes, to be sure, but still merely technology . . . nothing more.

Yet, even in my own modest career, I have seen firsthand how much it can accomplish. For example, a few of my televised stories from such places as Rwanda and Sarajevo, Somalia and Ethiopia, the West Bank and the Gaza Strip allowed millions of Americans to see and hear the grim and sometimes grotesque reality of genocide and war and famine and poverty. Having seen and heard such awful things, many hundreds of Americans have written over the years to say they had come to understand what had previously escaped them. How different is that from what I was learning in my living room listening to Lex and Murrow just talking?

Or how different is it from those summer nights just after the war when, after dinner, my Kentucky grandfather would head for his front porch, settle himself into an old cane-bottom chair, light up his pipe, and wait for a neighbor or two to come around for what he called digestive conversation? Sometimes a brother or two dropped by, but whatever the group's composition, friends or family or both, they were all accomplished front-porch talkers with a grand collection of idiomatic expressions whose origins I've yet to decipher. Anything lengthy—a woman's hair, for example, or a flashy Cadillac or a freight train rumbling endlessly past—was invariably as long as Pittman's dog. Ebullient folks were always happy as Henrietta and anyone deemed less than bright was usually dumb as a tire. Even then I appreciated such moments. With fireflies flickering, crickets and cicadas yammering out in the lengthening shadows, and the sweet aroma of my grandfather's pipe curling into the gathering darkness, I would sit just next to his chair, a little boy at his grandfather's knee, listening and quite often wondering if any other child in the universe was quite so fortunate as I.

If Franklin Roosevelt and Ronald Reagan would distinguish their presidencies with their masterful communication skills—like Ed Murrow, they simply talked to the country—it was no mere accident. All of them, and my grandfather, too, were descended from a long line of able practitioners: Americans.

Newsmen still find themselves in harm's way: Palestinian cameraman Nazih Darwazeh, here taping in the West Bank town of Nablus, was shot and killed there by Israeli troops on April 19, 2003.

Their Most Lasting Contribution

by Stanley N. Katz

IN THE EARLY 1970S, a friend and I decided that we wanted to write a history of the origins of the philanthropic foundation. Actually, we were put onto the subject by another friend who was just about to become a foundation president and confessed to me that he hadn't a clue as to how foundations had come into existence. We were just about as innocent, and submitted grant proposals for support of the project to all the major foundations. We quickly received brief, polite rejections written on heavy bond paper from all of them. "Your request," they said, is "out of program." We decided that somehow foundations were not our league. But one morning I received a call from McGeorge Bundy, then the president of the Ford Foundation, whom I had known as an undergraduate at Harvard. "You've got a great idea," he said, "and I am going to give you a little money to get going on it." "But it's out of program," I said. "Never mind," said Mac, "if Ford contributes, so

> "WHAT THEY WANTED TO DO WAS TO DISCOVER THE UNDERLYING AND SYSTEMIC SOURCES OF THE COUNTRY'S SOCIAL AND ECONOMIC PROBLEMS."

will everyone else." And so they did. And so I entered the wonderful world of philanthropy. Clearly foundations were something else again, and I have been studying philanthropy ever since.

Most nations never contribute genuinely unique ideas and institutions to world culture, but the United States has contributed several. Among them, none has been so important as philanthropy. At a time when U.S. power in a unilateral world arouses widespread apprehension about our country, it may be that our recognized leadership and innovation in philanthropy will be the countervailing force that restores the good image of our nation. We will be judged by the faithfulness of our people to what is best in our tradition, and philanthropy is at the core of that tradition.

Philanthropy is a term that is used loosely and casually. Mostly it is used to describe activities that are charitable. Charity, in its essence, is gratuitously

The Boston Symphony Orchestra travels to New York City for a performance at Carnegie Hall, opposite, a concert hall built with funds from philanthropist Andrew Carnegie. Carnegie was the wealthiest man in the world when he sold his steel mill in 1901 for $300 million. He spent the rest of his life giving the money away.

doing good for others. It is the giving of unsolicited gifts. It is benevolence and the tangible expression of good will to others. Most commonly charity has been thought of as the giving of money, food, or shelter to the poor—that is, almsgiving.

Charity is one of the world's oldest instincts and institutions. Indeed, it seems likely that every world culture has had its charitable traditions. Historically, most cultures are identified through their religious traditions, and over time all religions have promoted some notion of charity.

Americans are most familiar with the Christian and Jewish conceptions. Both the Hebrew Bible and the New Testament abound with injunctions to be generous and kind to others, especially the poor. Maimonides, writing in the twelfth century, said that the highest form of charity was helping the needy to become self-supporting: "He who urges and activates others to give Tsedakah [gifts to the poor] receives a greater reward than the donor himself." St. Augustine said that "it is only charity that distinguishes the children of God from those of the devil." But the Quran also commands Muslims to give to the needy, and to pay the zakat (the tax on the rich).

Andrew Carnegie, top, and John D. Rockefeller, bottom, both gave away much of their enormous fortunes. Carnegie believed that inherited wealth corrupted and donated $351 million to found 281 public libraries all over America; Rockefeller gave dimes to small boys on his birthday and, by the time he died, had given $530 million to various causes, largely to medicine, black educational institutions, and the University of Chicago.

Charity is thus central to benevolence. But it is a concept largely restricted to helping those in need who cannot help themselves. Indeed, all too often, even in American charitable practice, charity has been restricted to the "deserving" poor.

Philanthropy is a broader and different concept with distinctive origins in the United States of the late nineteenth century. It was originally the brainchild of the greatest entrepreneurs of the industrial age, Andrew Carnegie and John D. Rockefeller Sr. Both men were committed Protestants (although Carnegie opposed sectarianism) and actively charitable. Rockefeller started tithing (giving a tenth of his earnings to charity) with the first dollar he earned, and both men gave generously for charitable purposes as they began to amass their immense fortunes. Rockefeller gave pensions to the widows of former employees and cash to burnt-out churches. Carnegie donated church organs and helped out employees in need.

But they both came to see that writing checks was an inefficient method for alleviating the suffering of the world. No amount of almsgiving would stem the curses of illness, poverty, and ignorance that oppressed the people of the nation. What to do? They reached back into their business experience. They had both triumphed in the extractive and manufacturing boom of post-bellum America by applying modern business organizational methods, the knowledge of the second scientific revolution, and huge financial resources. Could not such methods be used to solve social and economic problems as well?

In this perception lay the roots of modern philanthropy. The early philanthropists viewed the existing charitable movement as dealing merely with the alleviation of manifold individual instances of distress, whereas what they wanted to do was to discover the underlying and systemic sources of the country's social and economic problems. Charity, they thought, merely treated the symptoms of the sick society; philanthropy could identify and root out the underlying causes of illness. They wanted to move from symptomolgy to pathology. The model of (then) modern medical science was very much in their minds, and it was no accident that much of Rockefeller's early philanthropy took the form of funding biomedical research in public health.

Carnegie and Rockefeller had used clerks in their business offices to write checks to widows and ministers, but they realized that they needed separate organizations to institutionalize philanthropy—to figure out how to distribute large sums of money that would both fund research into the causes of ignorance, illness, and poverty, and build the institutions necessary to carry out such reform. Quite independently they discovered and pioneered what we today call the private philanthropic foundation—an endowment given in perpetuity, governed by a policy-setting board of trustees originally appointed by the donor, and administered by a professional staff who could determine the best ways to invest philanthropic funds in research and reform.

Carnegie and Rockefeller each founded several different foundations and more or less left the investment of the endowed funds to trustees and staff. The trustees were self-perpetuating, which is to say that they chose their successors—the idea being that each generation of trustees would be in touch with the needs of its own age. The donors therefore did not dedicate the foundations to narrow purposes, recognizing that the pressing problems of each day might be radically different from one another. The legal purpose of these trusts was normally some variation of "to address the needs of humanity," and it was intended to be continually redefined by the trustees. And so the Carnegie Corporation and the Rockefeller

From its towering headquarters in New York City, on land donated by John D. Rockefeller, the United Nations, left, distributes funds worldwide.

Foundation were established in the decade before World War I.

Other donors quickly emerged and other foundations sprang into existence. Among the earliest were the Russell Sage Foundation and the Rosenwald Fund, but they were followed by others—the Ford Foundation just after World War II is one of the largest, followed by those endowed by other wealthy individuals such as Robert Wood Johnson, David Packard, William Hewlett, and, most recently, William Gates. Through philanthropic financial investments, foundation philanthropy has made a significant impact on the development of science and medicine, but it has also operated in the domains of social policy, technology, the arts, education, and almost every significant domain of life in the United States.

At a high school in Miami, Microsoft chairman Bill Gates, right, announces grants to support technology enrichment for teens in poor communities.

The fact that the foundations operate in the private sector has given them the freedom to invest in projects too risky or out of fashion for government action, and they have frequently funded innovative research that has produced an immediate impact—the eradication of whole diseases and the creation of children's and public television are good examples. But from the beginning, just after World War I, foundations discovered that their policy relevance might endanger their political survival. Thus we have had congressional investigations of foundation activity more or less every decade since World War I, and there is always some tension between foundation creativity and public accountability.

This comes about largely because we have tied philanthropy to the federal tax structure. Foundations are tax-exempt entities, free from paying most federal and state taxes. The critical argument has been that if these organizations are in effect subsidized (to the extent that they do not pay taxes), shouldn't they be accountable to the government? So far there has been little government regulation of the philanthropic sector, but the inherent reformist tendencies of philanthropy always run the risk of arousing political antagonism and administrative restrictions.

But of course philanthropy is much more than private foundations. Its fullest manifestation is the larger nonprofit sector—private tax-exempt institutions that serve public needs of all sorts. Many, but by no means all, of these are voluntary organizations. All of them adhere to the legal constraint that they cannot distribute surpluses to their members. They are legally charitable corporations, chartered by the state (simply upon application and at practically no cost), that exist for specific purposes. Significantly, they are not only tax exempt themselves, but those who contribute to their activities receive tax deductions from the federal government.

Except for tax-deductibility, for there were few taxes in the nineteenth-century United States, what we now call the nonprofit sector emerged with the nation itself. Alexis de Tocqueville's most famous observation on his visit to this country in the 1830s was that we were a nation of joiners, that we gathered together in voluntary private associations to accomplish everything from worshiping to singing to nursing. And we have continued to do that as associationalism has merged with philanthropy. The nonprofit sector is now huge, and it is supported to a great extent by philanthropy.

Private foundations of course support portions of the nonprofit sector, but individual support is even more significant. And so do the newer philanthropic entities we have developed to support the sector: United Way, community foundation, and national single-purpose fund-raising organizations such as the March of Dimes, the American Cancer Society, and innumerable others. Ironically, government itself has come to be a major supporter of nonprofit organizations by contracting with them to provide services (such as aspects of health care) that it would otherwise have to provide itself.

Through philanthropy America has created a private engine of public progress for the whole society. The philanthropic sector is composed of both donor and donee organizations, givers and recipients, but they are two sides of the same coin. The coin is our commitment to use private wealth in the public interest. What we have done with it is to create a complex system of financial support for a network of organizations that see to our cultural, social, and even economic needs. Ours is a tradition of relatively weak government and, on the whole, antipathy to the welfare state. But, at least at our best, we do not keep the state in its place in order simply to deprive citizens of full and healthy lives. Rather, we have organized the private nonprofit sector in such a way as to enable us to provide for one another, and to create positive partnerships with the state.

Philanthropy is thus one of the miracles of American history and life. It is central to the best things we have accomplished in this country—and it gives hope to new democracies around the world that a better life is possible without subjecting citizens to the threats of statism.

Hewlett Packard CEO Carly Fiorina helps pack boxes at the Second Harvest Food Bank in San Jose, California, left. It distributes more than 26 million pounds of donated food each year.

Inventor of the Modern Age

by David Halberstam

HENRY FORD WAS ONE of the great revolutionaries of the age, a stubborn, cantankerous, difficult man. Like so many other populists of the time, he despised much about the urban and suburban America he helped create; the cities of America were to his mind increasingly alien places populated by alien people he did not want to know. Yet if anyone helped create modern, dynamic, mid-century America, a society where the worker became part of an ever larger middle class, it was Henry Ford. Together with Franklin Roosevelt, who despised Ford as much as Ford despised Roosevelt, he was the architect of an America where the worker was infinitely more optimistic about his own life: it was Ford who created the mass production line where cars (and soon almost every other industrialized product) could be manufactured in record time, thereby cutting the cost; it was Roosevelt with his New Deal who had shrewdly adjudicated the needs and rights of labor with those of management, creating a new, more democratic form of capitalism that became the model for most industrialized nations.

Evidence of Ford's influence is all over the second half of the twentieth century. Late in Ford's life a young man once questioned him rather sharply about his surprisingly narrow, almost primitive views on education. "But sir," the young man had finally said, "these are different times—this is the modern age and . . ." At that point Ford cut him off. "Young man," he said, "I invented the modern age."

So he had. When he first began to manufacture cars, only the very rich could own them. People who owned cars did not often drive them themselves—they had chauffeurs, and the best

> "NO ONE HAD DONE AS MUCH TO USHER IN AN AGE OF MIDDLE CLASS AFFLUENCE. HE HAD BECOME, ALMOST INVOLUNTARILY, POINT MAN FOR A PROFOUND INDUSTRIAL AND SOCIAL REVOLUTION. . . ."

Motorists, opposite, take a spin in the country in a 1916 Ford Touring Car, brainchild of inventor and manufacturer Henry Ford, below. By introducing mass production and the production line into his factories, Ford made the automobile available to Americans of modest incomes.

chauffeurs, as a Detroit weekly newspaper noted, "came from the servant class." Ford changed all that. He modernized the process—he loved the process far more than the cars, and he would do anything to improve the process and almost nothing to improve the car. Mass production, he understood from the start, was the key: "Every time I reduce the price of the car by one dollar," he said of the production line for the Model T, "I get one thousand new buyers." When he started manufacturing the Model T, it took twelve and a half hours to produce a single car. For a time his greatest goal was to produce one car every minute. It took him twelve years to achieve that goal; five years after that, in 1925, he was producing a car every ten seconds. Before he (quite reluctantly) replaced it with a newer model, Ford had sold 15.4 million Model Ts.

He was, because of his success, stunningly rich, his personal worth placed at $646 million in 1946 dollars, though of course, money other than that used as an instrument to improve production, meant nothing to him.

His people were fairly typical immigrants who had arrived here in the middle of the nineteenth century, fleeing Ireland because of the potato famine. William Ford, his father, had arrived here with his tools and two pounds in cash. At first he made railroad ties; when he made a little money, he bought some land, a privilege denied men like him in the old country where ordinary people were doomed to be tenants, never land owners. He hoped that his son Henry, born here in 1863, would become a farmer. But Henry Ford hated farming; it was all drudgery and it bored him completely. Instead he was by instinct and intuition a mechanical wizard, brilliant at playing with every piece of farm machinery, the immigrant's son as a born, obsessive tinkerer. When at thirteen he was given a watch as a present, he immediately took it apart and then put it back together. He soon repaired watches for all of their friends. When he was a grown man someone asked him about his childhood toys. "My toys were all tools," he said. "They still are."

He couldn't wait to leave the farm and go to Detroit and make his name in the world of mechanical engineering. In one of his earliest jobs he worked as a shop apprentice, making $2.50 a week and paying $3.50 a week for room and board, and making up the difference by working as a watch repairman. He soon came up with a plan to mass produce watches— 600,000 a year. No one took him up on the idea, but it was an early sign of the mass production genius lurking inside him. For a brief time he returned to the farm; he was about to be married and needed some measure of security. But Ford quickly discovered that having been around the world of machines, he hated the farm even more. Back he went to Detroit. William Ford was puzzled: "He just doesn't seem to want to settle down. I don't know what will become of him," he said.

At the Ford factory in Highland Park, Michigan, opposite, auto bodies slide down a production line to be joined with chassis in 1917. By 1925, Ford was producing a car every ten seconds. Above, Ford the tinkerer dismantles a watch at his workbench.

In Detroit he was at first just one of many would-be inventors hoping to get in on the coming age of the gas engine. His first car was essentially a quadricycle, a small gas engine attached to two bikes. He sold the car for $200, and immediately used the money for supplies for his next car. At one convention his approached his personal hero, Thomas Edison, and explained his idea to Edison, who was immediately enthusiastic: "Young man, that's the thing! You have it—the self-contained unit carrying its own fuel with it! Keep at it!"

He continued to work on prototypes for new cars with increasing success; after one early drive around Detroit with a reporter he had passed a harness maker's shop. "His business is doomed," Ford said. In 1903, now forty, no longer an apprentice, he started the Ford Motor Company. He wanted a kind of people's car, one that ordinary working men and farmers could afford and enjoy. He also knew that the key to it was mass production. "Better and cheaper," he would say, "more of them, better and cheaper." He told one of his early financial backers: "The way to make an automobile is to make one automobile like another automobile; just as one pin is like another pin and one match is like another match when it comes from the match factory."

Ford demonstrates an early, 1896 version of his auto: the quadricycle, barely more than two bicycles powered by a small gasoline engine. His dictum, "Better and cheaper," allowed 15.4 million Americans to buy his Ford Model T.

In 1908, he finally brought out the car he had always wanted, the Model T, simple, durable, and strong; it was in the words of an early biographer Keith Sward, all bone and muscle—with no fat. With it, he ushered in the age of mass production. His manufacturing line became in Sward's apt phrase, "like a river and its tributaries," with all kinds of different sections gradually feeding into a main movable chassis; inevitably, it used fewer and fewer skilled workers. The first piece on the modern assembly line, as it started to develop in 1913 was the magneto coil assembly. In the past, one skilled worker made the entire magneto himself—about thirty-five or forty of them a day. Now even this one piece was produced by a sub-assembly line, twenty-nine different stages manned by twenty-nine different men, and the time required to make a magneto dropped overnight from twenty to thirteen minutes. It was a mere beginning. The entire manufacturing process became ever faster. The price fell, too, from $780 per car in the first two years, to $600, to $550 and finally, on the eve of World War I in 1917, $360. In 1908 when he brought out the first Model T he had a little over 9 percent of the market; six years later it was 48 percent. There was no doubt that he knew exactly what he was doing. "Mass production," Ford wrote later, "precedes mass consumption and makes it possible by reducing costs and thus permitting both greater use-convenience and price-convenience."

He did not age well. As he grew older he was increasingly a caricature of himself—it was hardly unique to his status as a maverick genius. He had always been a difficult, contentious man, sure of his theories in all areas because in his own world, the only world he really cared about, he was convinced that he had always been right. At first people had been amused by some of the weird things he said: Alcohol, he had once announced, was the real cause of the First World War—because of the tension between the beer-drinking German and with wine-drinking Frenchman. Those mutterings on subjects other than car production soon became less and less charming, and loonier and loonier. A man who had once seemed like a brilliant eccentric now seemed increasingly mad.

Though he was critically important as someone who had created a dynamic that had given ordinary workers infinitely better lives, his labor practices became ever more brutal; his factory was run by thugs who used sheer physical force to keep the men in line, and he himself became bitterly anti-labor. During the Depression, when so many ordinary Americans underwent terrible times, Ford spoke often about how the Depression was good for the country and that the only problem with it was that it might not last long enough. He refused to modernize his cars, and General Motors, with its ever more attractive Chevrolets, eventually passed Ford. He destroyed among others his own talented, somewhat gentle son, Edsel—it

was as close to a case of slow motion filicide as one could imagine. He regarded the government of the United States, under whose aegis he had so wondrously prospered, as one views a sworn enemy.

Yet his importance as a towering figure—and a uniquely American one—in the twentieth century should not be underestimated. No one had done as much to usher in an age of middle class affluence. He had become, almost involuntarily, the point man for a profound industrial and social revolution, an age that produced not just greater political democracy, but greater economic and social democracy, and workers who not only lived better and better but enjoyed more of the fruits of their labor. Other industrial manufacturers in all fields began to model their plants on his. During the post–World War II housing boom, when William Levitt, who developed mass produced housing in the suburb that bore his name and was aware that houses were too large to come rolling down a production line, simply reversed the process that Ford pioneered. Levitt mechanized his process as Ford had mechanized the automobile line, but he brought the workers, each of them responsible for the tiniest possible function, to the site. Thus were even houses mass produced and costs cut, as part of the revolution that Henry Ford had begun.

One of the most popular autos ever produced, the Ford Thunderbird arrived in 1955. This 1957 model beguiles a suburban couple.

RACHEL CARSON

The Unlikely Revolutionary

by Timothy Egan

THEY ARE OUT THERE now, crossing the Hudson between New Jersey and New York, riding the thermals along Florida's gold coast, chasing mice in cornfields not far from St. Louis, nesting in cities like Seattle and Minneapolis. The national symbol— the American bald eagle— rules the skies once more. Nature may bat last, as was said when an earthquake disrupted the World Series in San Francisco, but it usually loses in the end. Not so with the bald eagle.

An honest scientist, or any historian of the natural world, knows whom to credit in large part for the eagle's rise from the brink of extinction to healthy residency in nearly every state. It was a hero, they say, struggling while sick against long odds, but one who did not look the part. A birdwatcher who lived with her mother? Rachel Carson was much more, of course. Most simply, she was a scientist who could write. And with one book, *Silent Spring*, she changed the way Americans look at their backyard.

We were poisoning ourselves, laying down a carpet of pesticides at a time when science could do no wrong. The mission was to eradicate a host of insects considered a menace. But something else was set in motion in the indiscriminate aerial spraying: small birds and fish ate poisoned bugs, or took in the tainted water, forcing DDT and other toxins through the blood and up the food chain, until it got to the eagles. Their eggs, like those of songbirds, were thinned by the poisons, leaving not enough of a shell to continue the chain of life. Carson, writing for people who got their science in narrative form from the Book of the Month Club instead of scholarly journals, told a fable, heavily documented:

> "THE BOOK WAS A SENSATION, AND CAUSED A FUROR. IT IS HARD TO IMAGINE NOW, BUT IN CARSON'S TIME, IT WAS RARE FOR SOMEONE OF HER STATURE TO CHALLENGE AND ATTACK CONVENTIONAL WISDOM IN THE SCIENTIFIC COMMUNITY."

Bald eagles soar in America once again, opposite, largely thanks to the work of one woman: Rachel Carson, below. Her 1962 book Silent Spring *awakened the world to the dangers of indiscriminate use of pesticides and helped to launch the environmental movement.*

what are we doing to ourselves? And, appealing to populist sentiment dating to a revolution that kicked the British out of America, she asked: under what authority could life be so dramatically altered?

"Who has decided," she wrote, "who has the right to decide—for the countless legions of people who were not consulted—that the supreme value is a world without insects, even though it be also a sterile world ungraced by the curving wing of a bird in flight?"

She died of cancer barely eighteen months after *Silent Spring* was published in 1962. The book was heralded as the most significant volume on the natural world since Darwin's *Origin of Species*, and compared to *Uncle Tom's Cabin* in its effect on public opinion. It was also fiercely attacked. But in stirring a prosperous nation to look beneath the surface sheen of its surroundings, to try to see beyond their generation, Carson also set in motion the modern environmental movement. Six years after she died, the country had its first government agency devoted to protection of the land and living things, and a law that said before any piece of earth could be reshaped, sprayed, scoured, or cut, there had to be fair warning on what the consequences would be to the environment. What's more, every community could count dozens of people, from garden club activists to hook-and-bullet old-boy conservationists, who went

Smokestacks of the Homestead steel plant pump deadly fumes into the air over Pittsburgh in 1903. By the time Carson entered college here, Pittsburgh's air and water were the dirtiest in the country.

around with dog-eared copies of this *birdwatcher's* book, asking questions.

Rachel Louise Carson grew up Springdale, sixteen miles up the Allegheny River from Pittsburgh, in a drafty old clapboard house without indoor plumbing. Her father had purchased the surrounding sixty-four acres on Colfax Hill. This was Rachel's playground—the orchards, the pine forest, the rabbit warrens and flower meadows—and also her laboratory. She was born in 1907, the third child. Through her mother, Maria Carson, the girl learned to name flowers and birds, and developed a fondness of reading.

Pittsburgh was one of the great clanking, coughing engines of the American industrial age. But the people and land around the city paid a price for the title of Steeletown, USA: soot and ash fell from the sky and often blocked the sun, slag choked the rivers, and the air itself presented a long-term risk for anyone with respiratory problems. By the time Rachel entered Pennsylvania College for Women (later Chatham College), Pittsburgh had the worst air and water pollution in the country.

Rachel was shy, socially insular, dressed in homemade clothes, with a case of late teenage acne, as her biographer, Linda Lear, described her. In an essay written at age eighteen, Carson said she wanted to be a writer, and that her true love was the outdoors. She chose not to study the charismatic mega-fauna, as eagles, elk, and other big animals are sometimes called, but the banal—tiny stuff that appeared most active under a microscope. She got a degree in biology and decided to become a marine scientist. She went to Johns Hopkins for graduate work, and wanted to pursue a doctorate, but the Depression forced her out of college.

Carson found work at Harold Ickes's Interior Department, translating government science from the jargon of those in the field to readable prose, and as a freelancer. It was Carson's early genius to take the ordinary and make it sing. One piece on bats, "He Invented Radar—Sixty Million Years Ago!", was so popular the U.S. Navy distributed it for years thereafter.

A love of the sea, fostered first by the stories of Melville and Stevenson and then by wandering in the glorious muck of tidepools in New England, prompted her first book, *Under the Sea-Wind.* In studying the ocean, Carson realized that humans were a small part of the earth, but had the power to control almost everything else. Reviewers said she had combined poetry and science to bring forth a lyrical homage to the ocean. It was published just as World War II broke out, in 1941, and sold barely two thousand copies.

It took her ten years to bring out another book. But this time, the world embraced Rachel Carson. The second book, *The Sea Around Us,* won the National Book Award and was translated into thirty-two languages. At the time, 1951, Carson described herself as a biographer of the sea, but of course she had higher ambitions, sometimes only barely concealed. In accepting the book award, Carson said, "The aim of science is to discover and illuminate truth. And that, I take it, is the aim of literature, whether biography or history or fiction."

She was gaining confidence as a speaker and leader of a fledgling environmental movement. Her writing showed a scientist's love of precision, a novelist's love of conflict, and a crusader's sense of how to use the bugle. But the woman behind the prose was physically fragile, often deathly ill, suffering an appendectomy and a long and debilitating bout of shingles. The cancer would show up later. If she sensed life's brevity, she showed it in the stepped-up pace of her work.

Carson first became alarmed about DDT, a new synthetic pesticide, in the mid-1940s. She feared that the indiscriminate use of chemicals to kill insects would do more than lead to a world free of selective pests. It was, she feared, a monumental act of hubris. Could one thread of life really be yanked from the fabric without tearing out the whole? As a marine scientist, she was intimate with the small world and its interdependency. Throughout the 1950s, as the spraying programs grew with little government oversight or warning, Carson became increasingly concerned. She had received several letters from people troubled by evidence of a big crash in

A crop duster sprays DDT on an alfalfa field in California's Imperial Valley in 1947. The substance, which imperils many vertebrates, was later banned.

bird and fish life in areas that had been heavily sprayed.

"There would be no peace for me if I kept silent," Carson wrote to a friend.

Silent Spring was a somewhat slim volume, illustrated with sketches, and had Carson's usual blend of lyrical writing and detail-rich science. She started by asking, "What if?" summoning in the first chapter an image of a small town in a peaceful setting where birds failed to show up in spring, bees did not arrive to pollinate fruit trees, hens brooded but no chicks hatched, and the streams became lifeless.

"Over increasingly large areas of the United States," she wrote, "early mornings are strangely silent where once they were filled with the beauty of bird song."

Interspersed were chapters on cell biology, entomology, and groundwater mechanics—not the usual stuff of popular nonfiction. The book was a sensation and caused a furor. It is hard to imagine now, but in Carson's time it was rare for someone of her stature to challenge and attack conventional wisdom in the scientific community. And it was conventional wisdom that had government backing. Also, she argued for bugs, but did so in a clever way. Her book was not a case, per se, for mosquitoes and gypsy moths, rather it was an appeal to the dangers killing those bugs en masse posed to Norman Rockwell America—the fishing hole, the lover's glen, the farmer's dell. The bald eagle, endangered to the point of extinction when Carson's book landed in 1962, was another brilliant prop in her argument.

"You have made it literature," said William Shawn, the *New Yorker* editor who had long mentored Carson, "full of beauty and loveliness and depth of feeling."

The book prompted a nationwide campaign against her by the chemical industry. Her facts held up. Government hearings were ordered, and Carson was called as a witness. The attacks became personal. Ezra Taft Benson, who had been agriculture secretary in the 1950s when the government expanded its spraying program, wondered "why a spinster with no children was so concerned about genetics." Other critics also took issue with Carson's private life, noting with disapproval that she kept cats and loved birds, and lived with her mother.

Carson was scared, but her fear was over her health, which declined during the writing of *Silent Spring* and fell precipitously after the book came out. She had suffered viral pneumonia and developed an ulcer. Then, on the eve of publication, lumps were found in Carson's lymph glands. She began radiation treatments for a cancer that had been seriously metastasizing during the writing of the book. With wig and good cheer, she made television appearances and went before government committees. Time was precious. She weakened. There were so many things to see still, and so many people who wanted to hear her speak. She toured the Muir Woods, on the Pacific Coast, in a

Carson accompanies Audubon Society birders in a park. She lived to see her book published to great acclaim but died of cancer just eighteen months after its publication. Carson wrote that she was motivated by "anger at the senseless, brutish things that were being done" to the natural world.

Two-year-old Meg Tousey-Wyatt of Irvington, New York, and her father, Kevin Wyatt, plant trees during an Earth Day 2000 program at United Nations Headquarters. Earth Day is one of many environmental organizations and impulses borne of Silent Spring.

wheelchair, and continued with massive doses of radiation therapy. She died April 14, 1964, at age fifty-six.

The campaign to discredit Carson proved futile, and what she set in motion could not be stopped. The spraying and use of DDT were cut back dramatically and banned in many areas. In Carson's day there were only a handful of environmental groups, mostly on the margins of political power. Now these groups sit at the table of decision makers. The most powerful environment law ever passed—the Endangered Species Act of 1973—gives living things equal and often greater standing than ordinary commerce. Songbirds flourish again and the bald eagle is ascendant.

It would be inaccurate to credit Carson with the nation's environmental renaissance. She alone did not force a country to try and save its natural heritage. But along with Teddy Roosevelt, John Muir, and Henry David Thoreau, Rachel Carson belongs on the Mount Rushmore of American conservation. She stands out for many reasons. She was a woman and a biologist who had to fend off an entire industry while trying to rouse from complacency her fellow scientists.

Ever since she was a little girl imagining a world beyond the slag-choked banks of the Allegheny River, Carson wanted to be a writer. She was that, and something more: someone whose words not only outlived her, but changed no small part of the world.

WILLIAM F. BUCKLEY

The Rise of a New American Right

by Sam Tanenhaus

WILLIAM F. BUCKLEY, the most famous conservative intellectual of the last hundred years, is also the most elusive. Who is he exactly—what label can we pin on him? Author? Well, at last count he'd written fifty books, some of them very good, though he has spent no more than six months drafting any one (and often only six weeks). A political figure? True, he did once run for office—for mayor of New York in 1965. It was a splendid lark, as indicated by his first press conference. He was asked what he would do if by some miracle he actually won. "Demand a recount," Buckley replied, just in case anyone was seriously thinking of voting for him. In fact, 340,000 people did—a very respectable 13 percent. What's more, the campaign provided an important bridge from Barry Goldwater's disasterous presidential run in 1964 to Ronald Reagan's landmark election to the California governorship in 1966.

"BUCKLEY MADE HIS CASE WITH CALM LOGIC AND LITERARY FLAIR. HE MEANT BUSINESS, BUT HIS BUSINESS WAS PROVOCATION, NOT SELF-RIGHTEOUS ANGER."

Of course there is Buckley the pundit, with a pointed opinion about everything from airplanes (he used to fly them) to Zimbabwe. His syndicated columns—Buckley has been producing sharply argued commentary now for forty-one years and through nine presidencies—would fill twenty-five book-length volumes. And there is the punditry of *Firing Line*. Broadcast for thirty-four years (longer than any other program in history), it more or less invented the TV head-to-heads now copied, or vulgarized, in countless cable formats.

And don't forget Buckley the magazine editor, who founded *National Review*, the most influential conservative journal in American history and "a finishing school for apostates," as Buckley once said in his signature tone of comic worldliness, referring to such straying

Senator Barry Goldwater, opposite, a conservative Republican, acknowledges delegates to the party's 1963 national convention. William F. Buckley, below, supported Goldwater and became the conservatives' most articulate and witty spokesman.

talents as Arlene Croce, Joan Didion, John Leonard, and Garry Wills.

For the sake of brevity we can skip Buckley the spy novelist, sailor, concert pianist, lecturer, husband, and father.

The trouble is not just that he's done so much, but done it so well. Some find this infuriating because Buckley's tireless activity has often served to advance ideas they find outrageous, even reprehensible. But others are grateful. Imagine American politics without Buckley, who entertains and amuses even as he provokes. He is easily the best company to emerge from modern conservatism. If Goldwater was the movement's ideological torchbearer, and Reagan its "great communicator," then Buckley (who tutored both men) has been its peerless performer— always in front of us, challenging, provoking, teasing, often with the slyest of winks. Politics matters, he seems to tell us, but the best politics is living well. It's an important message for a conservative to transmit since the dogma of our age implicitly argues that conservatives don't know how to live—or let others live. They're censorious, narrow-minded, authoritarian.

It's certainly how most were seen, rightly, before Buckley bounded onto the political stage in 1951 as the twenty-five-year-old author of *God and Man at Yale*,

Buckley, right, grew up in Connecticut as one of ten children to a father who had gained his wealth in the oil business. At age twenty-five, he published God and Man at Yale, *a book that made him famous.*

still the most influential book to emerge from the modern conservative movement. Yale, he observed, "derives its moral and financial support from Christian individualists and then addresses itself to the task of persuading the sons of those supporters to be atheistic socialists." Buckley wasn't the first to say this. The Red-baiting press (Hearst, McCormick) had been on the case for years. And it wasn't news to Kansas preachers or rube congressmen. So why did Buckley's book cause such havoc? The answer was on the dust jacket: the boyish author peered out with the aristocratic clear-skinned beauty of the young F. Scott Fitzgerald, just above the summary of his campus triumphs: Skull and Bones, editor of the *Yale Daily News*, champion debater, class orator. This was no malcontent. This was Dink Stover, Mr. Yale. Why on earth did he have it in for the alma mater that had nurtured him so well? What was he so mad about?

The short answer: he wasn't mad. He was serious, which is not the same thing. Buckley made his case with calm logic and literary flair. He meant business, but his business was provocation, not self-righteous anger. It was his critics who seemed beside themselves, depicting Buckley as a would-be Torquemada or hooded Night Rider on the gallop. Only the journalist Dwight Macdonald, a left-winger and sometime campus rebel as irreverent as Buckley himself, saw what was really going on. Yale panicked not because it had been slandered but because it hadn't been. Buckley had simply told the truth. Old Blue had abandoned the old-time religion and its faith in Adam Smith's "invisible hand." So why not just say so? Instead came spluttering indignation, ad hominem attacks issuing from the president's office, rigged panels formed to exonerate professors of having imparted Keynesian heresies in "Economics 10." Macdonald's article in *The Reporter* got the comedy just right. The authorities at Woodbridge Hall, caught flatfooted by "Kid Buckley's" deft jabs, "reacted with all the grace and agility of an elephant cornered by a mouse."

Whether or not Buckley's argument held up (in some places it did, in others perhaps not), the bigger point was clinched. The "Liberal establishment," much as it might tout academic freedom (Buckley put the words in mocking quotes), was sneakily selling its own grim orthodoxy, and woe to him who dared dissent from it.

Buckley relished the commotion. He fully expected the other side to fight back. Even when they threw rabbit punches—as when Yale's president called him "a militant Catholic" who believed only scripture was fit to be read in the classroom (the book said nothing of the kind)—he kept his cool. "After each side has had its say," he had written in the foreword, "we are right and they are wrong." The counterassault only proved what he believed anyway: in mid-century America, "the conservatives, as a minority, are the new radicals."

And the future might favor them. Not that many were looking that far ahead. Buckley sprang into celebrity at the same moment when *Time* magazine declared the advent of a new "silent generation" whose ambitions reached no further than the commuter train from Greenwich to Wall Street and a sparkling new kitchen with shiny appliances. Yet here was a rebel on the right who demanded to be heard, not unlike Holden Caulfield, that other decrier of grown-up falsehood ("phonies") who blazed up from the dreary "consensus" of 1951.

Caulfield spoke for teenagers, those half-children, not-quite-adults who had been created by American abundance but felt like outcasts (Elvis Presley, Chuck Berry, and Marlon Brando carried the same message). Buckley spoke for a slightly older set, back from the war, experienced beyond their years, impatient

Loyola University student Brian Whalen, Republican leader of the Young Americans for Freedom finds political direction on a street sign, left.

Republican presidential hopefuls, including George H. W. Bush (left) and Alexander Haig (second from left) explain to Buckley and his co-moderator Robert Strauss (right) why they should earn their party nomination at a Firing Line debate in Houston in 1987. Firing Line was on the air for thirty-four years.

with regnant certitudes: the New Deal, "the arsenal of democracy," the "four freedoms." These innovations, exciting in their day, now rang with the hollowness of institutional pieties. America's "lonely crowd," as another seminal book of the day put it, was being told what to think not just by atheist Keynesians, but also by humorless social engineers, by secular clerics who deplored The Bomb but were strangely silent about the human soul, by "progressives" keen to thicken the girders of the welfare state.

Buckley, the enemy of liberal conformity, pointed to intriguing paradoxes. His own burgeoning career became a test case. Those so quick to defend First Amendment rights in the case of, say, Communists, seemed to think Buckley should be kept from saying what *he* thought. But he said it anyway, piercing the shroud of sameness with ingeniously apposite formulations. Thus: "I should sooner live in a society governed by the first two thousand names in the Boston telephone directory than in a society governed by the two thousand faculty members of Harvard University." Only a prig could disagree and not admire the wit behind it. Or the GOP ticket he proposed for 1968: "Reagan, [Senator Jacob] Javits—with perhaps the explicit

Republican president Ronald Reagan first came to the attention of the national public while campaigning for Barry Goldwater for the 1964 election. Buckley was a political ally to Reagan from that time on.

understanding that if President Reagan were to die in office, Vice President Javits [a liberal] would hurl himself upon the funeral pyre in grief."

Today, of course, Buckley is prized for this very contrariness and is said to be one of America's premier public intellectuals. It's true, though it doesn't do justice to his spirit. He's not so much an intellectual as an artist of controversy, thoroughly unlike his would-be heirs, the in-your-face bullies and shouters and no-spin-zoners. Buckley, even at his most combative, always listened—and if the joke was on him was the first to laugh.

As the United States neared the zenith of its hegemonic glory, Buckley reminded us of much that was neither healthy nor attractive about "American exceptionalism": the smug collective virtue, the relentless sincerity, the borderless coercive sympathy that viewed the entire planet as a slum-clearance project (as Buckley's colleague James Burnham once put it). Too few, he told us, appreciated the world as it was—God's world as Buckley was unashamed to call it. Was this world flawed? Absolutely. But we all knew that by now. It had been drummed into us since childhood. But just think how much might improve if we all treated each other better—as Buckley treated everyone he knew, allies and adversaries alike. "Right thinking"—*recta ratio*, as he put it in one of his treasured Latinisms—might do more for civility and generosity than all the ministrations of what Buckley and the gang at *National Review* called the Total State.

A remarkable change came over Buckley in the mid to late 1960s, around the time he ran for mayor and saw places (like the South Bronx) not normally on his itinerary. He became more sympathetic to the downtrodden and at the same time more reverent toward the World As It Is. This devotion began to infuse his work. The warmth flowed more naturally, and the humor grew more antic. What his soulmate Murray Kempton called Buckley's "genius for friendship" now was evident on the page and on the podium. He began to embody his particular conservative idea rather than simply defend it.

This is the Buckley best known today. Many who don't care for his politics, or aren't even acquainted with them, are held fast by his charming sailing memoirs and by his book-length journals on the fly (*Cruising Speed, Overdrive*), all of them odes to sociability, with their crystalline glimpses of his droll glamorous wife, his enchanted childhood on two estates (Connecticut and South Carolina), his revered parents, his nine siblings—some nearly as gifted as he, all fluent like he in Spanish (and some in French, too)—his many friends (of all political stripes), his connoisseur's love of Bach.

Waspish and wan, Buckley peers from the cover of Time headlined, "Conservatism Can Be Fun."

If this was conservatism, maybe America needed more of it. When Dick Gregory, the black comic and activist, was urged to tangle with Buckley in debate he said, "But I love that cat." Others did, too: the glinting eyes, the darting tongue, the drawled witticisms, the scrunched-up jacket, the clipboard and Bic pen, the ten-dollar words. *Time*'s 1967 cover story sent forth the message: Buckley's existence alone was Cartesian proof that "conservatism can be fun." Fun meant taking ideas seriously, but never oneself. Buckley spent a quarter century trying to get a conservative elected president. And when it finally happened, he took no credit. Nor did he say "I told you so" when the Soviet Union finally went under. He'd done his part, but others had done as much or more. The joyous struggle was its own reward.

So of course Bill Buckley wasn't mad in 1951. And he seldom has been since. It would have made no sense. He had received too many blessings. As he approached eighty, universally respected, even revered, he continued to go about his business—still writing a book a year, still pounding out his column and his Bach, still practicing the arts of friendship, all with the serenity of one who had earned his special place in the panoramic novel of our age, and also in the eyes of his God. Once, after trying to explain the basis of his abiding faith, he admitted he was "discomfited by the arguments of the disbeliever, for whom it is undoubtedly proper to summon what evidence he can to devastate the Christian God, to render as untenable as possible the Christian position.

Yet is he not working from the top down? Is he not inspecting a phonograph record and stating that it is impossible that from it audible musical waves can reach the ear? Is he scrutinizing a light bulb and asserting that it is more likely that by screwing it into a socket candlepower will result? And his is a logical position because he shirks the first premise of faith and rejects evidence of revelation. I, on the other hand, realize that by wrapping six copper wires around each other and feeding current at one end, six circuits will be completed, but I have no idea how or why that mysterious seventh circuit appears, and I comfort myself that neither do the engineers of Bell Telephone Company. And yet I am humiliated by the naturalist [i.e., the nonbeliever] because in our day and age, faith is unfashionable and intellectual humility is weakness, and I am a product of our age.

Buckley was twenty-four when he wrote those words, a World War II vet and Yale senior already fixed on his destined course. Others might ponder dark riddles. Buckley embraces the lucent mysteries of what used to be called Grace.

Buckley signs his book Elvis in the Morning at a Barnes and Noble bookstore in New York in August 2001. The prolific author averaged a book a year for many years.

CHAPTER SIX

THE COMING OF AN AMERICAN CULTURE

★

"The genius of American culture and its integrity comes from fidelity to the light. Plain as day, we say. Happy as the day is long. Early to bed, early to rise. American virtues are daylight virtues: honesty, integrity, plain speech. We say yes when we mean yes and no when we mean no, and all else comes from the evil one. America presumes innocence and even the right to happiness."

—Richard Rodriguez, in his 1991 essay "Night and Day"

The Egalitarian Spirit

by Robert MacNeil

COMING FROM CANADA to spend the summer of 1952 in Massachusetts, the first thing I noticed about Americans was their easygoing informality. The difference was slight, but obvious. Americans had thawed a subtle layer of the reserve with strangers I was used to.

A decade later, when I moved to the United States after eight years in Britain, the contrast was sharper. Compared to the British, Americans guarded their privacy less strictly; they were quicker to confide, more forward in friendship, more eager to share experience. If these descendants of Thoreau's mass of men were leading the lives of quiet desperation he had divined a century earlier, they hid it well. They projected confidence that, for a reasonable effort, they would share equitably in the evident prosperity of the times. They had faith in the implied social contract. I was taken with the openness and instant acceptance this confidence bred, and which I have enjoyed here ever since.

Fifty years later and now a citizen, I am still intrigued by this aspect of American character, its approachability and informality, and the mystery of the egalitarian spirit behind it—characteristics soon noted by foreign visitors as unique and identifiably American.

> "IN DRESS, IN MANNERS, IN LANGUAGE, IN EATING HABITS, WE HAVE JETTISONED OLD STANDARDS; MAKING LIFE LESS FORMAL, LESS STRUCTURED, MORE EASYGOING. . . ."

In the 1860s, the novelist Anthony Trollope wrote, "There is an independence which sits gracefully on their shoulders, and teaches you at the first glance that the man has a right to assume himself to be your equal." Trollope visited a poor frontier farmer, "in ragged blue trousers and old flannel shirt . . . who has worked out his independence, and shows it in every easy movement of his body."

Eighty years later, Simone de Beauvoir watched the soldiers who liberated Paris and wrote: "The easy-going manner of the young Americans incarnated liberty itself."

Peace and love permeate the famous music festival in Woodstock, New York, in 1969, opposite. Here, rich and poor mingled in the mud for three days in a spirit of egalitarianism. and equality.

The frontier's upper crust gather for a dance, circa 1820. Even then the lower classes provided the music, here a black fiddler. Life on the frontier—its dangers and privations, its loneliness and isolation—tended to make friends of neighbors.

How was it generated, this unique American personality? It can't all have been the spirit of the Revolution, or what Trollope called "the braggadocio of equality." The American experience had been unique for a century and a half before Independence and must have stamped the colonial character.

The enforced intimacy and shared indignities of the voyage to America would have broken down much reserve and prudery. What reserve could have survived two months below decks in those squalid ships? Once landed, the privations and dangers of life in the wilderness would have bred new forms of self-reliance and interdependence. So would the forms of self-government they instituted immediately.

Farmers make hay while the sun shines in 1875. Neighbors routinely gathered at harvest time, moving from farm to farm to make certain everyone got some help.

Inevitably, the little formalities of life in the old country would have been abbreviated. The colonists could not have held themselves to strict standards when life was more dangerous and the climate more extreme than anything they had known. They survived by adaptation and courage, and they prospered in making their own judgments. Such experience would shape human character, generation by generation.

After the British surrender at Yorktown, how did they so quickly internalize the new idea of liberty and transmute it into personal behavior that instantly stamped them as American? After all, the living conditions did not

Old cowhand or retired president? LBJ in retirement has the look of the Texas rancher he once was. His Great Society—a dream to provide abundance, justice, and liberty for all—brought Americans Medicaid and Medicare, civil rights laws, funds for education and Head Start, clean air and water standards, an increased minimum wage, food stamps, protective laws for consumers, PBS, and endowments for the arts and the humanities.

change appreciably. A modified British class system still prevailed. By breeding, education, and wealth, many fathers of the Revolution were colonial aristocrats, living gentle and cultured lives. The Liberty they talked was of a different order than was available for the toiling masses. Or was it? And how did the sense of equality filter down?

Owning land must have been the psychological foundation for everything. An impossible dream for most common people in the Old World, land had been the lure for immigration and settlement before the Revolutionary War, and was a reward for service in it. However brutal the life, farming land one owned gave an

American substance and dignity and the chance, by good husbandry, of accumulating wealth.

Besides land—with the old hierarchies shuffled off—there were philosophical messages that overturned eons of established thought. A man is not entitled to power simply because of his birth—king, aristocrat, anybody—but because of his own worth and achievement. Stunning! Hard to imagine any change in our thinking today that could so shake the foundations of our society as that did. But that wasn't all. In rejecting the king of England, they also finally rejected the established Church, thus enshrining the principle the dissenting Pilgrim Fathers had come to Massachusetts to protect: a man may make his own relationship with God—or none—with no intermediaries. At the height of Elizabethan paranoia about the threat of Catholicism, an Englishman could be fined £20, a fortune, for failing to attend a Church of England service. Many Scots-Irish Presbyterians emigrated from Northern Ireland because the British forced them to pay tithes to the Church of England. These feisty Ulstermen became the backbone of the Revolution.

An independent American was also freed from a fixed place in the Great Chain of Being, the medieval idea that still inspired Britain's rulers: social distinctions were divinely inspired; a person lived his life in whatever estate he was born, serf, peasant, guild craftsman, landowner, and so on up the caste system. Social mobility was restricted, economic competition discouraged, usury and capitalism considered dangerous to the state. While this rigid system had largely dissolved in Britain, in the late nineteenth century the scholar Matthew Arnold could write, "We have the religion of inequality." A hundred years before, Americans had thrown that religion out.

That set America off from the Old World, philosophically and psychologically, and the curious wanted to see it in action: America as a zoo, or a theme park for curious Europeans who came to observe the new species. Some jeered at the crude republican manners liberty sometimes produced. Others marveled at how it unleashed the creative and physical energies of the people. They watched as this ideology of equality and opportunity inspired millions of Europe's poor to cross the Atlantic, and moved other peoples to liberate themselves from colonial rule or despotic monarchies.

But did equality actually mean that even the poorest Americans could think themselves as good as anyone? Certainly, it did not cover slaves from Africa. It did not mean equality for women, or a universal franchise.

But it did mean social mobility. A person of ability could become anything, could aspire to the pinnacle of society, regardless of his birth. That pinnacle quickly meant wealth, because wealth bought everything that the European nobility had—except birth— and soon by marriage it could buy that, too. It made being rich very desirable, as de Tocqueville noted: "I know of no country, indeed, where the love of money has taken stronger hold on the affections of men."

But his sentence, interestingly, continues, ". . . and where a profounder contempt is expressed for the theory of the permanent equality of property." By 1835, when his *Democracy in America* first appeared, early socialist theories were surfacing in reaction to the brutal working and living conditions of the Industrial Revolution and capitalism. While socialist communities did spring up in the United States, the nation emphatically rejected equality of property in favor of equality of

Setting a standard of wealth toward which all Americans aspired, John D. Rockefeller was the world's first billionaire.

Middle-class Americans in mid-twentieth century aspire to the sophistication of the wealthy. Here, friends gather for a dinner party. Between 1947 and 1979, family income roughly doubled.

opportunity to get property. That was America's "religion" of equality and, like all religions, it was based on faith. That faith pushed human optimism onto a new scale, especially to Europe's huddled masses. Fused with personality traits already developed, that faith created what came to be recognized as the American character: less cynical and fatalistic, more optimistic, idealistic, and innocent; inventive in business and full of get-up-and-go; gregarious, outgoing, and generous-hearted; flamboyantly and boastfully patriotic; and convinced that this country was, even in God's eyes, exceptional.

That optimism was born out as America delivered a better life and released the talents of more people than any system, anywhere before.

Well, how does this religion of equality fare today? Better in some ways. In the last half century, America has made its promise of equality far more comprehensive, outlawing open racial discrimination and significantly liberating women. In a legal and often a social sense, the nation is closer than it ever was in 1776 to believing "that all men are created equal," although the sad residue of slavery still leaves African Americans behind in education, employment, and housing.

This surge of tolerance has been matched by a rush to make America even more completely the global citadel of informality. In dress, in manners, in language, in eating habits, we have jettisoned old standards, making life less formal, less structured, more easygoing—some of it inspired by our obsession with youth and commercial deference to the tastes of the teenage consumer. We have even come to look back, pityingly, as in the movie *Far From Heaven*, on social structures that appear, only fifty years later, ridiculously constrained.

But I also see American society now showing signs of retreating from the egalitarian spirit, ironically as other countries adopt it in their own fashion. Not as allergic to anything vaguely socialist as Americans are, people in Western Europe, Britain, and next door in Canada have evolved systems in which equal opportunity is taken to mean helping the weaker individual more generously than in this country. For example, every citizen of those countries is covered by national health care.

Education was an early glory of an American democracy determined to guarantee parents that their children would acquire the skills to rise and prosper. Education was fundamental to the promise of equal opportunity. Adlai Stevenson said in 1948, "The most American thing about America is the free common school system." Today the quality of education is distressingly uneven, too often following the geography of wealth and race. There are vigorous political efforts to privatize education more, thus diluting the principles of free and common.

Perhaps most interesting is the recent trajectory of wealth. This used to be pre-

eminently the middle-class nation, yet the middle-class standard of living is effectively declining, and the gap between the middle class and the rich continues to widen. In the decades after World War II (1947–79), family income grew roughly 100 percent across the economic spectrum. The middle fifth, or quintile, of American families saw their income rise 111 percent. In the next two decades (1979–1998), family income for the middle fifth rose 8 percent, while that of the top fifth rose 38 percent.

The growing income gap is symbolized by the ratio of earnings of CEOs of corporations to those of their average worker. In 1980, the CEO earned 40 times the average blue-collar wages. By 2000, it was 530 times!

The country is becoming a nation of the rising rich and a sinking middle class. The move to eliminate estate taxes, which was waged during George W. Bush's administration, threatened to further entrench what was already becoming a hereditary American aristocracy of wealth and power.

Whether these trends continue, or are challenged politically as straying too far from the spirit of equality, remains to be seen. Also uncertain is whether the new era of vulnerability and anxiety we entered on September 11, 2001, will permanently affect the national personality—whether easygoing confidence will remain the American trademark.

Teenagers hang out in a school hallway. "The most American thing about America is the free common school system," Adlai Stevenson said in 1948.

America Finds Its Voice

by Robert Kotlowitz

As LATE AS 1941, American public high school English classes rarely required students to read American writers. American writers were mainly the provenance of adventurous private-school English departments. In my own high school, in Baltimore, Maryland, we read *Julius Caesar* and *Macbeth* in homage to William Shakespeare and *A Tale of Two Cities* and *Silas Marner* to honor the narrative sweep and moral resonance of the nineteenth-century British novel. (Not that we had any notion of what moral resonance might amount to; it all had to be explained in class.) And it never occurred to anyone—least of all the students—to object to such a restrictive effort. We were all, teachers and students alike, totally intimidated by Anglo literary culture, with its proud traditions and romantic myths, to say nothing of its inbred air of superiority. There was something there that demanded uncriti-

> "CRITICS . . . HAD BEGUN TO EXAMINE AMERICAN LITERATURE AS SOMETHING ENTIRELY UNIQUE, . . . INDEPENDENT, VIGOROUS, AND ALWAYS WITH A STRONG VOICE OF ITS OWN."

cal respect, even if it was only for its sense of longevity.

For all practical purposes, there was no American literature in the classroom. There were some great names, of course—Hawthorne, Melville, William Dean Howells, Henry James, Edith Wharton, Theodore Dreiser, Willa Cather, Ernest Hemingway, F. Scott Fitzgerald, William Faulkner, Thomas Wolfe—but to read them we first had to discover their work on our own; they were simply not mentioned in school. And we did dicover their work, furiously scouring our public libraries for books to take home, and finding them. (It was one of the great American experiences; almost everyone found Thomas Wolfe and was galvanized on the spot by his ardent invocations of time and the spaces we live in.) We might have been yokels on any international scale, self-conscious and culturally shy, but we were also trying mightily to become civilized citizens

Author Ernest Hemingway, opposite, helped revolutionize American literature in the twentieth century. Previously, writing in the United States had looked toward Europe; Hemingway and others established a uniquely American voice.

of the world. Books would help us to reach that alluring goal.

Within a few years, the shared experience of Word War II changed all the terms. Millions of young Americans left their homes for the Armed Forces with a reasonable sense of commitment to the struggle, and then went overseas to fight, each in his own way, the greatest war in the world's history. By the time it was over and the young men came home, nothing would ever be the same again. America and Americans were irrevocably changed. Some fabulous energy had been released by World War II—call it democratization, egalitarianism, even the first muffled drumbeats of globalization—and it touched our national life at almost every point, including the culture in general and American literature, specifically.

In terms of our literature, other factors were also involved. To begin with, American criticism had sharpened. This process had been at work even before the war. Some of our critics, such as Edmund Wilson and Alfred Kazin, had begun to examine American literature as something entirely unique, with debts perhaps to other cultures, but still, in itself, independent, vigorous, and always with a strong voice of its own. And their influence began to spread. Serious readers paid attention; so, in some cases, did serious writers.

GI Bobby Hunter, opposite, finds solace in a book during the Allied push through Normandy in the weeks following the D-Day invasion of France in World War II. Willa Cather, here on the cover of Time, right, was another writer with a distinct American style.

There was also the launching of paperback books in the late 1930s. These books cost a quarter each. Everything would become commercially accessible to the reader over the next decade: classics, westerns, mysteries, contemporary novels, the best in current nonfiction, as well as massive anthologies of poetry. Then, after Pearl Harbor, the military joined with the publishing industry to produce the Armed Forces Service Library, which put millions of books into the hands of confirmed as well as new readers. (Each book was perfectly designed to fit into the deep pockets of a fatigue uniform. I went into combat in 1943 carrying Harry Kurnitz's smart little mystery, *Fast Company*, in one pocket and *The Pocket Book of Verse* in the other. It also occurred to me that they might help protect me against shrapnel.) The Armed Services Library was a brilliant concept, superbly executed. Wherever there were GIs there were books, and, more to the point, books that were read.

All of this, combined with a new sophistication that came from soldier/ civilian contact in often unexpected places in the world, helped to produce a new vigor in post-war American writing. Every year, fresh and feisty young writers enhanced the literary scene with growing strength, confidence, and ambition so

The Manhattan skyline rises beyond author Norman Mailer. His gritty World War II novel, The Naked and the Dead, *brought the GI's war home to Americans and established Mailer's reputation.*

intense that it can only be described as sublime. The roll call of those years is resonant and sometimes thrilling: Mailer, Jones, Styron, Welty, O'Connor, McCullers, Salinger, Vidal, Capote, Ellison, Baldwin, Updike, Kerouac, Miller, Williams, Malamud, Bellow, Roth. Is there anything to compare with it?

Recently, I went back for another look at three of the novels that had affected me deeply when I first read them at least a half-century ago. I was an ex-GI then, a former infantryman returned to college to finish his education on the GI Bill. The novels were Norman Mailer's *The Naked and the Dead*, James Jones's *From Here to Eternity*, and William Styron's *Lie Down in Darkness*. The first two are war novels, of

course, among the most powerful ever written and certainly among the most popular. The third is a dark, burnished tale about the mutual destructiveness of a Virginia family—father, mother, and daughter. All three were published within five years of each other; all three remain in print, after more than fifty years, in handsome paperback editions that are substantially more expensive than the original hardcovers.

I soon discovered that what was there when I first read all three is still there: a kind of explosive energy and range in the case of *The Naked and the Dead* that still astonishes; a brutal rawness tempered on every page by James Jones's love for his main character,

Robert E. Lee Prewitt, in *From Here to Eternity;* and in *Lie Down in Darkness,* Stryon's elegantly unfolding prose at the service of his strong narrative sense.

How sure of themselves these writers seemed to be. There is not a moment's revealed hesitation in their books (whatever was going on in their souls), no doubt or withholding, no diffidence, and no reticence, either. They had written novels in which the reader was not offered much by way of courtesy or discretion. It was all there, all-out, take it or leave it, right on the page; and it still is.

Yet, there is an aura of dreamy exhaustion, even romance, hovering over all three novels. Each, for example, carries the idea of death in its title, one explicitly, the other two metaphorically. Each is saturated with the idea—as a threat, as a reality, as the ultimate reality—most especially *Lie Down in Darkness,* which is not even a novel about a war. Writing in an era when American triumphalism was shaping the national sensibility, these three young men, who were still in their twenties, seemed to be almost in love with the idea of defeat. (Has there ever been a first-rate novel about war that wasn't?)

In the years that followed and the books that filled them, Mailer, Jones, and Styron always managed to remain unimpeachably themselves. But the hold that their books had over me fifty years ago is still strong. Strong enough, in fact, that it took me forty years to gather the confidence to write my own book about the war.

The energy that these books—and others—embody has turned out to be regenerative. It has been reinforcing itself for the past half-century. We feel it today, readers and writers alike. It helps to define our culture, it *is* our culture, as is the energy that has driven the best of American art in the past half-century, serious American music, certain movies, jazz, and both modern and classical American dance.

Perhaps we have produced more than our share of cultural litter since the end of World War II (the case can be easily made). Certainly we produce at least our share of cultural splendor, and the world—or most of it—seems to relish it. The essential fact is that we are yokels no more. Nor are we shy; far from it. We have become models for the world; we sell ourselves hard. Often we are hated for it, sometimes we are imitated and even loved, and always we are envied.

When England's Booker Prize committee recently considered inviting American novelists to be candidates for the prize, England's most sought-after literary honor, the committee soon decided against it. It was feared that American writers would run away with the award each year. That kind of success and power, we are just now coming to understand, exists today on a shockingly grand scale that was almost unimaginable fifty years ago.

Novelist James Jones chronicled the war in Hawaii and the attack on Pearl Harbor with From Here to Eternity, *later a popular movie.*

The Silver Screen as Looking Glass

by Janet Maslin

How DID WE GET from Buster Keaton to Ace Ventura? The history of America's twentieth-century self-image lies in the answer to that question. If you are what you emulate, then we have been courtly and comical; we have shown pioneer spirit; we've been screwball and trigger-happy; we've been Working Girls and Easy Riders. We have been Pet Detectives. And we have made all these things quintessentially American, even if they happened in a galaxy far, far away.

No single movie's rags-to-riches story can compare with Hollywood's own. Born of primitive technology and carried aloft by the American dreams of European immigrants, it became the century's most influential art form—not to mention its most thrilling. And film evolved into an enormously revealing mirror. Looking at the screen, we have found our proudest self-imagery and our worst nightmares.

> "BORN OF PRIMITIVE TECHNOLOGY AND CARRIED ALOFT BY THE AMERICAN DREAMS OF EUROPEAN IMMIGRANTS, IT BECAME THE CENTURY'S MOST INFLUENTIAL ART FORM—NOT TO MENTION ITS MOST THRILLING."

Because film is as varied as literature—and because, for increasingly visually oriented new generations, it is becoming just as important—it has offered near-infinite opportunities for audience identification. And the beauty of this medium's many genres is that they are not mutually exclusive. The same viewer who grows misty over *It's a Wonderful Life*, with its damply heartwarming evocation of American virtue, may be just as powerfully influenced by the *Godfather* films. They, too, after all, define family values.

The landmark films, the ones on which we model our outlook and expectations, aren't necessarily the greatest. After all, Sylvester Stallone's Rocky Balboa managed to become as conspicuous a cinematic creation as Charlie

New Yorkers line up for John Ford's The Grapes of Wrath in 1940, opposite. Movies have reflected America's culture since their beginnings. In the 1920s, when Buster Keaton was popular, below, Hollywood's movie studios produced about six hundred films a year.

Chaplin's Little Tramp. And the most seemingly American film images haven't always been native-grown. It took one Englishman directing another to produce one of our most perfect visions of paranoia: Alfred Hitchcock sending Cary Grant racing through a picture-perfect cornfield in *North by Northwest*.

The American films that have become definitive are the ones that best express and analyze our values. This is less a matter of morality than of message. Just as the screwball genre at its quick-witted, freewheeling best expressed Depression-era resilience, the fear-filled B-picture classics of the 1950s spoke to a Cold War terror of being body-snatched. The emblematic experiments of the 1970s get their staying power from the cultural youth-quake that they embodied. And the *Top Gun*–style machismo of teen-oriented, dynamite-filled 1980s action pictures spoke to a blow-hard, boastful atmosphere in the nation at large.

Most of us can look back to a single, seminal film that showed us how definitively a viewer can be influenced by the screen. For me, it was *Lawrence of Arabia*—not a film aimed at young ado-

lescents, but one capable of magnetizing them as powerfully as *The Catcher in the Rye* (or at least so it seemed to twelve-year-old me). There was a role model: the solitary, authority-flouting adventurer, running from an inner sense of shame and proving his grit with astonishing feats of stoicism. That the stoicism melted into masochism, and that in 1962 films could still captivate so fully and convey so much geopolitical information—those things were just icing on the cake.

From Keaton's comic grace to Bogart's wounded machismo, from the fizz of the *Thin Man* series to the sinew of a John Ford western, American cinema has provided endless archetypes and models. But on the way from *Pat and Mike* to *When Harry Met Sally*, the values, intelligence, and demeanor in those films changed, reflecting larger shifts in our society. Those who grow up watching grisly, over-heated sci-fi fantasies full of comic-book characters will move in a very different world from that of their parents—who grew up thinking, thanks to the movies, that married people slept in twin beds.

Changes in society, film content, technology, and marketing have been

Romantic comedies from Hollywood—like Pat and Mike, *top, and* When Harry Met Sally, *bottom—chart the changing relationships between men and women over the decades.*

Together for the first time
CLARK
GABLE
and
CLAUDETTE
COLBERT
in

1ST PRIZE
ACADEMY
OF
MOTION PICTURE
ARTS
SCIENCES

"It Happened One Night"
with WALTER CONNOLLY · ROSCOE KARNS
From the Cosmopolitan Magazine story by SAMUEL HOPKINS ADAMS
Screen play by ROBERT RISKIN
a FRANK CAPRA Production
A COLUMBIA PICTURE

COLUMBIA PICTURES

Swept away, Claudette Colbert swoons in the arms of Clark Gable in It Happened One Night, *a romantic story of love on the run. Such so-called screwball comedies of the 1930s helped take Americans' minds off the hardships of the Great Depression.*

deeply interwoven. When the mere image of a train on screen struck audiences as a miracle, film was precious simply because it existed. The America that it reflected was a place where leading men tipped their hats to ladies—unless they were as exotic as Valentino, in which case they vamped, ravished, and glowered.

Women were dainty, imperiled creatures, sweetness personified—unless they, too, aspired to an exaggeratedly wicked glamour. Either way, films and their performers sparkled with possibility, just as the nation itself stood on the brink of newly expanding business prospects. Only some of the history preserved at that time, like the Ku Klux

Klan in *Birth of a Nation,* is now tarnished in hindsight.

The roar of the 1920s could be heard even in the last silent films, as uncensored abandon filled the screen. Films of that period often had a sexy, hedonistic freedom. It would be undercut by the arrival of self-imposed Hollywood restrictions, all in the name of so-called decency. But the wit and energy of snappily articulate 1930s comedies let audiences read a great deal between the lines.

Our notions of male heroism, which took shape so grandly in the burgeoning Western genre, would evolve from Depression escapism to wartime toughness. Some of film's most stirring romances

Henry Fonda, star of Mister Roberts, emerges on deck. The Office of War Information supervised the content of films made during World War II. But by 1955, when Mr. Roberts was filmed, the agency was no longer needed.

were created under the shadow of World War II—and frankly, audiences did give a damn. The movies' ability to inspire and sustain viewers in a troubled world, and to transform their fears into fantasy, has always been one of Hollywood's most valuable functions.

The tensions of the 1950s also played out eloquently on the screen. McCarthyism contributed to the period's polarizing extremes. On the one hand, squeaky-clean family stories and Douglas Sirk soap operas dealt with the status quo of middle-class values; on the other, charismatic rebels and bikers made their mark. And their imprint lasted: these were the precursors of a revolution that would turn cinema inside out, just as it transformed the nation.

As the costly wide-screen epic dominated the late 1950s and early 1960s (and as the by-now-ailing musical enjoyed a new lease on life), the seeds of drastic change were already sown. Vietnam would eradicate the traditional, four-square war film and force filmmakers to illustrate a more subtle, less black-and-white kind of struggle. Racial inequality would become the subject of mainstream entertainment, thanks in part to the across-the-board appeal of an actor like Sidney Poitier.

Actor and dancer Gene Kelly directs Barbra Streisand in the musical Hello, Dolly!, *here filming on location in Garrison, New York, on the Hudson River.*

And even some of the late 1960s fairly conventional-looking filmmaking was a harbinger of something different. A whole new generation of inventive,

Clearly in need of a bigger boat, Richard Dreyfuss (left) and Robert Shaw confront their nemesis, the great white shark, in Jaws. The 1975 film alarmed summertime beach-goers the world over.

stereotype-shattering writers, directors, and actors would revolutionize the way Hollywood conducted business, and the way Americans looked to the world. The heady atmosphere evoked by artists like Robert Altman and Martin Scorsese was a visible extension of nationwide upheaval. All the old bets were off. We were ready to explore the new.

If the 1970s were an especially roiling time for the nation, the same held true for film. On the one hand, the blockbuster was born, and it threatened to stomp all over more specialized kinds of cinema. But the countereffect to that was the rise of a parallel universe: the world of the independents, where any-

one with a camera, a new idea, and a credit card had a chance. It's no coincidence that the indies began to thrive just as the disco-age homogenization and trashing of popular culture took hold.

By then, the advent of home video had begun to change the nation's moviegoing experience. *Citizen Kane*, once watched in a dark room with awe, was now something you could put in your pocket. The very conception of new films began to take into account this ancillary experience; if they hoped to be hugely popular, then they had to be big, broad, and cartoonish enough to hold the attention of someone talking on the telephone. The idea of mass-market films of real subtlety and sophistication all but died with that burst of progress.

Mainstream films of the 1990s sunk to the level of their most enthusiastic consumer: the horny teenage boy. A golden age of idiocy began, with bathroom jokes as its hallmark and dopey pranks its stock-in-trade. This is not to say that low humor á la Ace Ventura isn't funny; it's just to say that it's low. The overall, perhaps prosperity-linked, coarsening that affected music, television, clothing, and behavior in public places was most conspicuous. The audience for an Astaire-Rogers musical went to see something elegant and different. The audiences of the 1990s often saw their own worst selves on the screen.

Then everything changed. The early years of the twenty-first century have maintained business as usual at the low end of the movie spectrum, but they also seem headed toward a new brand of escapist fantasy. The gun-toting action hero of the disaster epic now looks like a dinosaur; instead, we have lately gravitated toward coolly futuristic daydreams with strangely

spooky heroes. Brute force is not the lure that it used to be. Brainpower, even when silly and self-important, counts for more.

And the most basic aspect of moviegoing is now different from what it used to be: what used to inspire amazement now fuels ambition. Half of our ten-year-olds can name the weekend's top-grossing hit. Behind-the-scenes video, directors' explanations, and endless outtakes are all part of the package. And what once looked like a mysterious craft has been democratized into a popular choice of career.

But however prevalent, numerous, and even commonplace films become, they will always offer our preferred stock of self-images. We will still turn to them to see ideals of love, loyalty, revenge, and even kindness, not to mention countless other forms of citizenry. And they will look back at us to see where the truth of these thoughts and feelings really lies. Films and audiences continue to speak a common language. Anytime someone says "this looks like the beginning of a beautiful friendship," we know exactly what that means.

America's ideals of romance change with the times: The classic love story Casablanca, bottom, with Humphrey Bogart and Ingrid Bergman, left audiences weeping; later, There's Something About Mary, top, provoked tears of laughter. Both reflect the America of their times.

The Sound of a Nation

by Robert Santelli

WHEN PUBLISHING MAGNATE Henry Luce proclaimed in his famous 1941 *Life* magazine editorial that the twentieth century was "the American Century," he was referring to this nation's economic and military power on the eve of World War II. But Luce could just as easily have been alluding to America's musical might. In that regard, too, the twentieth century belonged to America.

In the past one hundred years, more than a dozen popular music forms were either born or came of age in this country. Blues, ragtime, jazz, rhythm & blues, modern gospel, country, Cajun, rock & roll, bluegrass, zydeco, soul, funk, disco, and hip-hop taken together represent the most remarkable canon of popular music any country has ever produced at any time. Add in genres that evolved from the mother music forms such as swing, be-bop, and folk-rock, and this nation's popular music heritage gets even more substantial. Then there are the American contributions to classical music, the advent of Broadway and Hollywood musicals, a full-bodied catalogue of indigenous folk and Native American music, and a melting pot of imported musical styles—German polka, Spanish flamenco, Jewish klezmer music, Puerto Rican salsa, Jamaican reggae, and Mexican conjunto—all brought to this country by immigrants and, over time, Americanized.

Music runs through the veins of our nation. Songs chronicle our history and shape it, too. For us, music is a lifeblood, an endlessly necessary nourishment. It defines our spirit and sense of place. It does far more than entertain us. Music has had more to do with our essential character—as complex as it is—than even film, our other precious cultural resource. Over the past fifty years in particular, pop music has had a profound effect on what we wear, how we speak, and what we buy. Music influences our thoughts

> "MUSIC RUNS THROUGH THE VEINS OF OUR NATION. SONGS CHRONICLE OUR HISTORY AND SHAPE IT, TOO."

At the Cotton Club in Harlem, bandleader Cab Calloway performs with his orchestra in 1935, opposite. American music has developed from many influences and roots, including the black slave culture, Native Americans, Europeans, and Jews. TV host Dick Clark, below, promoted one style: rock & roll.

about youth, sex, politics, war, and peace. It articulates our fears and hopes and dreams. Today, America is a nation of beats and rhythms, a culture consumed by sound.

Consider for a moment America's greatest music makers: Stephen Foster, Scott Joplin, John Philip Sousa, George M. Cohan, Louis Armstrong, Duke Ellington, George Gershwin, Jerome Kern, Irving Berlin, Charles Ives, Jelly Roll Morton, Richard Rodgers, Oscar Hammerstein, Lorenz Hart, Bessie Smith, the Carter Family, Jimmie Rodgers, Ella Fitzgerald, Aaron Copland, Woody Guthrie, Cole Porter, Robert Johnson, Billie Holiday, Benny Goodman, Bing Crosby, Charlie Parker, Louis Jordan, Hank Williams, Muddy Waters, Miles Davis, Elvis Presley, Johnny Cash, Marian Anderson, Judy Garland, Mahalia Jackson, Frank Sinatra, Bill Monroe, James Brown, B. B. King, Chuck Berry, Buddy Holly, John Coltrane, Pete Seeger, Sam Cooke, John Cage, Smokey Robinson, Bob Dylan, Brian Wilson, Philip Glass, Aretha Franklin, Jimi Hendrix, Paul Simon, Bruce Springsteen, John Adams, Tupac Shakur, Kurt Cobain. It is an awesome list, and it is very incomplete.

Music and America are inseparable. Americans of every color and ethnic background have embraced music as a vital national—and personal—experience. For us, music is inherently democratic. It speaks to us in a common language; it connects us despite our cultural diversities; it sidesteps class and other social barriers. We value the simplest folk songs as much as we do the most artistically complex concert piece—maybe more. The best rock & roll songs are nothing more than a couple of chords and an avalanche of attitude. Country music is made up of simple song-stories of human emotions: love, pain, sorrow, and joy. Jazz is no easy music form to master, but beneath the most innovative improvisations can usually be found the blues, like country, a musical primer of our most basic feelings.

What is it that makes American music unique? How did song become such a significant factor in history and culture? First off, it wasn't always that way. Although music was present in America ever since settlers began arriving on these shores, a national music, or any semblance of it, was slow in forming. European music dominated not just high culture in America, but also folk, religious, and popular culture through the eighteenth century. The privileged attended recitals and concerts in which European music was performed, while Scottish and English settlers without pedigree sang ballads from the old country in their frontier homes. In church the hymns the congregation used to praise God also were from across the Atlantic. Puritans sang from the *Ainsworth Psalter*, a book of psalms brought to Plymouth from

The Carter Family, top, pioneered country harmony, singing songs from the eastern mountains. Jazz singer Billie Holiday, bottom, lived— and sang—the blues.

England in the early 1600s. More than a century later, on the eve of the American Revolution, William Billings published *The New England Psalm Singer*, the first book of original American music. It was a long time coming.

Even when colonists sought to sing nonreligious songs about their American experience, most of the time the melodies were borrowed, if the lyrics weren't. One of the more popular tunes during the American Revolution was "Yankee Doodle," a jeering song sung first by the British, then pirated by the American rebels to playfully satirize their commander, George Washington. Other songs were taken from the English folk canon and made American by altering the lyrics. Such hybrid songs, or broadsides as they were called, were sold on street corners in colonial cities. When the musically enterprising colonists sought to create both melody and lyrics, the results were seldom memorable.

West African men and women forcibly taken from their villages and sold in the colonies as chattel did the same thing as their white masters: they brought their music with them, harboring it in their heads and hearts. European music stressed melody and harmony; African sounds were heavy with rhythm. When black and white music in this country finally collided with two hundred years of pent-up force and unabated passion—as they would in the early years of the twentieth century—the result was a spectacular explosion of sound and song. In fact, the most fundamental foundation of our nation's music experience—the one thing that distinguishes it from that of all other nations—is the creative tension that comes from the tug and tangle of our black and white roots.

In the seventeenth, eighteenth, and much of the nineteenth century, black and white music, although always influencing and flirting with each other, mostly existed on separate planes. Slaves sang in the fields, while white colonists usually preferred their music in church and in formal social settings. Black and white music inched closer together in the early 1700s during a period known as the Great Awakening, in which colonists with a missionary's zeal sought to make Christians out of slaves. Those brought into the church were taught European hymns, most of which were structured and stiff, ill-suited to the African-derived, free-wheeling vocal tradition preferred by slaves.

American slaves celebrate a wedding early in the nineteenth century. Their ancestors brought rhythms and harmonies from Africa; their descendants added themes of Christian suffering and hope.

Becoming followers of Christ didn't guarantee blacks a better life, at least not in this world. But the Christian concept of salvation and a place in God's kingdom of heaven sat well with slaves whose earthly condition was miserable. On Sunday, slaves went to one church, whites to another. Eventually, rhythm and improvisation crept into the way blacks worshiped. Emotions, strong and deep, altered singing styles, and traditional hymns were deconstructed. Some evolved into spirituals, religious songs that had an African-American point of view and were sung with a raw beauty and a ray of hope.

One hundred years later, in the 1830s, black and white music and culture came closer together in secular music, too, in the form of the minstrel show. But the results were a national disgrace, undoubtedly the darkest part of American music history. Yet, looking back, it isn't all that surprising that minstrelsy, the musical ridicule by white actors and singers in burnt-cork blackface of everything black, became one of the most popular forms of entertainment in antebellum America. Ours was a segregated country, torn by racism and an incessant belief in white superiority. Minstrel shows were merely the reflection of the culture from which they had sprung.

In their concert finery, the Jubilee Singers of America's Fisk University visit England around 1890. They were invited to perform for Queen Victoria.

If the minstrel show, with its "jump Jim Crow" mentality and crude comic sketches depicting blacks as little more than plantation buffoons, offered anything useful to America, it was the introduction of black music and culture—even if it was exaggerated and warped to northern white audiences unfamiliar with southern black plantation life. Stephen Foster, a white Pittsburgh tunesmith, penned songs such as "De Old Folks at Home" and "Oh! Susanna" about the black experience, and in the process created a popular music sound that mixed black music and culture with white notions of entertainment. Sheet music was the way music was sold before the creation of the phonograph, and "Oh! Susanna" reputedly sold over 100,000 copies in 1848, the year it was published, an astonishing number given the fact that the song told the tale of two black lovers separated by circumstance.

The Civil War and the emancipation of slaves ended most white interest in minstrel shows. Blacks, on the other hand, embraced minstrelsy as if it had been theirs all along, and, in a way, it had. Itinerant black singers and dancers blackened their faces in the white minstrel tradition and entertained black audiences not so caught up in the shame of minstrelsy that they couldn't laugh at themselves. At the same time, other blacks took the spiritual out of the church and onto the concert stage. The Nashville-based Fisk Jubilee Singers sang spirituals for appreciative white audiences up north and in Europe in the late nineteenth century, marking the first time American black music had been taken seriously in cultural circles.

Although America hadn't quite realized it yet, the possibilities that came from the often uneasy but always fruitful relationship between black and white music were boundless. It took a European to remind the nation of its musical wealth. In 1893, Anton Dvorák, teaching and lecturing in America, debuted his *New World*

Symphony, which was inspired by indigenous American music. Dvořák's work, coupled with music composed by Bostonians George Chadwick, Edward MacDowell, and Amy Beach, loosened the grip Europe had over the American conservatory. As the twentieth century dawned, other American composers began to look within their own culture for musical ideas. What they found were themes undeniably American, as evidenced by the music of the quintessential American classical composer Aaron Copland, ("Appalachian Spring," "Billy the Kid," "Rodeo"), Charles Ives, and others.

With the new century came a startling new fact: For the first time more Americans lived in cities than in the country. Improvements in transportation spurred on the modernization of America. The country was on the move, as was its music. With immigrants streaming into New York, black southern sharecroppers migrating north, and easterners heading west, the nation was a hot, exciting jumble of possibilities. What followed was nothing less than a hundred-year romp of musical experimentation, innovation, and integration.

Out in the country was where blues and hillbilly music were born. But both musical forms needed to go to the city to thrive. The blues went to Memphis, Chicago, and New York; hillbilly, which would later be called country & western and then simply country, headed to Nashville. In the big city, tradition tangled with technology, and art with commerce,

as the blues and early country went from being rural-based folk music forms to popular music commodities, reaching the masses and making money, thanks in large measure to the phonograph and the radio.

The phonograph personalized music; performers could sing just for you in the comfort of your own home, and they could do it again and again. The radio democratized music, making it available to just about everyone with a turn of the dial. The need for national expression found its outlet in popular music and its means through technology. So much was happening so fast. American musicians and composers responded, creating a catalogue of song as broad and as far-reaching as the nation itself.

It wasn't only African Americans who contributed mightily to the growing body of American music in the early twentieth century. Jewish immigrants escaping religious persecution in Eastern Europe made their mark on the music and the business of music, in New York and, later, California. As the minstrel show transformed itself into vaudeville and the early musical, Jewish songwriters eager to earn a living in the arts seized opportunities to shape twentieth-century American music. Tin Pan Alley, originally in a section of Manhattan around 28th Street and Broadway and later around 42nd Street

Old-time mountain music fills the hall at the Grand Ole Opry in Nashville in 1956.

and Broadway, was where songwriters, song pluggers, publishers, and producers, many of them Jewish immigrants and their offspring, huddled around pianos in cramped offices, writing lyrics and plotting out melodies inspired by the contemporary sights and sounds of American pop culture.

Jerome Kern and Irving Berlin blazed the path others would follow, including George Gershwin, who some music historians consider the twentieth century's greatest songsmith. All three men were Jews, living and working in New York; they not only possessed rare musical gifts, but understood with equally rare clarity what Americans wanted to listen to and, in a way, needed to hear.

Kern was born in New York, but cut his musical teeth in London. In the early years of the twentieth century, Kern wrote dozens of songs, many of which found their way onto Broadway, where the evolving American musical was a finding a home. He contributed to *Showboat*, America's first masterpiece musical, staged in 1927. In part inspired by the *Showboat* film that followed its Broadway run, Kern also began contributing songs to Hollywood musicals. Composing the music for such classics as "Ol' Man River," "Smoke Gets In Your Eyes," "The Last Time I Saw Paris," and "Long Ago and Far Away," Kern became one of America's most important music writers for stage and film.

Irving Berlin, whose birth name was Israel Baline, was born in Russia and

Lyricist Oscar Hammerstein II (standing) and composer Jerome Kern helped invent the Broadway musical comedy, above. Kern is a product of New York's so-called Tin Pan Alley, right, the heart of the music publishing industry at the turn of the twentieth century.

emigrated to New York with his family in the 1890s, where he forged a career in song despite not being able to read or write music. Many of his songs stressed sentimentality and cheerfully celebrated life. "Alexander's Ragtime Band," "Easter Parade," "God Bless America," and "White Christmas"—all classic songs America came to love and cherish—brought Berlin fame and fortune and beautifully demonstrated the power of a pop song in American culture.

George Gershwin counted Kern and Berlin among his most important influences, along with jazz and other forms of black music. The son of Russian Jews, Gershwin was born in 1898 in New York. A gifted composer and a pianist, Gershwin merged elements of jazz and pop with classical music in such an astounding way that the results were beyond category, proven by the hybrid brilliance of "Rhapsody in Blue," the composer's 1924 gem. During his short career—tragically, he died of a brain tumor in 1937 at age thirty-nine—George Gershwin, often along with his lyricist brother, Ira, impacted American music like few others. From the wonderful sounds of "Swanee," which Al Jolson turned into a million-selling hit in 1919, to gems such as "Someone to Watch Over Me," "I Got Rhythm," "Embraceable You," and the music for *Porgy and Bess*, America's first successful opera, Gershwin pushed American music to new heights. Reflecting on Gershwin's

GEORGE GERSHWIN'S AMERICAN FOLK OPERA
PORGY and BESS
PRODUCTION DIRECTED BY ROUBEN MAMOULIAN

A THEATRE GUILD PRODUCTION

Porgy drives his goat cart down Catfish Row on the cover of the program for Porgy and Bess, *the folk opera by George Gershwin. It was based on a play by DuBose Heyward that chronicled the lives of poor blacks in Charleston, South Carolina.*

musical accomplishments, Irving Berlin once remarked, "The rest of us were songwriters, but George was a composer."

The Tin Pan Alley era produced other great composers: Cole Porter, Richard Rodgers, Lorenz Hart, Oscar Hammerstein, and Howard Alden. Together they created a body of popular music so rich and accessible amid the modernization of America, the toils of immigrants, and the struggle for identity that this could truly be called the nation's golden era of pop songs.

The Depression stifled America's fledgling music industry, but only temporarily, and demanded that the nation's pop music forms reinvent themselves in order to remain relevant. That they did. Traditional or Dixieland jazz, that rich, bluesy music of wildly expressive cornets, clarinets, and hot rhythms created in the streets and gambling parlors of New Orleans in the early 1900s, succumbed to a new swinging form of jazz in the 1930s, led by the likes of Duke Ellington and Benny Goodman. Country music came out of the mountains and valleys of Kentucky and West Virginia every Saturday night and celebrated its homespun sounds on the Grand Ol' Opry radio show.

Productions like *Showboat* and *Oklahoma!* captured onstage and in front of Hollywood cameras another part of our musical soul, describing for us common themes of community and self-determina-

On New Year's Eve, 1938, bandleader Benny Goodman, top, plays for revelers at the Waldorf Astoria, New York. Elvis Presley, bottom, sings for a rapturous crowd in the late 1950s.

tion. And then there was Woody Guthrie, Chaplin-esque in his demeanor and a hobo at heart, but always around with a song for the oppressed and the forgotten side of America. Guthrie wrote hundreds of songs, passionately depicting the struggles of the working man, and in the process extending the reach of folk music to include elements of social and political protest.

World War II changed everything about America, including its music. When the fighting was over, a new class of American emerged: the teenager, who demanded an identity of his own and a chance to celebrate it, mostly with music. Rock & roll, a rebellious surge of sexual freedom, youth, innocence, and rhythm, coiled and ready to spring each time the radio blared, became the soundtrack of young America—and remained so for nearly a half century. It began with Elvis Presley, a young white kid born in Tupelo, Mississippi, where he was baptized, with black blues and the joyous sounds of gospel. At age thirteen his family moved to Memphis. Then, in 1954, Elvis undermined everything considered proper about American pop music and set on course a new form, rock & roll, yet another blend of black and white music that would not only revolutionize how Americans listened to music and why, but also what we expected from it.

The arrival of Elvis caused quite a stir. How was it that a kid whose sneers and sexually audacious moves onstage could be followed with the kind of soft-spoken politeness that had him answering questions posed to him with "yes, sir" and "no, ma'am"? How could he rip through early rock & roll songs with a vengeance and still be a mama's boy? How could he ooze innocence one moment and scare the bejesus out of parents and civic leaders the next? Was he a black man in white skin? A white man with black blood? Was he ambitious, or just plain possessed?

Elvis didn't know he had the answers to questions concerning America's ongoing debates about race, reckless youth, and sex, but he did—or at least his music did. In short, rock & roll cared not about racial barriers that prevented black equality in a white society. It thumbed its nose at convention and codes of conduct. It glorified youth. It promised independence and a bold new way of thinking about things. Rock & roll was as American as any musical form could possibly be.

The tidal wave that rock & roll became swept over and through the 1960s, 1970s, and 1980s, changing almost everything in its path. Along the way artists like Bob Dylan, originally a Woody Guthrie–wannabe, matured and became the most articulate singer-songwriter of his generation, and Bruce Springsteen, originally a Dylan-wannabe, depicted the fragmented American Dream in song and demonstrated the power of rock & roll night after night in clubs, concerts halls, and then arenas and stadiums across the country.

Dylan and Springsteen gave rock & roll a conscience. What began as teen-driven dance music in the 1950s, fueled with gooey lyrics and simple yet catchy melodies and rhythms, matured, through the pens of Dylan and Springsteen, into songs with meaning and purpose. Dylan brought folk into rock and created a splendid hybrid: probing, poetic lyrics that dealt with injustices like racism and poverty as well as the threat of nuclear holocaust. Springsteen roamed America's darkened streets and highways, chronicling blue-collar lives wrecked by broken promises and bad luck—often against a raging rock backbeat.

There were many other artists and heaps of bands that sang their songs and rock & rolled, contributing to an astounding body of music that became the sound of modern America as it pushed toward the twenty-first century. Rock also had plenty of company: soul and hip-hop, for example, continued the process of musical reinvention in the black community, creating songs that were fresh and full of new ideas. The sacred and the secular clashed in soul music, while beats became bigger than melodies in hip-hop, and rap lyrics pushed the limits of free speech.

In a nation where most everyone comes from somewhere else and diversity is the rule rather than the exception, it is comforting to know that music binds Americans like nothing else. Songs open up our past, comment on our present, and inspire our future. Woody Guthrie once said that he was born to sing. As a nation, we can say the same thing.

"The times they are a-changin'," sang Bob Dylan, a musical descendant of Woodie Guthrie, top. Pop singers Eve (right) and No Doubt's Gwen Stefani, arrive at the BET awards in Las Vegas in 2001, bottom.

The Divide That Unites Us

by Samuel G. Freedman

IN THAT SPRING of 1906, the spring when a one-eyed black preacher named William J. Seymour showed up there, the frame building of the Azusa Street Mission hunched alongside the Los Angeles stockyards. Its whitewashed walls still bore the scorch marks of some earlier fire. The altar consisted of a wood plank laid across two chairs. And a sign hung outside: FOR SALE.

Something happened on Azusa Street that spring, and continued happening for three and half more years. At ten o'clock each night and twice more by daylight, Seymour grasped his palm-sized Bible and told of God healing the sick and broken, God conjuring new language from the mouths of the faithful. So they came, the people of this city inventing itself, the Mexicans and Chinese, the Okies and Negroes, even a rabbi named Gold.

Skeptics came, too, in the form of reporters. Early on in Seymour's revival, the *Los Angeles Times* placed an article beneath a headline warning, "Weird Babel of Tongues: New Sect of Fanatics Is Breaking Loose." The correspondent went on to describe the Azusa Street pilgrims "breathing strange utterances and mouthing a creed which it would seem no one mortal could understand." He could not resist commenting, too, on the spectacle of white people at worship "imitating the crude Negroisms of the South," as if such integration was the most offensive spectacle of all.

Azusa Street is America, and America is Azusa Street. To say that is not to elevate a single, specific moment into the emblem of a polyglot nation. Narrowly speaking, after all, the events in the mission gave birth to but one part of the nation's religious experience, the Pentecostal movement. They reflect the American whole no more or less than a roomful of

"[THE] 'WALL OF SEPARATION' MIGHT BE MORE ACCURATELY IMAGINED AS A FLEXIBLE AND POROUS PARTITION, A MEMBRANE TESTED AND POKED BY CITIZENS."

Moved by the spirit, two African-American women, opposite, shake their tambourines and take part in a popular American ritual: worship. Forty percent of American adults worship somewhere every week. A stop sign, below, enjoins passersby to take time for church.

Quakers ruminating or an adherent of Santería lighting a candle to the Seven African Saints.

Yet in a broader way the Azusa Street revival offers an archetypal expression of religion in American life—populist and protean; confounding and repellent; and, most of all, impassioned. This nation has welcomed believers from Amish to Sikhs, and it has provided the fertile ground for the invention of entire faiths, Mormonism and Christian Science, Conservative Judaism and the Nation of Islam. America has nurtured the outsized personalities of founders and prophets, faith-healers and snake-handlers, swindlers and charlatans and false messiahs. This country, without a state religion, celebrates its own version of a saint's day each January in marking the birthday of the Reverend Martin Luther King.

"Religion in America takes no direct part in the government of society, but it must be regarded as the first of their political institutions," Alexis de Tocqueville wrote more than 150 years ago in *Democracy in America*. "[F]or if it does not impart a taste for freedom it facilitates the use of it. Indeed, it is in this same point of view that the inhabitants of the United States themselves look upon a religious belief. I do not know whether all Americans have a sincere faith in their religion—for who can search the human heart?—but I am certain they hold it indispensable to the maintenance of republican institutions. This opinion is not peculiar to a class of citizens or to a party, but it belongs to the whole nation and to every rank of society."

Such vitality arose, paradoxically, not from the endorsement of religion by the Founding Fathers but rather from their principled ambivalence about it. The stimulant of religious life in America is tension. When the First Amendment established the freedom of religion from the state, it simultaneously established the freedom of the state from religion. What Thomas Jefferson envisioned as a fixed and impermeable "wall of separation" might be more accurately imagined as a flexible and porous partition, a membrane tested and poked by citizens both faithful and secular in the tussling of public life. If religion in America is kept honest, if it is held accountable for its excesses and scandals, then it is kept honest in part by the critique of nonbelievers. Radical Jewish immigrants held banquets on the fast day of Yom Kippur to mock their pious brethren. Sinclair Lewis anticipated every Jim Bakker to come in *Elmer Gantry*. The spokesman for Americans United for Separation of Church and State is a minister.

Americans can choose from among "many mansions" in their worship. Jewish children study the Torah, top. W. R. Tinker will handle deadly snakes at a revival meeting, bottom. Shakers, opposite, perform their trembling dance.

Among the faithful, too, competition reigns. Mormon missionaries pound sidewalks in the Bronx. Jehovah's Witnesses ring doorbells, flourishing the latest copy of *The Watchtower*. Muslims convert Latino Catholics. Protestants convert Asian-born Buddhists. Yuppies study Kabbalah or whirl in the Sufi zikr. So many famous people raised as gentiles discover in midlife they have Jewish roots that the playwright Wendy Wasserstein confesses, tongue in cheek, that she has just found out she is really a WASP.

And all of this traffic in souls contributes to the larger vigor. The state-sanctioned Church of England attracts less than 5 percent of the nation's Anglicans on a typical Sunday. In the American marketplace of mosque and ashram, synagogue and chapel and cathedral, 40 percent of adults worship somewhere each week. Far fewer vote in a nonpresidential election. Which to Randall Balmer, a scholar of American religion at Barnard College, gets at a larger truth. "We Americans tolerate politics, but we're passionate about religion," he says. "You have two centrist political parties and you have a religious parliament, this huge spectrum from left to right. The real energy in America is in the religious sphere."

As Ballmer suggests, religion is too varied and intense and untidy to belong to any precise ideological point. It defies the secular impulse to divide public life into liberal and conservative, Democrat and Republican. At the very same time the late Cardinal Bernardin of Chicago inflamed reproductive-rights activists for his stance against abortion, he incensed Cold Warriors by campaigning against nuclear arms. Those who perceive faith as an inherently conservative force, abstemious and repressive and intolerant, conveniently forget the Civil Rights movement, a crusade that would have been impossible without the liberation gospel and organizational structure of the African-American church. Those who worry when a political leader like President George W. Bush proclaims divine sanction for military endeavor might not realize that it was the Jehovah's Witnesses who brought and won the Supreme Court case ensuring a citizen's right not to salute the flag.

These varying and vying claims, all made in the name of the Almighty, do share one common presumption: American exceptionalism. "Wee Shall finde that the God of Israell is among us," John Winthrop wrote aboard the *Arbella* in 1630. "Wee must Consider that wee shall be as a Citty upon a Hill, the eies of all people are upon us." This urge toward perfection gives the United

Faith healer Oral Roberts stirs up a crowd of believers, right. Oral Roberts University in Tulsa began accepting students in 1965. Today more than five thousand are enrolled.

States its moralistic side, its preachy tone, its true believer's arrogance. Not for nothing did French president Jacques Chirac, in the days leading up to the Iraq invasion of 2003, compare American piety unfavorably to Western European secularism. Yet the same impulse toward what Judaism calls *tikkun olam*, the prophetic injunction to heal the world, has informed religious figures in their roles as abolitionists, settlement-house workers, granters of sanctuary to illegal immigrants.

The failings of organized religion in America, of course, afford more than ample evidence of human frailty and institutional mendacity. The Catholic Church was sullied in the early twenty-first century by pedophile priests and a hierarchy that protected them. A former leader of the National Baptist Convention, the largest denomination of black Christians, pleaded guilty in the late 1990s to massive fraud and embezzlement. When the convicted and disgraced junk-bond impresario Michael Milken wanted to rehabilitate his reputation, he endowed a number of Jewish institutions in the Los Angeles area.

Still, even in the most tawdry moments, sometimes something redemptive can be found. In the late 1980s, the New York Times dispatched me to South Carolina to report on the implosion of televangelist Jim Bakker's $129 million empire. What began with the disclosure of his affair with a church secretary had opened into a wider pattern of misuse of funds. It was a sordid tale, replete with an air-conditioned doghouse and gold-plated bathroom fixtures bought with the tithes of the gullible. All I needed to know about Bakker's appetites was on the menu at the pizzeria in his theme park, Heritage, U.S.A. "Jim's Special," as one particular pie was entitled, carried all nine toppings.

One night during that trip to South Carolina, though, I drove over to the small, pine-shaded sanctuary called the Upper Room. It contained the sort of plastic bin used for sweepstakes drawings, and the bin was filled with prayer requests and family snapshots, so much honest yearning for a miracle. Into the room walked an uncommon sight for the Deep South, even in 1987—a middle-aged, married couple, he black and she white. Here in the Upper Room, not so differently from at the Azusa Street Mission long before, the color line disappeared. "We've come here to rejoice and we've come here in sadness," the wife told me. "And always our prayers have been met."

Archbishop Bernard Cardinal Law seeks strength at a hearing in a Boston courtroom in August 2002, left. The hearing involved defrocked pedophile priest John Geoghan.

On Becoming American

by Amy Chua

I THINK OF MY FATHER as the quintessential American. Both he and my mother were Chinese, but grew up in the Philippines. They were children during World War II, and lived under Japanese occupation until General Douglas MacArthur liberated the Philippines in 1945. My father remembers running after American jeeps, cheering wildly, as U.S. troops tossed out free cans of Spam.

My father was the black sheep in his family. Brilliant at math, in love with astronomy and philosophy, he hated the small, back-stabbing world of his family's can business and defied every plan they had for him. Even as a boy he was desperate to get to America, so it was a dream come true when the Massachusetts Institute of Technology accepted his application. My parents arrived in Boston in 1961, knowing not a soul in the country. With only their student scholarships to live on,

they couldn't afford heat their first two winters and wore blankets around them to keep warm.

Growing up in the Midwest, my three younger sisters and I always knew that we were different from everyone else. Mortifyingly, we brought Chinese food in thermoses to school; how I wished I could have a bologna sandwich like everyone else! We were required to speak Chinese at home—the punishment was one whack of the chopsticks for every English word accidentally uttered. We drilled math and piano every afternoon and were never allowed to sleep over at our friends' houses. Every evening when my father came home from work, I took off his shoes and brought him his slippers. Our report cards had to be perfect; while our friends were getting rewarded for Bs, for us getting an A-minus was unthinkable. In eighth grade, I won second place in a history

> "I FOUND STRENGTH AND CONFIDENCE IN MY PECULIAR FAMILY. WE STARTED OFF AS OUTSIDERS TOGETHER, AND WE DISCOVERED AMERICA TOGETHER, BECOMING AMERICANS IN THE PROCESS."

The Bay Bridge helps frame Chinatown in San Francisco, opposite. Nearly every large American city boasts a Chinatown, the legacy of decades of Chinese immigration. For many recent Asian immigrants, America has been a land of opportunity: In 2000, the median income of Asian-American households was higher than that of any other racial group.

A team of Chinese immigrants helps build the Northern Pacific Railroad across the American West. Many faced fierce discrimination—even violence—and the Chinese Exclusion Act of 1882 banned new immigrants from entering the country.

contest and brought my family to the awards ceremony. Somebody else had won the Kiwanis prize for best all-around student. Afterward, my father said to me: "Never, never disgrace me like that again."

When my friends hear these stories, they often imagine that I had a horrible childhood. But that's not true at all; I found strength and confidence in my peculiar family. We started off as outsiders together, and we discovered America together, becoming Americans in the process. I remember my father working until three in the morning every night, so driven he wouldn't even notice us entering the room. But I also remember how excited he was introducing us to

tacos, sloppy joes, Dairy Queen, and eat-all-you-can buffets, not to mention sledding, skiing, crabbing, and camping. I remember a boy in grade school making slanty-eyed gestures at me, guffawing as he mimicked the way I pronounced "restaurant"—I vowed at that moment to rid myself of my Chinese accent. But I also remember Girl Scouts and hula hoops; poetry contests and public libraries; winning a Daughters of the American Revolution essay contest; and the proud, momentous day my parents were naturalized.

Asians weren't always welcome in the United States. In the mid-nineteenth century, the Chinese laborers who helped build the transcontinental railroad faced widespread contempt and animosity as well as periodic mob violence. Anti-Chinese sentiment grew so intense it became a campaign issue. In 1882, the U.S. Congress passed the Chinese Exclusion Act, banning Chinese—along with prostitutes, criminals, and lepers—from entering the country. As late as World War II, while my father was cheering on American troops in Manila, the U.S. Supreme Court in *Korematsu v. United States* upheld the government's policy of evacuating Japanese Americans from their homes into internment camps.

By the late 1960s, however, the Civil Rights laws and the 1965 Immigration Reform Act had lifted many barriers, legal and social, for Asian Americans. For my father, as for so many other Asians who arrived during that period, determination and hard work translated directly into success. My father got his Ph.D. in less than two years, became a tenured professor at the age of thirty-one, and won a series of national engineering awards. In 1971, he accepted an offer from the University of California at Berkeley's prestigious Electrical Engineering and Computer Science department, and we packed up and moved west. My father grew his hair and wore jackets with "peace" signs on them. Then he got interested in wine collecting and built himself a one-thousand-bottle cellar. As he became internationally known for his work on chaos theory, we began traveling around the world. I spent my junior year in high school studying in London, Munich, and Lausanne, and my father took us to the Arctic Circle.

But my father was also a Chinese patriarch. When it came time to apply to colleges, he declared that I was going to live at home and attend Berkeley (where I had already been accepted), and that was that—no visiting campuses and agonizing choices for me. Disobeying him, as he had disobeyed his family, I forged his signature and secretly applied to a school on the east coast I had heard people talking about. When Harvard accepted me, my father could not have been prouder. I later graduated from Harvard Law School as well. He was equally proud when his next daughter graduated from Yale College and then from Yale Law School. He was proudest of all (but perhaps also a little broken-hearted) when his third daughter left home for Harvard, eventually to get her M.D./Ph.D. there.

America tends to change people. When I was four, my father had said to me, "You will marry a non-Chinese over my dead body." I married a Jewish American, and today my husband and father are the best of friends. When I was little, my parents had no sympathy for handicapped people. In much of Asia even today, disabled people are seen as

Asian-American girls explore a beach. Historian Harold Evans has written that the Asians now, "if anything, seem more American than Americans."

shameful, so when my youngest sister was born with Down's syndrome, some of my relatives encouraged us to send her away to an institution in the Philippines. Instead, my mother immersed herself in books about learning disabilities and became involved in organizations for the handicapped. Today my sister Cynthia still lives with my parents in Berkeley, volunteers at a hospital, and holds two Special Olympics gold medals. When I was growing up, my parents had no interest in politics. The main unit of organization for us was the family. I suppose that's still true, but my parents are far more civic- and politically minded today, with my father even occasionally quoting the Constitution.

I see this as part of a broader trend. The United States has generally offered more economic than political opportunities for Asian Americans. This is not to say that Asian Americans have always enjoyed economic freedom or that Asian Americans today are all successful. In the mid-nineteenth century, Asian women were brought to the United States to work in bars and brothels while Asian men were relegated to running laundries, working as domestic servants, and taking up other low-status jobs that white men would not accept. Even

New York mayor Rudolph Giuliani joins Asian Americans among the crowd at the city's 1999 Gay Pride Parade.

today, the label "Asian-American" and the stereotype of "model minority" mask tremendous ethnic and economic disparity. Large pockets of Asian Americans, particularly Southeast Asian refugees, live in extreme poverty. More than two-thirds of Cambodians and Laotians in the United States are on welfare. From Los Angeles to New York, America's Chinatowns are filled with sweatshop laborers.

At the same time, for millions of Asian Americans, especially those who, like my parents, came to the United States to pursue higher education, America has been the proverbial land of opportunity. According to Census 2000, the median income of Asian-American households is over $55,000, the highest median income of any racial group. Forty-four percent of all Asian Americans age twenty-five and older have a bachelor's degree or higher, compared to 26 percent for the general population. Roughly one out of every seven Asian Americans has an advanced degree. Just 4 percent of the population, Asians are disproportionately represented at the nation's most prestigious universities, typically comprising about 20 percent of the entering freshman class at Harvard, Stanford, and Yale, and almost 30 percent at MIT.

Asian Americans have enjoyed markedly less success in the domain of politics and leadership. Although formal constraints are largely gone, many Asian Americans continue

to experience discrimination, exclusion, social vulnerability, even violence. They are underrepresented in political office, in university faculty positions, and in top corporate jobs. Historically small in numbers, often stymied by language barriers, Asians Americans have never been a potent political force in the United States. This finally may be changing. More and more Asian Americans are applying to law schools, engaging in public advocacy, and running for government office. Although progress is slow, the number of Asian-American journalists, television anchors, judges, and elected officials is steadily growing.

A tiny part of me regrets that I didn't marry another Chinese person and worries that I am letting down four thousand years of civilization. But most of me feels tremendous gratitude for the freedom and creative opportunity that America has given me. My two daughters, like my father, are thoroughly Americans, full of original contradictions. At ten and seven, they speak fluent Chinese and are going to learn Hebrew. One is a prize-winning pianist, the other a rebellious, dazzling violinist.

My daughters don't feel like outsiders in America. I sometimes still do. But for me, as for my father, that is less a burden than a privilege.

FAIRMONT PLAZA
SILICON VALLEY FINANCIAL CENTER

The Technologist's Utopia

by Michael Lewis

SILICON VALLEY no longer traffics in silicon. It isn't even much of a valley. But it is still a distinctively American place, as curious for the way of life it has invented as it is for its more famous technologies. It began as a quiet rebellion against the economic status quo, and it has never quite ceased rebelling. It's the world around it that's changed, and turned it into the sort of place that needs its own name.

For the thirty years leading up the 1990s boom, Silicon Valley was chiefly a refuge for technical people—engineers, research scientists, inventors, would-be technology entrepreneurs—who came both for the weather and for better treatment than they had received from mainstream corporate America. Their lives echoed the broader California experience. The gold rush had acted as a kind of global magnet for people who were not deeply attached to their circumstances, and gave rise to a tradition of people migrating west to escape the prison of

> "SUDDENLY IT WASN'T JUST GADGETS SILICON VALLEY WAS EXPORTING; IT WAS EXPORTING, INADVERTENTLY, SOCIAL ATTITUDES."

some established order or some embarrassing mistake, to seek a new fate. But the engine of this great migration, particularly from the late 1960s, was the underground railroad built by the American Engineer for the American Engineer. Technical men who might have spent their careers suppressed by the established order, chained to a toolbox inside some giant corporation, instead came to Silicon Valley, where there was no established order and no giant corporations. Just possibility.

Silicon Valley became the technologist's utopia. The technical men paved over the orchards south of San Francisco and fashioned a little local economy that exalted their skills. They created big high tech companies (Intel, Hewlett Packard), startling high-tech innovations (the microchip, the personal computer), and a culture that rewarded technically minded people as they never before had been

Buildings of Fairmont Plaza in San Jose, California, opposite— the heart of Silicon Valley—soar as high as the valley's technocrat's dreams. Here in the 1990s new technologies and newer ideas combined to create the newest in social attitudes and work innovations. Even street signs, below, bore witness.

rewarded. Above all, they celebrated the innovator: no place was ever so well designed to accommodate people bent on finding new and more efficient ways of doing old things. Outside the Valley there was an inglorious tradition of corporations and financiers robbing the innovator of his ideas and energy. Inside the Valley the innovator was sometimes robbed, too, but more often he wound up in a big house on the hill. Valley business culture—the only culture the Valley has ever had—insisted that the fellow who had the new idea retain some ownership in it, and share its returns. This and a lot of other peculiar new ideas about life and work that flourished inside the Valley had no obvious effect outside the Valley. The place was still a sideshow in a great economy, and the people in it still saw themselves as bit players. No one paid them much mind. But then the Internet went boom.

Sun Microsystems looks for help in April 2000. The company makes and sells software, servers, storage systems, and workstations, products and services that didn't exist a few years ago.

One consequence of the technology craze of the late 1990s was to establish Silicon Valley as an arena of American ambition of the first rank. Silicon Valley had existed long before it made its quixotic bid to take over the universe but it never had been viewed in the same light as Hollywood or Wall Street, the other places in America people meet to eat each other. The struggle for supremacy inside Silicon Valley had never reverberated in the outside world the way that it did in those other places. Once the Valley went

boom—once it became the place where the greatest American fortunes were made, quickly—it took only moments for its ideas to infect the other arenas of American ambition. Nobody had much noticed that a whole way of life, a parody of the American way of life, had arisen in Silicon Valley. Now they noticed.

From early 1996 to the middle of 2000—when the boom turned on a dime into a bust—the Valley imposed itself upon the outside world, in an entirely new way. The little local business culture that the American Engineer had created for himself turned out to have global appeal. Suddenly it wasn't just gadgets Silicon Valley was exporting; it was exporting, inadvertently, social attitudes. The same shiftless, protean quality that made Silicon Valley such a fertile place for new technology also made it a wildly successful laboratory for social experiments. One of my favorite Silicon Valley social inventions was its view of corporate loyalty. It didn't exist. Until the technical men got their wrenches around the relationship between man and corporation, the U.S. economy assumed that it was valuable for a worker to subordinate his interests to those of his employer. The technical men asked: why? Who does this strange custom benefit? Certainly not the innovator.

Where the new thing was always preferred to the old one, loyalty had always been a dubious virtue; during the boom it became almost a vice. The high-tech worker who devoted too much time and energy to one company was regarded by everyone outside that company with suspicion. Why was he so comfortable sitting around? Did he have lead in his pants? Why hadn't he set out to invent the new business that would destroy his old one? Forced to choose between two otherwise similar job applicants, one who had spent ten years working his way up a single corporate ladder and the other who in that same decade had bounced around seven different ventures in search of lightning to bottle, a Valley employer instinctively preferred the latter.

The American Engineer's utopia was a fantastic exaggeration of what the average European thinks when he thinks of America: mercenary, frantic, dynamic, soulless, ever-changing, a bit nuts, un-European. Take the Silicon Valley attitude toward time, for instance. It was an exact inversion of the European attitude. The Valley dismissed the past and worshiped the future. All the power in the Valley resided not with the man who had done something but with the man who held, or seemed to hold, the idea that would determine what came next. This state of affairs arose almost unconsciously from the Valley's single-minded pursuit of new technology. New technology always implies the inadequacy of what it seeks to replace; a museum of old computers is a museum of inferior computers. And if you are looking to create something new, a disregard for the old thing it will displace is a tactical advantage: it is easier to excel in creative destruction if you don't particularly care for the thing that will be destroyed.

The impulse to suppress the power of money over human affairs was another of the Valley's radical social ideas that got an airing in the late 1990s. This sounds an odd thing to say about a place so devoted to money-making, but it is nevertheless true. Even before the boom, the influence of capital in the technology industry had been reduced: the guy with the good new idea—and the gumption to implement it—enjoyed a certain leverage over the banks that supplied him with the capital he needed. During the boom it wasn't unusual to see bankers and venture capitalists pleading with some twenty-six-year-old in short sleeves to take their money. In this one arena of American ambition, money and the people who controlled access to it came to be treated as less valuable than the people who put the money to use. The Valley has systematically stolen power from capital and bestowed it up on labor. Indeed, one of the mysteries of the Internet bust is that it is being blamed on Wall Street investment bankers, when Wall Street investment bankers were merely the help.

But will it fly? Michael Moshier, CEO of Millennium Jet, models the Solo Trek XFV personal helicopter as it begins its initial test phase after three years of development, right.

Even getting fired can be fun in Silicon Valley. Web developer Dave Gantenbein networks at a "pink slip party" staged to help those who have lost their jobs in the once-booming valley. In April 2000, Silicon Valley was producing sixty-four new millionaires per day.

It's tempting to believe that what happened in Silicon Valley in the late 1990s could happen only in late 1990s. Just now, in the messy aftermath, a lot of people are busy pretending that the Internet boom was a freak event, unconnected to anything that came before or after it. But that doesn't do justice to the event, or the place that triggered it. The boom wasn't an aberration; it was a caricature. The value system of the Internet boom was a simple exaggeration of the values that the American engineer built into his little local economy. And so when people ask what will become of Silicon Valley now that the boom's a bust and the money is gone, they ask the wrong question. The money is not really gone— and never will be gone. In America there has arisen a place uniquely well designed to attract and reward people who dream up new and better ways of doing things, and such people will always attract capital and bend it to their quixotic will. For the innovator there is no ordinary, sane, normal commercial path to follow. He will always be making it up as he goes along. He will always get away with as much as he can. It's just a question of how much the rest of us will let him get away with. And because we live in a world that defines progress as technical innovation, we will eventually let him get away with murder all over again.

The Way We Eat Today

by Julia Reed

IN THE SUMMER OF 1934, when Gertrude Stein mulled over an invitation to return to America from Paris to deliver a series of lectures, the thing that worried her the most, according to her companion, Alice B. Toklas, was "the question of the food she would be eating there." A French friend had recently visited and reported that American fare was "very strange indeed—tinned vegetable cocktails and tinned fruit salads, for example." The ladies came anyway, and managed somehow to forgo the offensive tins in favor of "unrivalled t-steaks and soft-shell crabs," wild rice, and "ineffable ice creams"—all of which rightfully remain among the best America has to offer.

Though their trip was a success, and Miss Toklas, "to the delight of my French friends," thereafter received regular shipments of the American wild rice, they were right to be afraid. The 1930s were not exactly the heyday of American cookery, but then the same could be said of most of the twentieth century. When the

> "WE HAVEN'T CREATED A NEW CUISINE, WE'VE SIMPLY RETURNED TO OUR RATHER IMPRESSIVE CULINARY ROOTS."

Misses Stein and Toklas set sail, such culinary "improvements" as canned foods and processed meats were all the rage; the first chain grocery stores had opened in the 1920s, reducing shoppers' reliance on the local butcher and farmstand, or, indeed, the family vegetable plot. Jell-O had already been invented (at the turn of the century) and the first fast-food restaurant, White Castle hamburgers, had opened its doors, in Wichita, Kansas, in 1921.

After World War II, when women entered the work force in droves, convenience became the nation's primary culinary goal—but, ultimately, at the great expense of taste. In 1959, in the *New Yorker*, A. J. Leibling wrote a screed against "food that does not know its own mind": processed cheese that isn't "cheesy," lobster tails "frozen as long as the Siberian mammoth" so that they aren't "lobstery," synthetic vanilla extract that isn't

Canned goods dominate a 1935 grocer's shelves, opposite, and Coca-Cola is already a popular drink. The Jell-O ad, below, appeared in 1925, but the product itself was first on the market in 1897. Its first flavors: strawberry, raspberry, orange, and lemon.

"vanillary." I was born a year later, in 1960, and it wasn't long before I knew exactly what he meant. There was no escaping, in restaurants or at home, such canned "taste treats" as fruit cocktail and the ever-popular "cling peaches"—which weren't really tastes at all, but textures drowned in sugar syrup. I did not discover, until I was almost ten and my next-door neighbor put in an asparagus bed, that the brine-soaked gray-green mush that came out of the Green Giant's can bore absolutely no relation to the crisp, pencil-thin stalks with the delicate flavor I grew to love. Likewise, I think I was an adult before I tasted, unadulterated, the wild rice Miss Toklas was so fond of (I have since made the excellent wild rice salad she included in *The Alice B. Toklas Cookbook)*. Until then, I thought "wild rice" meant the blend of wild and white rice that came out of Uncle Ben's box to be cooked with a sodium-dominated seasoning pouch.

The only "fresh" vegetables that were consistently sold in the grocery stores in my Mississippi hometown were highly transportable, nonseasonal items like potatoes, iceberg lettuce, and artichokes, so we had them, a lot, along with carrots I later found out had been bred to have blunt ends so they wouldn't puncture the plastic bags they were shipped in. Our local "fancy" restaurant was the dining room at the Downtowner Motor Inn, but every town had one just like it, serving up endless plates of bland roast beef, sliced on

When convenience reigns, taste suffers. With women increasingly forsaking the kitchen for the work force, foods such as canned vegetables reached American tables.

trolleys by interchangeable men in paper chefs' hats. The meat was usually overdone and always accompanied by a soggy, foil-wrapped baked potato, a clump of curly parsley, and an alarmingly bright, dyed-red apple ring.

My own personal culinary low point came after I spotted a picture of sliced Spam with pineapple sauce in a Betty Crocker children's cookbook. It looked so exotic—so modern!—that I begged my grandmother to buy it for me so I could surprise my horrified family with it at a Mother's Day lunch I insisted on making. Needless to say, we never had Spam again. The good news is that during the thirty-five years since, a whole lot of other Americans have given up on the stuff. There has been a counterrevolution of sorts against mass production and the space-age convenience that gave us everything from instant, freeze-dried mashed potatoes and glutinous instant gravy to brand names like Tang and Cheese-Whiz, Wonder Bread and Cool Whip. Now, increasingly, we squeeze our own orange juice and whip our own cream; we can buy artisinal breads, cheeses, chocolate. Homemade mashed potatoes have become so revered that it is a rare restaurant menu that doesn't include them. We used to identify our vegetables by their brand names (Del Monte, Bird's Eye); now we know their real ones (Scarlett Runners, Kentucky Wonders, Silver Queen).

We haven't created a new cuisine, we've simply returned to our rather impressive culinary roots, the last vestiges of which Alice B. Toklas wrote about. Many ranchers have gone back to breeding cattle the old-fashioned way, on pesticide-free grass and grain, without growth hormones or antibiotics, so that our "t-steaks" can again be described as "unrivalled." Soft-shell crabs (and countless other of our coastal treasures, from Monterey Bay prawns to Appalachicola oysters) pop up on restaurant menus the minute they're in season; generations of children who grew up knowing ice cream as the sucrose soft-serve stuff so universally popular may now taste the "ineffable" delicacy served to Miss Toklas (and made for George Washington—among his possessions at Mount Vernon was a "Cream machine for Making Ice"). Most important, we finally learned, in the words of Mario Batali, that "one of the most important things a chef can do is minimize the distance between the dirt and the plate."

In short, we embraced what has come to be known as "American Regional Cooking," a cuisine that, to paraphrase the southern food writer and historian Damon Fowler, was founded on English cooking, enriched and nourished by native ingredients (especially corn), and transformed in the hands of African cooks. This combination was further enhanced by the plentiful produce of our agricultural economy and the striking influence of the many cultures the country embraced—from the early French and Spanish and Cajun populations that helped create the cuisine of Louisiana, to Greek and Italian and German, Mexican and Chinese.

It was in the early 1970s that the pendulum began to swing. In 1973, Reay Tannahill published a book called *Food in History*, in which she rather mildly observed that "the consistent quality and price which recommended branded goods to the customer was to lead ultimately to a standardization in almost all food products which many people believe has now gone too far." One of those people was Alice Waters, a twenty-seven-year-old former Montessori schoolteacher from New Jersey who, in 1971 with a group of friends, opened the ground-breaking Chez Panisse in Berkeley, California. Waters, like so many before her, had her eyes opened during a college year abroad in France, where it was still possible to buy carrots with pointed ends, and where fine dining did not have the overwrought implications it had at home. In America, culinary sophistication meant home cooks desperately striving to duplicate the stylized, studio-lit spreads in *Gourmet* magazine and whisking up virtual vats of bechamel sauce, or "Continental" restaurants featuring high-toned, vaguely European-sounding dishes like veal Oscar and chicken Kiev, green beans amandine and duck a l'orange.

Waters, on the other hand, served American food cooked in the French manner, offering a single menu each

No Wonder Bread here: Fresh from the oven, artfully baked and displayed loaves and buns await a baker's customers.

Vines grow beneath the dangling weight of Cabernet Sauvignon grapes in California's Napa Valley. American vineyards now compete successfully in world markets. Their rise coincided with the arrival of "New American" or "California" cuisine, styles of cooking that take advantage of native ingredients and regional specialties.

night. Chez Panisse's first dinner included duck with olives, a simple salad of baby greens, and a prune tart. A year later, when Jeremiah Tower took over as head chef, the real revolution began. "I looked around and said we're sitting right in the middle of this beautiful place. Why are we slavishly trying to follow the old cookbooks?" At that point Waters still offered pâté en croute and wrote out many of the menus in French, but one night Tower cooked an eight-course "Northern California Regional Dinner," which included "cream of fresh corn soup, Mendocino style, with crayfish butter" and "Big Sur Garrapata Creek smoked trout steamed over California bay leaves" served with California wines. It "marked," Waters wrote in the *Chez Panisse Menu Cookbook* published in 1982, "a turning point in the restaurant's focus . . . and truly set a precedent which has been followed since."

Diners expecting grandeur arrived to find simple offerings that highlighted the excellence of the ingredients: ripe, just-picked tomatoes dressed only in extra-virgin olive oil (who knew olive oil had taste?), watercress and oranges dressed with sherry vinegar and walnut oil (who knew walnut oil existed?), charcoal-grilled oysters with chervil butter (who knew you could grill oysters?). There was great finesse, of course, and a classical beurre blanc or demi-glace found its way into the odd recipe. But the restaurant offered a straightforward elegance and seasonal focus that had been lacking in America for more than a century. What Waters and Tower accomplished was not unlike an admiring guest's description of Thomas Jefferson's White House menus, "republican simplicity united with epicurean delicacy."

Other American chefs had paved the way for the new/old cooking that was initially called "New American" or "California" cuisine." The great James Beard had been an early proponent of native ingredients and hearty but elegant cooking, and his good friend Helen Evans Brown published an influential book called *The West Coast Cookbook*. Craig Claiborne promoted high-style American, and later, Southern cooking, in his newspaper columns and books. And, of course, there was Julia Child. "Julia was a wonderful character on TV, and she got a lot of people interested in food, but she really didn't influence our cuisine that much," says Jason Epstein, the former Random House editorial director who had dinner at Chez Panisse one night and offered to publish Waters's cookbook on the spot. "Not a lot of home chefs or even restaurant cooks could—or wanted to—imitate what she was doing."

On the east coast, Larry Forgione, at An American Place, had much the same influence. Like Waters, Forgione had spent time in Europe, but as a chef, and when he opened his own place in Manhattan (whose very name was a sign that American cuisine had finally arrived), he couldn't find the ingredients he'd grown to rely on: plump chickens and tiny green beans, mushrooms that tasted like something other than cork. "It started to dawn on me—why do they have everything and we have nothing? Why don't we have chanterelles in the United States? We have oak trees, don't we?" Forgione sent people off to hunt for wild domestic mushrooms and talked farmers into raising heirloom fruits and vegetables and chickens he christened "free range," a moniker that became the norm on menus across the country.

These days, small farmers, driven to boredom from growing single, shippable crops and near-bankruptcy by the economics of selling to big wholesalers, are thriving. Manhattan's Union Square Market, which opened in 1976, now draws farmers from as far away as Vermont and offers one thousand varieties of fruits and vegetables, including blue potatoes and black radishes, three hundred kinds of peppers, and at least thirteen types of onion. Thomas Jefferson would be proud—at Monticello he was famous for his peas and grew, among a whole lot of other things, nineteen kinds of lettuce (his salad of "mixed garden stuff" was the original "field green" or mesclun salad). Long before Alice Waters raided her neighbors' gardens for the tables of Chez Panisse, and Forgione's

Chanterelle mushrooms, relatively new to American markets, are ready for a recipe. With improving American cooking has come more plentiful and varied ingredients: The Union Square Market in Manhattan offers a thousand varieties of fruits and vegetables.

foragers trekked off after mushrooms, Jefferson hired his own foragers to hunt down the things he wanted. He once wrote his friend John Hartwell Cocke: "If you should have any Sea-Kale to spare I will thank you for some to replenish my bed."

His steward reported that Jefferson spent up to $50 for a single day's marketing while at the White House ("Mr. Jefferson's salary did not support him while he was president") and his almost nightly dinners for at least a dozen featured such novelties as french fries and hot pastries filled with ice cream. Jefferson's then-exotic macaroni and cheese pudding succumbed to "mac 'n' cheese" in a box (whose "mac" is a uniform elbow-shaped noodle and whose "cheese" comes from a packet full of electric orange powder), but the real thing is back now, popularized by Forgione and countless others. Smithfield ham is back, too, and stone-ground grits (chefs not only list the provenance of their vegetables and meats—they also proudly name the mills where their grits are ground), along with applewood-smoked bacon, cedarplanked salmon, homemade ketchup, Virginia spoonbread, and berry shortcakes. A seemingly modern concoction like a warm green bean salad with nasturtium buds is actually an eighteenth-century Shaker recipe. Not only are chefs celebrating our early heritage, they've gained enough distance to put modern spins on more recent icons like wedges of iceberg lettuce (I recently had a marvelous version with bacon jerky and buttermilk dressing at Charleston, South Carolina's Peninsula Grille).

By the turn of the twentieth century, "modern" American cooking had reached maturity. There had been a brief period when all the new young chefs got carried away by all the newly available ingredients and tried to outcreate one another. Fortunately, the dining public could stand only so much of such silliness as five-spiced salmon on a bed of kiwi and quinoa with a raspberry vinegar reduction, and things settled down. Cooks draw on their native talents and regions, so that in Santa Fe, notable Chez Panisse alum Mark Miller has elevated southwestern regional cooking to an art form at his Coyote Café, and in New Orleans, Paul Prudhomme (and lots of others) serves exquisite gumbos and etouffees and luscious bread pudding. Danny Meyer says that when he opened his Union Square Café in the early 1980s, the mark of a "luxury dining experience" was "raspberries on the menu in January." Now chefs know better—and home cooks do, too. They have enormous varieties of seasonal produce available to them in such upscale emporiums as Dean & Deluca and such mainstream ones as the Walmart Superstore, where the now-ubiquitous bags of mesclun are big sellers. Millions of middle-class Americans have become sophisticated chefs—inspired not just by cookbooks or even by the many American food magazines. There is an entire network, the Food Channel, devoted to

An American staple: a macaroni-and-cheese casserole. Even Thomas Jefferson enjoyed the dish at his home in Virginia.

nothing but choosing and cooking and eating food, which has an audience of more than 78 million U.S. households.

The way we eat now—locally and well—reminds me of the best of my childhood culinary experiences. Not the ones involving lunch-box Twinkies and Betty Crocker cake mixes, but those involving the thick porterhouse steaks and Gulf oysters on the half shell at Doe's Eat Place, where hot tamales introduced to the Mississippi Delta by itinerant Mexican workers were (and are still) also on offer. The Southern Italian immigrants brought to the Delta as indentured servants to pick cotton gave up that line of work as soon as they could and opened restaurants serving spaghetti and meatballs with deep red "spaghetti gravy," but also just-caught, pan-fried catfish with hushpuppies. (They had quickly become even more "southern.") Then there was the fried chicken, okra, and tomatoes; summer squash casserole; mustard greens; and corn pudding from the inimitable black female cooks at Sherman's Grocery Store, where they also sold homemade lemon icebox, pecan, and coconut cream pies and delicious pork barbecue sandwiches to go.

Meals like that have their roots in a time when Americans didn't make grand tours of Europe only to come back and mourn their culinary lot in life. Finally we have returned to that time. There were two kinds of early American travelers to Europe. The first was exemplified by Jefferson, who took lessons from even the humblest cooks and came home to share what he'd learned. "You must ferret people out of their hovels, as I have done, look into their kettles, eat their bread," he wrote to General Lafayette. "Later you shall be able to apply their knowledge."

Almost one hundred years later, when Mark Twain began his European sojourns, American cuisine had evolved to the point where he was always homesick for it. He wrote of his longing for "a mighty porterhouse steak an inch and a half thick, hot and sputtering from the griddle, dusted with fragrant pepper, enriched with melting bits of butter of the most unimpeachable freshness and genuineness . . . some smoking hot biscuits, a plate of hot buckwheat cakes." A trip in 1878 left him so bereft that he "made out a little bill of fare, which will go home in the steamer that precedes me, and be hot when I arrive." What followed was a list of more than sixty items including Virginia bacon, broiled; Blue points, on the half shell; Philadelphia Terapin soup; San Francisco mussels, steamed; canvas-back duck, from Baltimore; Missouri partridges, broiled; apple pie; apple dumplings, with real cream; peach cobbler, Southern style; butter beans; sweet potatoes; green corn, cut from the ear and served with butter and pepper; hominy; succotash; soft-shell crabs; and Connecticut shad.

That kind of traveler might miss many of those same things today. Happily, he or she will be able to return home to find them.

On his seventieth birthday, Mark Twain and a party of his friends and family enjoy a fine dinner at Delmonico's Restaurant on Fifth Avenue in New York.

In addition to serving as the host of the PBS series *Masterpiece Theatre*, **Russell Baker** is a Pulitzer Prize–winning commentator and memoirist. Mr. Baker covered the White House, Congress, State Department, and politics for the *New York Times* and wrote the "Observer" column for the paper's op-ed page for thirty-six years. He has published more than a dozen books and is a member of the American Academy of Arts and Letters.

Lee Bollinger is president of Columbia University in New York City and a member of the faculty of its law school. He served as law clerk for Chief Justice Warren E. Burger on the U.S. Supreme Court before joining the faculty of the University of Michigan Law School in 1973. He has since served as the provost of Dartmouth College and president of the University of Michigan. Mr. Bollinger has received several awards for his strong defense of diversity in higher education, including the National Humanitarian Award from the National Conference on Community and Justice.

Ben Bradlee was the managing editor and executive editor of the *Washington Post* for twenty-six years, which included the Watergate scandal and the publishing of the Pentagon Papers. (Jason Robards won an Oscar for his portrayal of Mr. Bradlee in *All the President's Men*.) Mr. Bradlee has written *A Good Life: Newspapering and Other Adventures*, his memoirs, and two books on President Kennedy.

Amy Chua is a professor of law at Yale University and the author of the *New York Times* bestseller *World on Fire: How Exporting Free Market Democracy Breeds Ethnic Hatred and Global Instability*. Ms. Chua lives in New Haven, Connecticut, with her husband and two daughters.

Timothy Egan is a national enterprise reporter for the *New York Times*. In 2001, he won the Pulitzer Prize as part of a team of reporters who wrote a series of articles on how race is lived in America. Mr. Egan is the author

of three books, including *The Good Rain: Across Time and Terrain in the Pacific Northwest*, which has been a regional bestseller for ten years and was rated in a poll by the *Seattle Post-Intelligencer* as one of ten essential books ever written about the region.

A long-time commentator for NPR, **James Fallows** is the national correspondent for *The Atlantic Monthly*. He has published six books and has won the American Book Award (for *National Defense*) and the National Magazine Award (for writing about Iraq). In the 1970s, Mr. Fallows was chief speechwriter for President Jimmy Carter and, in the 1990s, he was the editor of *U.S. News & World Report*. Mr. Fallows writes frequently for *Slate* and the *New York Review of Books*.

A contributing correspondent to *Religion and Ethics Newsweekly* on PBS, **Samuel G. Freedman** is the author of four acclaimed books, most recently *Jew Versus Jew: The Struggle for the Soul of American Jewry*, which won the National Jewish Book Award for non-fiction in 2001 and made the *Publishers Weekly* religion best-sellers list. Mr. Freedman was a staff reporter for the *New York Times* from 1981 to 1987 and continues to contribute to the paper on a freelance basis. A tenured professor at the Columbia University Graduate School of Journalism, he lives in Manhattan with his wife and children.

Bill Geist is an Emmy Award–winning correspondent and commentator for CBS News *Sunday Morning* and various other CBS News and CBS Sports programs. He is a *New York Times* best-selling author of six books. Mr. Geist won an Emmy Award for his report on the sixty-sixth anniversary of the famed Route 66. Before joining CBS in 1987, Mr. Geist was a reporter and columnist for the *New York Times*.

Cynthia Gorney is associate dean at the Graduate School of Journalism at the University of California, Berkeley, and a former reporter for the *Washington Post*. She is the author of *Articles of Faith: A Frontline History of the*

Abortion Wars. Ms. Gorney's articles have appeared in many magazines, including *The New Yorker,* the *New York Times Magazine, O: The Oprah Magazine, Bazaar, Health, Mother Jones, Parenting,* and *Vogue.*

Vartan Gregorian is the twelfth president of Carnegie Corporation. He served for nine years as the president of Brown University and is currently professor emeritus of history. He was president of the New York Public Library for eight years. Mr. Gregorian was born of Armenian parents in Tabriz, Iran, and was educated in Iran and Lebanon before attending Stanford University in 1956. In 1986, Mr. Gregorian was awarded the Ellis Island Medal of Honor, and in 1998, President Clinton awarded him the National Humanities Medal.

Félix F. Gutiérrez is a visiting professor of journalism at the University of Southern California's Annenberg School for Communication. His publications on diversity and the media include five co-authored books, most recently *Racism, Sexism, and the Media: The Rise of Class Communication in Multicultural America.* Mr. Gutiérrez previously was senior vice president of the Newseum and the Freedom Forum.

David Halberstam, the general editor of *Defining a Nation,* is the author of nineteen books, including *The Best and the Brightest, The Powers That Be, The Children, The Fifties,* and most recently, *The Teammates.* He began his journalistic career in 1955 as the only reporter on the smallest daily in Mississippi and covered the early days of the Civil Rights movement for the Nashville *Tennessean.* Mr. Halberstam was awarded the Pulitzer Prize in 1964 for his early pessimistic reporting from Vietnam for the *New York Times.* He is a member of the elective Society of American Historians.

James Hoge is the editor of the esteemed *Foreign Affairs,* a bimonthly magazine on international affairs and foreign policy. He has been an editor and publisher of major metropolitan newspapers since the 1970s, shepherding the *Chicago Sun-Times* to six Pulitzer Prizes and the *New York Daily News* to one. Mr. Hoge is also chairman of the International Center for Journalists.

Kenneth T. Jackson is the president of the New-York Historical Society and the Jacques Barzun Professor of History and Social Sciences at Columbia University. Mr. Jackson edited *The Encyclopedia of New York City* and wrote the prize-winning *Crabgrass Frontier: The Suburbanization of the United States.*

Michael T. Kaufman spent forty years at the *New York Times* working as a foreign correspondent in many countries, deputy foreign editor, metropolitan columnist, and chief obituary writer. Mr. Kaufman has written six books, most recently *Soros: The Life and Times of a Messianic Billionaire.*

Stanley N. Katz is the director of the Princeton University Center for Arts and Cultural Policy Studies and is president emeritus of the American Council of Learned Societies, the leading organization in humanistic scholarship and education in the United States. Mr. Katz is a professor at the Woodrow Wilson School of Public and International Affairs at Princeton University, where he also serves as the faculty chair of the undergraduate program.

The author of the acclaimed books *There Are No Children Here* and *The Other Side of the River,* **Alex Kotlowitz** has written extensively about race, poverty, and children. He is a former staff writer for the *Wall Street Journal,* and his writing has appeared in *The New Yorker* and the *New York Times Magazine.*

For many years, **Robert Kotlowitz** was the head of programming for WNET/Thirteen, New York's public television station. Before that, he was the managing editor of *Harper's* magazine. Mr. Kotlowitz is the author of four novels and a memoir of World War II, *Before Their Time.* His articles have appeared in the *New York Times Magazine, Esquire,* and *Harper's.* He is now working on a documentary film about Berlin, the result of a stay at the New American Academy there as a Prize Fellow.

Nick Kotz, a Pulitzer Prize–winning journalist and author of five books, lives and raises cattle on a farm in Broad Run, Virginia. Mr. Kotz won the Pulitzer Prize in 1968 for his reporting on unsanitary conditions in the meat-packing industry for the *Des Moines Register.*

Anthony Lewis was a *New York Times* columnist from 1969 to 2001. He is the author of *Gideon's Trumpet, Portrait of a Decade,* and *Make No Law.* In 1955 and 1963, he received the Pulitzer Prize for national reporting.

Michael Lewis is the author of the best-selling books *The New New Thing, Next, Moneyball,* and *Liar's Poker,* which was a number-one *New York Times* national bestseller in hardcover and paperback. Mr. Lewis has served as senior editor and campaign correspondent of *The New Republic* and has hosted a series on presidential politics for National Public Radio. His articles have appeared in *The New Yorker, Slate,* and *Foreign Affairs,* and he has filmed and narrated short pieces for ABC's *Nightline.*

Robert MacNeil is a journalist and author. He is the former co-anchor of the *MacNeil-Lehrer NewsHour* on PBS. Mr. MacNeil's books include three novels and three memoirs, the latest of which is *Looking for My Country: Finding Myself in America,* published in 2003.

Janet Maslin is a book critic for the *New York Times.* Formerly the *Times's* chief film critic, she began reviewing films for the *Boston Phoenix* in 1971 and later for *Newsweek.* Ms. Maslin has also written about music for various publications, including *Rolling Stone.* She is a member of the board of directors of the Jacob Burns Film Center in Pleasantville, New York.

A West Point graduate, master parachutist, and army aviator, Lieutenant General **Harold G. Moore** commanded two infantry companies in the Korean War and was a battalion and brigade commander in Vietnam. After retiring from the army in 1977 with thirty-two years of service, he served as the executive vice president of a Colorado ski resort for four years before founding a computer software company and co-authoring the acclaimed *We Were Soldiers Once . . . and Young.* He and his wife, Julie, divide their time between homes in Auburn, Alabama, and Crested Butte, Colorado.

A former Washington bureau chief and editorial page editor, **Martin F. Nolan** wrote for the *Boston Globe* for more than forty years. He was a member of the investigative team that won the *Globe's* first Pulitzer Prize in 1966. He was also a Pulitzer finalist in 1985 and 1991. A former fellow at Duke, Harvard, and Stanford, Mr. Nolan has written for *The Atlantic Monthly,* the *New York Times,* the *San Francisco Chronicle,* and other publications.

Anna Quindlen is the author of four best-selling novels, including *One True Thing,* which was made into a major motion picture, and her recent bestseller, *A Short Guide to a Happy Life.* In 1992, Ms. Quindlen won a Pulitzer Prize for commentary, and she has alternated with George F. Will in *Newsweek's* popular column, "The Last Word." While a columnist for the *New York Times,* Ms. Quindlen became only the third woman in the paper's history to write a regular column for its op-ed page.

Julia Reed has been senior writer at *Vogue* magazine since 1987. Ms. Reed is a contributing editor at *Newsweek* and a contributor to the *New York Times Magazine,* where she writes the food column. She writes frequently about American politics and southern culture for the *Sunday Telegraph* in London. She also is a regular guest on CNBC's *The News with Brian Williams* and MSNBC's *Hardball with Chris Matthews.*

Richard Reeves is a syndicated columnist and the author of a dozen books including *President Kennedy: Profile of Power, President Nixon: Alone in the White House,* and *American Journey: Traveling with Tocqueville* *in Search of Democracy in America.* He is a former chief political correspondent of the *New York Times* and has made several award-winning documentary films.

Sam Roberts has worked as a reporter, columnist, and editor at the *New York Times* for twenty years and before that at the *New York Daily News.* He is now the deputy editor of the *Times's* Week in Review section and the host of the *Times's* nightly public affairs television program on NY1 News. Mr. Roberts is the author of *The Brother: The Untold Story of the Rosenberg Case* and *Who We Are.*

Robert Santelli is the director and CEO of Experience Music Project in Seattle. He is the former vice president of education and public programs at the Rock and Roll Hall of Fame and Museum in Cleveland and the author of *The Big Book of Blues* and other books on American popular music. Mr. Santelli writes for numerous publications, including *Rolling Stone,* and is the co-producer and writer of the thirteen-part public radio series *The Blues.*

Founding editorial director of *USA Today* and a former president of the American Society of Newspaper Editors, **John Seigenthaler** founded the First Amendment Center at Vanderbilt University in 1991. Mr. Seigenthaler served as the editor, publisher, and CEO of the Nashville *Tennessean,* having started there as a cub reporter forty-three years before his retirement. He left journalism briefly in the 1960s to serve as administrative assistant to Attorney General Robert F. Kennedy.

Vanity Fair contributing editor **Sam Tanenhaus** is writing a biography of William F. Buckley Jr. His previous biography, *Whittaker Chambers,* won the Los Angeles Times Book Prize in 1998. Mr. Tanenhaus's essays and articles have appeared in the *New York Times,* the *New York Review of Books, The New Republic,* and more than a dozen other publications.

Jeremiah Tower is one of the world's foremost authorities on food, wine, and travel. He began his career as

chef and co-owner of Chez Panisse in Berkeley, California. From 1984 to 1998 Mr. Tower ran several other successful restaurants (most notably Stars) in San Francisco, Hong Kong, Singapore, and Seattle. In 1996, the James Beard Foundation named him "Outstanding Chef in America." He is the author of two previous books, *Jeremiah Tower's New American Classics* and *Jeremiah Tower Cooks.* Most recently, Mr. Tower hosted the PBS series *America's Best Chefs.* He currently lives in New York City and Italy.

A native Mississippian, **Curtis Wilkie** worked as a national and foreign correspondent for the *Boston Globe* for twenty-six years. He is the co-author, with Jim McDougal, of *Arkansas Mischief* and the author of *Dixie: A Personal Odyssey Through Events That Shaped the Modern South.* Mr. Wilkie's articles have appeared in many national magazines, including *Newsweek* and *The New Republic.*

Roger Wilkins is the Robinson Professor of History and American Culture at George Mason University. He served as assistant attorney general during the Johnson administration and shared the Pulitzer Prize with Woodward, Bernstein, and Herblock for the coverage of the Watergate scandal while on the editorial staff at the *Washington Post.* He has also written for the *New York Times* and the *Washington Star.* Mr. Wilkins wrote the acclaimed autobiography *A Man's Life* and co-edited *Quiet Riots: Race and Poverty in the United States.*

A former reporter for the *New York Times,* **James T. Wooten** is the senior correspondent at ABC News. Much of his career has been focused on covering politics and war. Mr. Wooten is the author of three books and numerous magazine articles, and he has been awarded several prizes for his work, including the Ernie Pyle Award for combat reporting, the Overseas Press Club award for foreign correspondence, and most recently, the John Chancellor Award for excellence in journalism.

INDEX

INDEX

PHOTO CREDITS

Jerry Alexander/Getty Images: 294

Lee Balterman/Time Life Pictures/Getty Images: 82

Alfred Batungbacal/Time Life Pictures/Getty Images: 95

Tom Bean/Getty Images: 50

Ken Biggs/Getty Images: 150

Margaret Bourke-White/Time Life Pictures/
Getty Images: 96, 119, 123b

Per Breiehagen/Getty Images: 60

Horace Bristol/Time Life Pictures/Getty Images: 107

Bruce T. Brown/Getty Images: 285

John Bryson/Time Life Pictures/Getty Images: 81

Larry Burrows/Time Life Pictures/Getty Images: 94

C Squared Studios/Getty Images: 207

©Geoffrey Clements/CORBIS: 190–191

Steve Cole/Getty Images: 63

Jerry Cooke/Time Life Pictures/Getty Images: 212

Gary Cralle/Getty Images: 278

Myron Davis/Time Life Pictures/Getty Images: 116

Loomis Dean/Time Life Pictures/Getty Images: 227

John Dominis/Time Life Pictures/Getty Images: 230

Alfred Eisenstaedt/Time Life Pictures/Getty
Images: 114a, 225, 228, 232, 248–249

Eliot Elisofon/Time Life Pictures/Getty Images: 106

Bill Eppridge/Time Life Pictures/Getty Images: 72

Getty Images: 2–3, 4–5, 6–7, 8–9, 10–11, 12, 24–25, 26,
28, 30, 31, 32b, 34, 35, 36, 37, 38, 39, 40, 41, 42,
44–45, 45, 46, 47, 52, 56, 57, 59, 62, 64–65, 66, 67,
68, 69a, 69b, 74, 76, 77, 78, 80, 83, 86, 87, 88, 89,
100–101, 102, 103, 104, 105, 110, 111, 120, 122,
122, 123a, 124, 125, 126, 127, 128, 129, 133b, 134,
136, 138, 142, 144, 146, 147, 148, 149, 152–153,
153, 154, 155a, 155b, 158, 160, 161, 162–163, 163,
164, 165, 167, 172, 174, 175, 176, 177, 181, 184,
186a, 186b, 187a, 187b, 188, 189, 192, 193, 194,
195a, 195b, 196, 197, 198, 200, 201, 202, 203, 205,
206, 208, 209, 210, 211, 214a, 214b, 216, 217, 226,
229, 231, 237, 238–239, 240, 242–243, 243, 244,
245, 246, 247, 254, 258–259, 259, 260, 262, 263,
264a, 264b, 265, 266, 268a, 269, 270b, 271a, 271b,
272, 273, 274a, 275, 276, 277, 280, 281, 282, 283,
284, 286a, 286b, 288, 289, 290, 297

Bob Gomel/Time Life Pictures/Getty Images: 92

Peter Gridley/Getty Images: 308

Henry Grossman/Time Life Pictures/Getty Images: 252

Brian Hagiwara/Getty Images: 296

Carl Iwasaki/Time Life Pictures/Getty Images: 79

David Job/Getty Images: 224

Yale Joel/Time Life Pictures/Getty Images: 267

Shelly Katz/Time Life Pictures/Getty Images: 234–235

Robert W. Kelley/Time Life Pictures/Getty Images: 84

Wallace Kirkland/Time Life Pictures/Getty Images: 137

Santokh Kocharr/Getty Images: 151

John Lawrence/Getty Images: 135

Library of Congress, Prints and Photographs Division,
(LC-USZ62-113629): 204

Thomas D. McAvoy/Time Life Pictures/Getty Images: 75

Franklin McMahon/CORBIS: 156–157

David McNew/Getty Images: 49

Ryan McVay/Getty Images: 293

Paul Merideth/Getty Images: 143

Vernon Merritt III/Time Life Pictures/Getty Images: 235

Francis Miller/Time Life Pictures/Getty Images: 274b

Ralph Morse/Time Life Pictures/Getty Images: 98

Rob Nelson/Time Life Pictures/Getty Images: 133a

Peter Pearson/Getty Images: 55

Lynn Pelham/Time Life Pictures/Getty Images: 178, 180

Hy Peskin/Time Life Pictures/Getty Images: 121

Charles Peterson/Getty Images: 270a

Private Collection: 27, 48, 53, 61, 112a, 118, 139, 173,
199, 255, 256a, 256b, 257, 261, 291a, 292

Gary Randall/Getty Images: 54

Erik Rank/Getty Images: 295

Bill Ray/Time Life Pictures/Getty Images: 29

Jon Riley/Getty Images: 215

Frank Scherschel/Time Life Pictures/Getty Images: 251

Paul Schutzer/Time Life Pictures/Getty Images: 182

Mark Segal/Getty Images: 51

Pete Seward Photography/Getty Images: 132

Art Shay/Time Life Pictures/Getty Images: 233, 253

George Skadding/Time Life Pictures/Getty Images: 109

W. Eugene Smith/Time Life Pictures/Getty Images: 268b

Dick Swanson/Time Life Pictures/Getty Images: 97

Time Life Pictures/Getty Images: 32a, 99, 113a, 166,
168, 169, 170a, 170b, 171, 236, 250

Terry Vine/Getty Images: 130

Art Wolfe/Getty Images: 58

Alex Wong/Getty Images: 115a, 183

Peter Yates/Time Life Pictures/Getty Images: 108

NATIONAL GEOGRAPHIC

Published by the National Geographic Society
President and Chief Executive Officer John M. Fahey, Jr.
Chairman of the Board Gilbert M. Grosvenor
Executive Vice President Nina D. Hoffman

Vice President and Editor-in-Chief, Book Division
  Kevin Mulroy
Design Director, Book Division Marianne R. Koszorus

One of the world's largest nonprofit scientific and educational organizations, the National Geographic Society was founded in 1888 "for the increase and diffusion of geographic knowledge." Fulfilling this mission, the Society educates and inspires millions every day through its magazines, books, television programs, videos, maps and atlases, research grants, the National Geographic Bee, teacher workshops, and innovative classroom materials. The Society is supported through membership dues, charitable gifts, and income from the sale of its educational products. This support is vital to National Geographic's mission to increase global understanding and promote conservation of our planet through exploration, research, and education.

For more information, please call 1-800-NGS LINE (647-5463) or write to the following address:
National Geographic Society
1145 17th Street N.W.
Washington, D.C. 20036-4688 U.S.A.

Visit the Society's Web site at
www.nationalgeographic.com.

ISBN 0-7922-6144-5

First Edition
Printed through Dai Nippon Printing Co., Ltd.
  in Korea

10 9 8 7 6 5 4 3 2 1

TEHABI BOOKS

Tehabi Books developed, designed, and produced *Defining a Nation* and has conceived and produced many award-winning books that are recognized for their strong literary and visual content. Tehabi works with national and international publishers, corporations, institutions, and nonprofit groups to identify, develop, and implement comprehensive publishing programs. Tehabi Books is located in San Diego, California. www.tehabi.com

President and Publisher Chris Capen
Vice President of Operations Sam Lewis

Senior Art Director Josie Delker
Production Artist Kendra Triftshauser
Editor Sarah Morgans

Director, Corporate Marketing Marty Remmell
Director, Corporate Publishing Chris Brimble
Corporate Sales Manager Andrew Arias

Tehabi Books offers special discounts for bulk purchases for sales promotions and use as premiums. Specific, large-quantity needs can be met with special editions, custom covers, and by repurposing existing materials. For more information, contact Andrew Arias, Corporate Sales Manager, at Tehabi Books, 4920 Carroll Canyon Road, Suite 200, San Diego, California 92121-3735; or, by telephone, at 800-243-7259.

Diverse images help to define a nation. Pages 2–3: An 1852 lithograph finds the U.S. Capitol, flags flying, proudly atop its hill in Washington, D.C. Pages 4–5: Like an alien, a visitor to New York City in 1958 views the city through sidewalk binoculars. Pages 6–7: Tight jeans cling to the rear ends of cowboys watching a rodeo in California. Pages 8–9: Stuffed and mounted, a swordfish leaps over a diner's booths, and storm clouds gather over a lonely Nebraska byway, pages 10–11. Overleaf: Springtime cherry blossoms, delicate and fragrant, frame the Jefferson Memorial in Washington, D.C.